# The RV Handbook

## FOURTH EDITION

# Other Products by Trailer Life

### The RV Handbook, 4th Edition

This comprehensive guide gives you user-friendly information on handling, maintenance, accessories, and technical advice for understanding and operating all kinds of RVs. Designed to be used as a quick-reference guide or a generously illustrated textbook, *The RV Handbook*, 4th edition, contains helpful checklists, photos, schematics and charts, as well as valuable information on avoiding towing errors, correct hitching techniques, crowd-free camping, electrical systems, improving fuel economy, the latest tech trends in RV manufacturing, and common mistakes. Great for either the seasoned RVer, or a novice hitting the road for the first time, they will find proven RV tips, tricks, and techniques to save time, money, and frustrations in *The RV Handbook.*

*8⅔ × 10¾, 288 pages*
*$29.95, plus S/H     ISBN: 0–9824894–2-0*

### 10-Minute Tech, Volume 3

Taken directly from *Trailer Life* and *MotorHome* magazines, 10-Minute Tech, Volume 3, provides a collection of useful, handy, and simple tips written by RVers for RVers. Filled with hundreds of time- and money-saving ideas from the people with the most experience—other RVers. Guaranteed to keep you amazed and entertained, these clever ideas will help you solve simple and complex problems, such as how to maximize vital storage space in your RV to smart ways to minimize cleaning and maintenance time, and handy hints to help you have fun in the great outdoors. Whether you're a seasoned RVer or just starting out, these ideas are sure to bring more enjoyment to your life on the road.

*7¾ × 9½, 174 pages*
*$29.95, plus S/H     ISBN: 0–934798–80-X*

### Trailer Life RV Parks & Campgrounds Directory

The *Trailer Life RV Parks & Campgrounds Directory* is the most widely recognized and used RVing directory in North America. Updated every year, the *Directory* lists information on thousands of RV parks and campgrounds. It is the official directory of the Good Sam Club and the primary source to find all of the Good Sam discount locations. The *Directory's* Exclusive Triple Rating system has set the industry standard. Each year new inspections are performed on all private RV parks and campgrounds, encouraging parks to do even more to earn the *Trailer Life RV Parks & Campgrounds Directory's* highest recommendations. For over 37 years it continues to provide essential, comprehensive RVing information to make your trip planning easier and save you money. If you are looking for an easy-to-use and helpful informational reference, you need the *Trailer Life RV Parks & Campgrounds Directory.*

*8 × 10¾, 1,736 pages*
*$24.95, plus S/H     ISBN: 0–934798–96–9*

## Trailer Life Directory Campground Navigator DVD

*The Campground Navigator DVD* includes all of the information found in the annual *Trailer Life RV Parks & Campgrounds Directory*. The easy-to-use *Campground Navigator* software includes comprehensive details, thousands of RV parks and campgrounds, all the Good Sam Club discount locations, detailed street maps, driving directions, and a searchable database of RV park amenities that mean the most to RVers. The *Campground Navigator* is a compact, powerful travel-planning tool. No matter where you are, you can turn on your PC, call up the *Campground Navigator* and plan your next stop or adventure.

*Trailer Life Directory Campground Navigator DVD*
*$59.95, plus S/H*     *ISBN: 0–934798–99–0*

## EXIT NOW: Interstate Exit Directory

Take the guesswork out of your RV travels with Trailer Life Books annual *EXIT NOW: Interstate Exit Directory*, a spiral-bound, easy-to-use co-pilot telling you exactly what's at every exit on every U.S. interstate. Color-coded listings and information help you locate essential services and travel amenities along interstates, making your trip planning safer, smarter, and easier than ever. *EXIT NOW* is arranged by interstate—not by state, so you don't have to flip pages when you cross state lines, and it even includes critical driver alerts—telling you about steep grades, highways converging together, sections of interstate where it's a long distance between gas stations, and sometimes-dangerous left exits. Look no further than *EXIT NOW* as a must-have resource for every road trip.

*9 × 10⅞, 577 pages*
*$24.95, plus S/H*     *ISBN: 0–934798–97–6*

Books are available from fine bookstores everywhere. Or, you may order directly from Trailer Life Books. For each book ordered, simply send us the name of the book, the price, and shipping and handling (California residents please add appropriate sales tax).

**Mail Orders to:**
Trailer Life Books
64 Inverness Drive East
Englewood, CO 80112

You may call our customer service representatives if you wish to charge your order or if you want more information. Please phone, toll-free, Monday through Friday, 6:30 A.M. to 6:30 P.M.; Saturday, 7:30 A.M. to 1:30 P.M., Mountain Time, 1–800–766–167.

Or, visit us online at www.trailerlifedirectory.com.

# The RV Handbook

## FOURTH EDITION

# Dave Solberg

**TRAILER LIFE** BOOKS

Senior Director of Production and Editorial: Christine Bucher
Senior Director of Marketing: Kim Souza
Production Manager:  Carol Sankman
Editor:  Dave Solberg
Production Editor:  Rena Copperman
Interior Design and Production:  Robert S. Tinnon
Technical Illustrations:  Randy Miyake
Cover Design:  Doug Paulin, Robert George
Prepress Specialist:  Milt Phelps

This book was set in Scala, Scala Sans, and Museo Sans.

Printed and bound in the United States of America
by Ripon Printers

10 9 8 7 6 5 4 3 2 0

ISBN 10:  0-9824894-2-0

ISBN 13:  978-0-9824894-2-0

This book is dedicated to my family:

My parents who showed me the wonderful outdoors and instilled in me the love of RVing as a child, with numerous camping trips to Glacier National Park, Washington D.C., Gettysburg, and even New York City.

To my wife for putting up with two decades of "everything RV" and for putting my nose out when it caught on fire from blowing out a s'more!

And my granddaughters for "Braving The Great Outdoors" in our Winnebago Brave on our now-famous camping trips. One little tip . . . take your cell phone out of your swimming suit pocket BEFORE getting into the water!

# Contents

# Preface

It is said that people retain approximately 10 percent of what you tell them. With over 3,000 components in the typical RV, even the best dealer walk-around will leave you yearning for more.

Most RV buyers take for granted the amount of education and training it takes to fully appreciate all that RVing has to offer. After all, we already know how to drive and we function very well in homes that have the same amenities, right?

Wrong! Very little of our day-to-day activities prepare us for the unique characteristics that an RV offers. In fact, in recent warranty and service support studies an overwhelming majority of RV-related breakdowns were actually misunderstandings of how a system or appliance works, or was caused by the owner's actions.

Welcome to *The RV Handbook*, 4th edition, designed to help educate and provide a guide for anyone looking to purchase an RV or get more enjoyment out of the one they already have. The original *RV Handbook* was penned by renowned author Bill Estes over twenty years ago, with the 3rd edition published in 2000. Since that time, there have been monumental improvements in every aspect of the RV industry, from engine power to the way in which we watch our televisions.

As indicated in editions 1 through 3, what this book is *not*, is a step-by-step repair manual. That task is left to another valuable book offered by Trailer Life, *Trailer Life's RV Repair & Maintenance Manual*, which has taken a more technical approach to troubleshooting and repairs. Bill drew on his decades of contact with readers of *Trailer Life* and *MotorHome* magazines to help select topics for the earlier editions. With today's technology, a click of the mouse provides an abundance of chat groups, forums, and Web sites dedicated to providing information on every aspect of RVing. It is from these sources, as well as over 1,000 seminars conducted at shows and rallies around the country, on which I have based my topics. However, unlike the chats and forums, the information provided in this book is less opinion and more industry-approved information meticulously researched and obtained from experts.

And, as a final note, I would like to thank all those industry experts, especially Bill Estes and Bob Livingston, who made this book possible. . . . Let's roll!

# Credits

I equate rewriting this handbook to the old classic of raising a child—it takes a community, an RV community in this case. The list of acknowledgments and credits just might eclipse the handbook itself . . . and wouldn't that be entertaining? However, I do need to identify some key contributors who not only helped with information, but provided professional graphics, photos, and charts that they had created. You know the saying—Don't reinvent the wheel!"

Michelin
Speaking of Wheel, thank you to Doug Jones and the staff at Michelin for not only providing graphics, charts and photos, but also for technical editorial as well. Carla, thanks for the XONE cutaway!

RV Safety & Education Foundation (RVSEF)
Dedicated to safety & education, RVSEF has provided crucial information on weights, towing, fire, and personal safety. Walter Cannon, Executive Director of RVSEF travels the country conducting seminars, weighing RVs, and assisting on several safety committees. A must have for every RVer is the RVSEF Safety Training Program available at: www.rvsafety.com

Winnebago Industries
You'll notice several of the outstanding photos by Tom Humberg in this edition and a special thank you to Tom Pilgrim in the Service Training Department keeping me straight on the electrical sections. Also a thank you to Chad Reece in Marketing for the access to company photos and documents, but also taking the extra shots needed.

Blue Ox
These people know towing! I've had the pleasure to work with them and the educational teams for over 15 years and there is a true passion to education in this group! You'll find towing information, tips sheets, and photos that they have provided throughout this book. Thank you to Jay Heese, Miranda, and the technical advisors at Blue Ox.

Roadmaster
Thanks to my new contacts at Roadmaster, David Robinson and Bob
Vondra for providing not only photos, but the Braking Laws chart as well.

Protect All
Ken Neuman helped proof the General Maintenance chapter and also
provided photos.

Workhorse
Alan Stegich provided photos of the Workhorse chassis and some great
maintenance information thoughout the owner's guide and service manuals.

Trojan Battery Company
Lore McKenna, Jeff Goodner, and the technical staff at Trojan Battery Company provided a wealth of information regarding maintaining,
storing, and charging deep cycle batteries.

Oakwood Campground
Lee Speaker runs one of the cleanest campgrounds in North America
nestled in the beauty of rural Iowa. Many of the photos of RVs in campsites,
pressure regulators, rubber roofs and more were taken of the
wonderful guests she has. If you're ever in the Midwest, do yourself a favor
and experience the wonderful hospitality that is Oakwood Campground!

And all the companies that provided photos such as Fleetwood, Monaco,
Coachmen, and others.

# The RV Handbook

FOURTH EDITION

# CHAPTER ONE

# CHOOSING THE RIGHT RV

**Step 1: The Usage**
**Step 2: The Budget**
**Step 3: Watch Your Weight—Ratings**
**Step 4: Shop 'til You Drop**
**Step 5: The Need**
**RV Classifications**
**Construction Methods**
**A Closer Look**
**What's Important**
**Comparing Models**

**A**ccording to the Recreational Vehicle Industry Association (RVIA), a recreational vehicle is "a motorized or towable vehicle that combines both transportation and temporary living quarters for travel, recreation, and camping."

Just like buying a house or an automobile, there are some important facts we must identify before we even start shopping. After all, it would be as much of a waste of time looking at a single bedroom home for a family of six as a farmer looking to haul feed with a Corvair.

Taking the following steps will narrow the search and make the RV experience much more enjoyable.

## STEP 1: THE USAGE

How do you plan to use the RV? In recent years we have seen a shift in the way people are using their RVs. More and more people are using an RV to support a lifestyle or hobby such as ATVing, going to flea markets, or golfing, rather than waiting to retire and buying something just to travel. Identify the need to better determine the usage **(Figure 1.1)**.

## STEP 2: THE BUDGET

Determine how much you can spend, how much you have to put toward a down payment, and what you can comfortably afford for monthly payments. You'll save a lot of time looking at the units you can afford and avoid getting disappointed with champagne tastes and a beer budget. Keep in mind your budget must also include after-the-sale expenses such as insurance, fuel, and storage, which will be covered later.

## STEP 3: WATCH YOUR WEIGHT—RATINGS

Watch your weight, not personally, but rather your RV weights. Later on we'll cover the language of RVs and what GVWR, GAWR, and GCWR mean and how they can affect your buying decision. Knowing what you will be putting inside your RV, what you'll need for a tow vehicle, and what you are planning to tow are extremely important.

**FIGURE 1.1** Identifying how you plan to use the RV, your budget, and how many people that will be regularly traveling with you are important first steps in choosing the right RV.

## STEP 4: SHOP 'TIL YOU DROP

Shopping for an RV can be confusing and sometimes frustrating. There are over 100 RV manufacturers, offering dozens of models, even more floor plans within those models, and even more options within those floor plans! Due to space limitations and cost, not all floor plans or options are represented for viewing at a show or dealership. Make sure you research thoroughly, keep good records of what you liked and did not like, and drop those that don't fit.

## STEP 5: THE NEED

For current RV owners looking to buy a different unit, the need is much clearer. Your current unit doesn't fit your needs, or there is some new "whiz-bang" item you can't live without. For the first-time buyer, there are many more questions and a lot more research that is required because they will have little or no RV experience to draw from.

### HOW AM I GOING TO USE THIS VEHICLE?

As stated earlier, more RVs are being purchased to support a lifestyle or hobby. It allows owners to park closer to their activities, carry more supplies, and bring larger items such as ATVs, motorcycles, and even horses (Figure 1.2).

Whatever the reason, identify how you will use the RV, what you will carry, how many people you will take, and for how long. This will help narrow the literally hundreds of choices down to the models that will fit your needs the best.

### What Camping Style?

What type of camping do you intend to do? It may be primitive, off-the-beaten-path camping, or luxury camping with full hookups and amenities. Primitive camping usually means limited or no facilities and requires more battery power, larger freshwater and holding tanks, and other "dry camping" features. Weekend campers will often compromise on size, storage space, and other amenities in exchange for a smaller investment in an occasionally used unit. Luxury camping and full-timing requires more space, more storage, bigger engines, and more power. (Some people's idea of "roughing-it" is only two plasma TVs!)

Identify the type of camping you will be doing, where you will be going, and what you need to take with you, or what you can or will do without. First-time buyers may want to rent and try a few local campgrounds to help get an idea of the different types of camping amenities.

### How Many People?

It may be fun for kids to sleep on a fold-down sofa, or even a tent outside the RV, but not for most adults. Who will you be going with, where do they sleep, and where do they eat? It's also important to differentiate between occasional travelers and those coming along on a regular basis. Remember, occasional guests can compromise on bathroom space, sleeping accommodations, and even eating outside on a picnic table. If you are spending more time on the road with more people, you'll want to compromise less and pick a model or floor plan that has more room Another consideration that is a combination of camping style and how many people is the amount of entertaining you may wish to do. There are dozens of RV clubs that hold rallies and caravans across the country, and a popular event is inviting other members over to play cards, do crafts, or other socializing events. (It's hard not to cheat at cards in a typical booth-style dinette!)

### Where Will It Be Stored?

Answer this question before you start shopping for an RV. If you plan to store it at home, do you

**Figure 1.2** Do the math! Know what you need to take and what the RV you're looking at can safely carry.

have limitations for length, width, or height? Is it legal to keep your RV in your driveway, yard, or street? If you want it covered, how much will it cost, how accessible is it, and does it have electricity to maintain batteries?

## BUDGET

Now that you've determined how an RV will fit into your lifestyle, you will need to know how it will fit within your budget. Sometimes the amount between what you want and what you can afford to spend is too great. There are several ways to finance a new or used RV: lending institutions, through a dealer, or your local bank or credit union. Many lenders specialize in RV loans, and dealers keep close tabs on the best rates and the strength of the institution to assure you get

the best overall financing option. Some RV manufacturers and RV clubs offer financing as well.

Once you determine a budget you can start to narrow the choices into categories, once again paying close attention to what is important or necessary, and what you can afford. Often, luxury items and high-line options can put the price of a unit out of your budget range while offering you little to satisfy your RVing needs. These items can be larger chassis and engine options, additional slide-outs, and high-line interior furnishings. Many of these items will be covered later in our discussion. However, work with your dealer to thoroughly research what options are necessary and what you can afford. Many times your RV needs will exceed your budget for a new unit. In this case, a used unit may offer the amenities you want.

As we mentioned before, you need to budget for after the sale—items such as insurance, yearly license, fuel, maintenance, campground fees, storage, propane, and other items. A yearly budget-plan starter kit is available in the Appendix.

## RV INSURANCE

Just as there are different types of RVs and different ways we use them, there are specialized insurance policies that cover our RVs properly. Policies for full-timing, replacement-cost coverage, purchase-price guarantee, and diminishing deductibles are just a few of the policies that are available through a provider that is familiar with the industry. Coverage for an RV may be less than you might expect, depending on the amount of time it is used, if it is stored during the winter months, and the policy you choose. Most dealers work with one or more specialty companies, or you can find them at RV rallies and shows across the country. The Good Sam Club offers an RV-specific insurance program that is very competitive with others. Whatever company you are working with, ask questions about coverage for content in your RV and in your towed/tow vehicle, liabilities during storage, and road service.

## DRIVER'S LICENSE

In noncommercial applications, most RVs do not require a specialized or professional license known as a Commercial Driver's License (CDL). This subject has been a hot topic on Internet forums, with discussions ranging from no special license to CDL requirements.

Each state regulates the type of license needed for drivers of all vehicles; therefore it is recommended that you contact your State Department of Transportation (DOT) Motor Vehicle Division's Driver's License Examination Station to verify the appropriate requirements. Some states require a special license for vehicles over a certain weight (usually 26,000 pounds) or length, such as California, which at the time of this printing requires

a noncommercial Class B license for vehicles over 40 feet but not longer than 45 feet. Keep in mind, road-use laws, such as license requirements, towing regulations, and speed limitations, are all subject to individual DOT enforcement and highway patrol officer interpretation. Therefore, it's wise to contact your local authorities for clarification and to keep a written copy of the description for verification (see Appendix, page 223).

Most states now consider RV delivery to dealerships a "commercial" classification as well as business usage, which would require a special license. Again, consult your local DOT representative for clarification.

## WATCH YOUR WEIGHT—RATINGS

Before you start shopping, it's important to understand weight ratings and what they mean to your decision-making process. Please refer to Chapter Two, "Understanding Weight" of this handbook.

When shopping for a motorhome, the chassis manufacturer sets the gross vehicle weight rating (GVWR) of a specific chassis, and the RV manufacturer designs and builds according to those specifications. Some lighter chassis options may have limited carrying capacity and may not be suitable for longer trips. Going to a heavier chassis is usually a substantial jump in price, so determine your usage, the amount of items you need to take along, and do the math. However, the lighter chassis may suit your needs if you decide not to travel with full water (8.3 pounds/gallon), propane (4.2 pounds/gallon) and only have two people instead of full sleeping capacity (154 pounds/person factored into the cargo-carrying capacity [CCC]).

When shopping for a travel trailer, the GVWR will determine what type of vehicle you need to tow that much weight. Trailers vary from the lightweight pull-behind type, which can be towed by most trucks and even some automobiles, to the larger fifth-wheel trailers that weigh more than 14,000 pounds.

## SHOP 'TIL YOU DROP

Once you've decided on the need, budget, and type of RV, it's time to start shopping **(Figure 1.3)**. With literally hundreds of models and floor-plan designs to choose from, RV shopping can be confusing and sometimes overwhelming. Having worked over 100 shows, I find one of two experiences occurs:

1. After looking at so many choices, potential owners get so confused and frustrated that they take that big bag full of brochures and throw it in the garbage, and their idea of "roughing it" becomes a cheap motel.

or

2. They design an RV that really doesn't exist, combining floor plans and features from several different models they liked.

That's why it's important to document every unit you look at, even the ones you didn't like. And make sure you compare the exact features. Keep in mind that a base RV can be outfitted with dozens of expensive options, and some manufacturers choose to offer "price leaders," units that are bare bones and require additional options.

Here are just a few items that will drastically increase the final cost:

**Chassis**—The heavier the chassis, the more weight-carrying capacity and the higher cost. Check to make sure the engine size, GVWR, towing capacity, and carrying capacity are comparable.

**Generator**—A number of varieties of power options are available, as well as fuel sources, such as gasoline, diesel, and propane. Determine the amount of power required and the proper fuel source.

**Air Conditioner**—Although this is usually a standard item, some "price leaders" list these as a separate option or come standard with just one unit.

**Model Year**—A simple change in model year usually means an increase in price because goods and operating costs increase.

**FIGURE 1.3** Shopping a large RV show can be a great way to see the most units at one time, but be prepared by bringing a detailed checklist of what you want (see Appendix).

You get the idea: Since RV lifestyles differ, appliance requirements, electrical needs, and carrying capacity will be different for each owner. Identify your needs and compare options.

### Make a List

As mentioned before, RV shopping can be confusing, so get a notebook and make a list. Document the model year, manufacturer, model, and where you saw it.

If attending a show, get the show program, and use the map to identify the dealer and location of each of the units you are evaluating. It's easy to get completely turned around in a large convention center.

Get a brochure and use a felt-tip pen to highlight the features you really like and floor plans that are at the show. Usually a brochure will help identify construction techniques and show additional floor plans or configurations that would be more to your liking. With all the floor plans and options available in today's market, it is impossible for a dealer to carry every model and color. Make sure you ask.

### Shopping for Used Units

There are many avenues for finding a used unit in today's market, starting either at a dealership or private party. The Internet provides a wealth of shopping experiences with forums, online-based resellers, and eBay. Although it should save you some money, shopping for a used unit could be as time consuming as shopping for new, sometimes even more. Once you've identified your needs and RV lifestyle, you'll spend more time looking for the right floor plan that's in good shape and at the right price.

Caution must be exercised when looking for a used unit to make certain it has been maintained properly, does not have any water leaks or damage, and all systems work properly. One method used to ensure a thorough inspection is the "Good Sam Certified pre-owned RV" that bears the Good Sam approval. A rigorous inspection of over 100 points is conducted by certified RV technicians and backed by a warranty. For information, visit www.goodsamclub.com and click on "Good Sam Certified RVs" under the "Buy or Sell RV" listing.

Most RV dealers will also perform a series of tests to make sure all systems are working so that you enjoy your RV experience with fewer issues. An extended warranty and an emergency road assistance program are also good options when buying used as they will cover large-item repairs, breakdown assistance, and some offer 24-hour technical assistance. Again, Good Sam offers Good Sam ERS, an emergency road service that offers 24-hour toll-free technical assistance, a nationwide towing network, and other roadside benefits.

### Shopping the Internet

With today's technology, there are literally thousands of RVs being sold by private individuals all over the country. Before the Internet, those units could only be seen by and sold to local buyers. However the Internet brings the nation and even the world closer to products and offers private owners several avenues to sell their own units. We won't go into specific locations or URLs, since they can change quickly, but take caution and research the Web site for feedback regarding scams and fraud.

It's highly recommended to use a private-seller Web site offered by those respected in the RV Industry, such as RV clubs that have established an excellent track record for legitimate sales. Online-auction Web sites can sometimes offer great deals; however, you have no scam or fraud protection and limited ability to physically inspect the unit prior to purchasing. Don't buy blind; do your homework.

Ask for specific photos and maintenance records. Get the vehicle identification number

# USED RV EXTERIOR CHECKLIST

**FRONT**

☐ Check the windshield for rock chips or cracks. A rock chip can easily spread to a full-length crack, requiring a costly windshield replacement. Carefully inspect all edges and corners for small cracks that would indicate a stress area, such as an improper installation of the windshield, molding, or even a screw protruding from a different install.

☐ Visually inspect the entire edge of the windshield, looking for gaps or irregular spacing as windshields set in fiberglass front caps can settle and are prone to leaks.

☐ Inspect the engine compartment (front-engine models) for aftermarket installations that would restrict airflow to the radiator. Look for any noticeable fluid leaks, corrosion, or "hot spots" on exhaust pipes. Older models could be prone to exhaust leaks or warping due to excessive heat and improper cool-down procedures. A qualified mechanic can bring the engine to operating temperature and check for exhaust leaks and/or excessive temperature issues.

**SIDEWALL**

☐ Look for irregularities in the sidewall, such as warps, bulges, and soft areas that would indicate water leaks or delamination. Delamination is a separation of one or more materials used in the construction of a sidewall or roof structure in an RV. This can be caused by moisture penetration that dissolves or weakens the bonding agent or separating layers in lauan or plywood. It can also be caused by improper or insufficient adhesion, creating air pockets that later separate.

☐ Examine outside storage areas for moisture leaks and especially rusty welds, steel bracing, and hinges. Do the compartment doors close and latch easily, do the locks work, and the struts hold the door open if applicable?

☐ Inspect the entrance door for proper alignment, ease of operation, and closure. Usually a test drive is the best method to find if it has a wind leak or rattle.

☐ Check for sagging of the body at the rear of the unit or along the floor line. Run a string line from the front to the back; this could indicate frame fatigue or structural damage.

☐ Look for sagging in the body line at the rear of the vehicle. Run a string line from the front to the back and notice any sharp declines that would indicate frame damage or foundation fatigue.

☐ Check all exterior lights and service-center functions.

☐ If equipped with one or more slide-outs, operate the room extended and retracted, looking for smooth operation, any binding, and restricted operation. Also check all surrounding seals and especially the roof as debris accumulating on the top can be drawn in and ruin the rubber gasket.

**ROOF**

☐ Check the roof for soft pockets that would indicate a moisture leak, sagging around air-conditioning units, or loose /wrinkled outer skin. This is generally reserved for rubber membranes or TPO material.

---

### USED RV INTERIOR CHECKLIST

☐ Look for evidence of water leaks on the ceiling and sidewalls.

☐ Check inside the cabinets where the ceiling meets the sidewall, around the air conditioners, windows, and back cabinetry. Look for discolored fabric, wrinkled wall board, rusty trim or screws, and bulging areas in paneling or countertops.

☐ Examine upholstery and carpet for wear, matting, and any discoloration.

☐ Look for signs of a soft floor, especially in areas exposed to heat from a muffler or catalytic converter underneath. Walk down the aisle applying pressure every 12 inches looking for a noticeable sag or noise. Extreme heat or even normal fatigue of wood and block foam in the floor can cause an aggravating spongy floor.

☐ Have an expert perform a "qualified" test of the house batteries. (See Chapter 8)

☐ Test all appliances for proper operation and have a certified technician perform a propane leak, or water-column test.

☐ Run the refrigerator for at least 6 hours on all modes to verify proper function and cooling capabilities.

☐ Check the water-heater function and the anode rod, if applicable.

☐ Check all plumbing for leaking faucets, water-pump operation, and pressure.

---

(VIN) or manufacturer's serial number and contact the manufacturer to verify the unit was not totaled or even stolen.

### Price

When shopping for a new unit, the Manufacturer's Suggested Retail Price (MSRP) with all standard features and options should be clearly posted in the unit. However the final price may be affected by dealer-installed items and extended warranties. Make a list and compare features such as the weight ratings, standard versus option items, and dealer-installed items. The final price can be greatly increased simply by upgrading to a heavier weight chassis or a different engine size. Each year, *Motorhome* and *Trailer Life* magazines publish the *RV Buyer's Guide*, which lists most of the models,

pricing, and comparison features. This is a good place to start, but shopping the dealer lot and shows is still the best way to dig deeper.

When shopping for a used unit, use the *NADA RV Guide* or *Kelley Blue Book*, which can be accessed online. These will guide you through a series of checklists to verify options and mileage that could affect the price. This will give you an average and high retail value to start your negotiations. Do your homework, compare like units, chassis specifications, and options, and you will be better prepared.

### RV CLASSIFICATIONS

You know how you are going to use your RV and what you can afford, but what are all these different classes and what do they mean? Classes A, B, C, and now even B+ and Super C? The following is a definition of the different RV classifications and some discussion on the advantages or challenges with the specific type.

## CLASS A MOTORHOME

The Class A motorhome is a unit in which the drivetrain and chassis rails are supplied by a chassis manufacturer and the cab, roof, and sidewalls are all built by the RV manufacturer **(See Figure 1.4)**. There are several sub-categories within the Class As, starting with the conventional units that are typically smaller, less expensive, and have limited storage compartments than the basement and diesel-pusher Class A models. Fewer manufacturers are offering this style of unit; however there are numerous used models to choose from.

Next is the popular basement model introduced in the mid 1980s that features a foundation that raises the floor and provides lower storage compartments, thus the "basement." The advantage of a basement-style motorhome is more storage, often complete pass-through for larger

items, and a flat interior floor with no step up to the driver's and passenger compartment found in the conventional models.

At the top is the diesel pusher, which features a diesel engine designed at the back of the coach and offers the utmost in power and luxury. The diesel-pusher models usually offer more engine power, especially in horsepower and torque, providing additional weight-carrying capacity, heavier towing, and improved handling and performance. We'll discuss comparing gas versus diesel later in this section.

## CLASS C MOTORHOME

For years, the Class C motorhome was popular with the weekender or small family due to the smaller size and affordability **(Figure 1.5)**. A Class C unit starts with the drivetrain, chassis rails, and the cab with all dash instrumentation supplied by the chassis manufacturer. Many RV manufacturers choose to design an overhead bunk, utilizing the space over the cab for additional sleeping capacity or an entertainment center; however the bunk is not the

**FIGURE 1.4** Class A Motorhome

**FIGURE 1.5** Class C Motorhome

determining factor to the classification because several models opt for a more streamlined design. In recent years, manufacturers have been offering increased weight capacity and powerful drivetrains, and the Class C unit offerings have grown to accommodate more than just the weekenders and to compete more with Class A floor plans. Many owners like the convenience of a driver's and passenger door, the lower profile design, and the shorter floor plans for maneuverability and towing.

A sub-category of Class C units is the micro-mini motorhome **(Figure 1.6)**. The first one was built by National RV in 1972 during the height of the first national gas crisis. It was a hybrid of a small Toyota pickup and a slide-in truck camper, which created a wave of fuel-efficient micro-minis in the industry. In the early 1990's, Toyota discontinued the popular chassis and the micro-mini was no longer available. However, there are literally thousands of used units on the market. Check the weight-carrying capacity and the actual weight of the unit when considering one of these units.

Lately manufacturers have been marketing a new category within the Class C line dubbed the

**FIGURE 1.6** Micro-Mini Motorhome

"Super C." Like the typical Class C, these units start as a cutaway chassis—sort of, since they are usually on a very large chassis platform with engines that rival the Class A units or even semi-tractor front designs. These units are designed to compete in the Class A market with full-length floor plans, multiple slide rooms, and high-line amenities; therefore manufacturers are marketing them in the Super C category rather than a typical Class C.

## CLASS B/CAMPING VAN CONVERSION

Typically a Class B RV utilizes an existing automotive-style van and customizes the inside with compact living amenities, such as a stovetop, a small refrigerator, and a dining table. Some models have an extended roof height by cutting the roof and adding a fiberglass top cap to provide more headroom. These compact units are ideal for dual use as an everyday second vehicle and an RV on shorter trips. Other advantages are the ability to generally fit in a parking spot and its towing capabilities **(Figure 1.7)**.

As with the Super C marketing, some manufacturers are listing units as a B+ RV. Several

of the express delivery companies have been using a new front-wheel-drive delivery van that has made its way to the RV, which we'll discuss in more detail in the chassis section. However, for clarification here, these compact shell units are being customized by RV manufacturers with amenities that rival most Class C units and therefore are being marketed as B+ RVs to set them apart from the traditional customized van. Besides the obvious difference in room and livability, one important feature of the B+ models is the dual rear wheels that provide additional weight-carrying capacity and stability.

## SPORT UTILITY/TOY HAULER

Another RV description that has entered the market in recent years is the popular toy hauler RV, which can be motorized or towable **(Figure 1.8)**. A built-in "garage" or storage area is designed to hold motorcycles, ATVs, or other sports-related vehicles and they usually have a fold-down rear wall that acts as a ramp. These units still fall under the RVIA general classification for their body type such as Class A or fifth-wheel.

**FIGURE 1.7** Class B/Camping Van Conversion

## TRAILER

While most motorhome owners tow a vehicle commonly referred to as a dinghy or "toad" for auxiliary transportation, the trailer enthusiast can simply unhook the trailer and use the tow vehicle in a large variety of ways **(Figure 1.9)**.

The tow vehicle can be purchased or sold separately, which can be a major economic consideration. A trailer is usable only when stopped or parked, while occupants can move around more freely inside a motorhome, although it is recommended that all passengers remain seat-belted while driving.

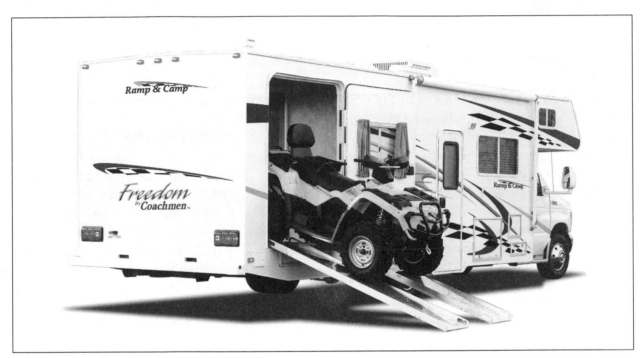

**FIGURE 1.8**   Toy Hauler

**FIGURE 1.9**   Travel Trailer

**FIGURE 1.10** Fifth-Wheel Trailer

## FIFTH-WHEEL TRAILER

Fifth-wheel trailers range from about 8,000 pounds to 18,000 pounds, plus the weight of fluids and personal effects **(Figure 1.10)**. In the more compact fifth-wheelers, a major difference between conventional models is sleeping accommodations. The smaller models provide a full-time bed in the raised forward section, which can be a real advantage when compared to a convertible bed. Headroom varies considerably, but most compact fifth-wheels require stopping while using the front section. Most of these models provide adequate living accommodations with little wasted space.

The larger (26–40 foot) fifth-wheel models provide the ultimate in livability and functionality and are popular with full-time RVers. Most include up to three large slide-outs and standing room in the front bedroom; the larger models come with all the appliances, furnishings, and audio/video entertainment features you would find in a luxury home.

As with any fifth-wheel trailer, they require a pickup truck for towing. It is important to match the proper truck to trailer, which is covered later in this chapter.

## FOLDING CAMPER TRAILER

Folding camper trailers usually feature a tent or canvas construction for pull-out or pull-up extensions and are relatively inexpensive, yet offer some unique floor plans for sleeping capacity **(Figure 1.11)**. Typical folding trailers offer two pull-out double bed platforms and a dinette that folds down into another sleeping area.

Some of the advantages of this type of unit are not only price, but, with the lighter-weight design, many can also be towed with just about any size car or truck and stored easily. Setup is quick, usually 15 to 20 minutes, which means teardown is about the same. This unit can get back into the woods easily for more "back country" camping. The challenge

**FIGURE 1.11** Folding Camper

of the folding trailer comes from the compromise of space and amenities as well as noise and movement during inclement weather. They just are not as sturdy and as well insulated as the hard-sidewall units. Their primary use is by families who want the feeling of the tent along with the convenience of camping "off the ground."

### PICKUP CAMPER

Several ingenious designs are available within the "slide-in" pickup camper classification. The lengths vary from smaller units that fit into small import trucks to large units for full-sized pickups. Living space in these campers is relatively compact due to the limitations of the truck bed and designing around the wheel wells. However, manufacturers have developed models with slide-outs, fold-outs, and even crank-up ceilings to dra-

matically increase the living space and comfort. These units are ideal for getting off the beaten path and parking next to your favorite hunting or fishing site. Plus, the camper can be removed and the truck used for everyday driving. It is an inexpensive way to get into RVing if you already have a truck that can handle the weight.

### CONSTRUCTION METHODS

For years, RV manufacturers used wood framing, loose-fill insulation, and an aluminum outer skin in roof and sidewall design. Some entry-level RVs still utilize this construction method since it requires less skill, fewer tools and jigs, fewer precise measurements, and therefore is more economical to build.

These units have less structural integrity and are usually equipped with lighter and/or fewer

**FIGURE 1.12** "Mesa" Sidewall Skin

amenities. Every RV has its purpose and place in the market.

Often these units feature a ribbed or "mesa" outer material made of aluminum or fiberglass. This is usually found in the travel-trailer market **(Figure 1.12)**, with most manufacturers using fiberglass due to the reduction of black streaks common to the aluminum skins.

Today, we see manufacturers using steel framing for risers and outriggers in the foundation, and aluminum for sidewall and roof framing. A one-piece fiberglass outer skin covers most of the industries' sidewalls and helps not only resist the elements, but also provides additional structural integrity when laminated to the framework and interior block-foam insulation.

The fiberglass skin can be purchased in a variety of finishes from a dull matte finish to the high-gloss "automotive" finish that has become popular on most motorized RVs. The high-gloss look is obtained when a fiberglass manufacturer adds several layers of a clear gel-coat finish to the

outer layers. While it provides an automotive-like shine, it can highlight sidewall imperfections such as waves or framework "bumps." Keep in mind, the extra gel coat adds nothing to the structure or longevity of the coach; it's simply for looks.

Due to weight limitations and new technology, most manufacturers have switched from steel framework in the sidewall and roof to aluminum. The process generally goes as follows: **(see Figure 1.13)**:

### STEP 1

The outer fiberglass skin is pulled onto a table or roller assembly where an adhesive is applied.

### STEP 2

A ¼-inch wood backing material is added, while some manufacturers purchase the fiberglass with

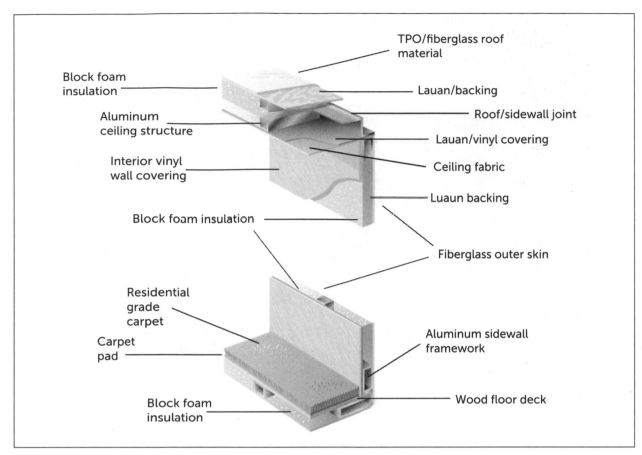

**FIGURE 1.13** Typical Sidewall Construction

a preapplied backing material to save this step while still providing structural integrity.

### STEP 3

Prewelded aluminum framework is placed on top of the sidewall material and block-foam insulation is cut to fit into the openings. Some manufacturers route the block foam to embed the framework leaving ½ inch of insulation outside the framework.

### STEP 4

More adhesive is applied and the interior paneling is placed on the top.

### STEP 5

The entire sidewall is then placed in a vacuum device known as the *Vacubond*. The Vacubond process draws all of the air and moisture out and laminates all of the layers for a specified amount of time.

Some manufacturers run the sidewall through a set of pinch rollers during each application; however, both methods produce a solid final product.

### STEP 6

Windows, doors, and other openings are cut out and the finished sidewall is sent down the line for assembly.

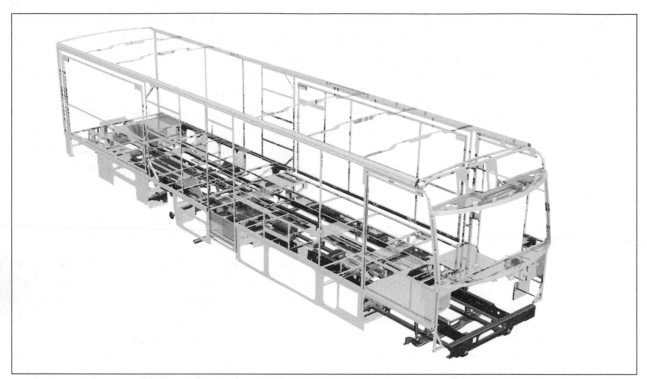

**FIGURE 1.14** Winnebago Industries "SuperStructure"

Since most RV manufacturers have a difference in their design/construction philosophy, it would be impossible to describe all the variations of roof to sidewall engineering techniques, substructure design, and structural integrity **(Figure 1.14)**. However, if you ask the right questions, and take the time to inspect the out-of-the-way spaces, you'll start to see the different materials and construction methods used. Unlike today's automobiles, they are not all made the same!

**QUESTIONS TO ASK**

*How is the weight of the roof transferred to the sidewall?* Pre-engineered interlocking-joint construction provides superior weight transfer and stability with less movement during travel.

*How is the sidewall fastened to the floor?* Sidewalls that are designed to sit or interlock with the metal perimeter framework of the foundation provide superior weight transfer. Sidewalls that

merely hang over the side and are fastened with screws rely on interior walls for additional support.

*What type of foundation supports the floor and ultimately the weight of a slide room?* Steel risers, outriggers, and perimeter framework help not only hold the weight of the floor, sidewall, and roof, but also reduce twisting and distortion that can affect slider-room performance.

*What material is used on the roof?* For years, aluminum was used for the roof material due to its durability and structural integrity. However, it posed challenges such as black streaks down the sidewall and punctures or dents. Some manufacturers switched to an ethylene propylene diene monomer (M-class) (EPDM) or rubber membrane, while others opted for a one-piece fiberglass material similar to the sidewall.

The stiff design of the fiberglass adds to the structural integrity of the roof, requires less maintenance, and has limited expansion and contraction due to temperature changes. This is, once again, a price-point consideration that falls into the category of need versus budget. I know what you're thinking—only four questions? Nope.

Throughout this book you will be guided through various exercises and evaluations to help determine the right model, floor plan, and amenities for specific RV lifestyles.

## A CLOSER LOOK

Let's say you wanted to build or remodel your home. Building a home requires exhaustive research into foundation design; framing; insulation; load-bearing walls; roofing materials; not to mention the subcontractor certification of heating, ventilation, and air conditioning (HVAC); plumbing; and electrical. In an RV we take that all for granted.

Use the same attention to detail in picking out carpet, fabric, and furnishings as you would in your home. Heavy-grade carpeting and a thicker pad not only provide additional comfort but also won't wear as quickly. Heavy-grade fabric provides less fading and holds stitching better.

Quality cabinetry will utilize solid framework that is fastened with screws versus staples, glue, and a paneled face. Look closely at the type of hinges, drawer pulls, and drawer guides. Check inside cabinets for water lines, propane lines, and wiring to see how they are routed. Are the electrical lines and appliances secure with plug-in or automotive- and residential-style connections?

An often-overlooked item in RVs is the bedroom mattress. I have yet to find a box spring in an RV as of this writing. It's not because of weight or cost, it's much simpler than that—box springs don't bend; therefore it's almost impossible to get them into the average RV.

Plus, many manufacturers simply cover a single piece of foam with little or no inner support. If you are going to spend any amount of time sleeping (comfortably) in your RV, it's recommended that you look for a mattress that has innerspring support, pillow top comfort, or opt for the "Sleep Number" type air mattress.

Less-expensive units will have more stick and paneled construction methods in cabinetry, storage compartments, and furniture. Look closely at the fit and finish of interior cabinets, trim pieces, and dash instrumentation. Once again, solid-oak cabinetry, heavy-duty carpets and fabrics, and residential-style furniture are going to hold up better to rigorous wear but will cost more, and you must decide if the price is worth the benefit.

## WHAT'S IMPORTANT?

Too often RV buyers get caught up in floor-plan design, brand name, or even prestige without looking at the construction techniques, quality of materials, and livability. (After all, it has quad slides, 400 hp, AND air horns!) Spend the same amount of time looking at details such as cabinetry, carpeting, bedding, and window treatments, the same things you would scrutinize in buying or building a home. Then determine what's important.

### A CLASSIC EXAMPLE

If you need a shelf that will sit next to a washer and dryer and hold detergent, you go to a home improvement store and buy a particle-board model for $19.95. However, if you need one to house a 200-pound TV in the living room next to a designer chair, you'll spend $1,000 on an armoire. Both are shelves, and both do the job required, however they are very different. The same holds true for RVs: different uses mean different units.

## COMPARING MODELS

### TRAVEL TRAILERS VERSUS FIFTH-WHEEL TRAILERS

There are only two advantages of a travel trailer over a fifth-wheel in my opinion: the lower cost, which allows you to try out the RV lifestyle with less of an investment, and the lower GVW rating means you can generally tow it with an SUV rather than needing to buy a "hauler."

Fifth-wheels generally tow better with a heavy-duty hitch, a larger "footprint," and without the extra tongue length.

The upper bedroom rides over the truck bed, providing a shorter overall length in a similar floor plan. The fifth-wheel is designed for extended use or even full-time camping with more storage capacity, larger or longer floor plans, and more interior space.

## FIFTH-WHEEL VERSUS MOTORIZED

If you already have a truck that is capable of towing the weight of a fifth-wheel, you'll save considerable money on buying just the camper section of your RV. However, keep in mind that trucks have a specific towing capacity and a typical half-ton vehicle is not rated for the larger fifth-wheel weights. Check your towing capacity by finding the towing guide for your make and model.

Some owners like the automotive ride of their tow truck and feel overwhelmed with the size of a motorhome. Others like to tow the fifth-wheel to a camping spot by a lake, then bring a boat back later with their truck. It really depends on how you plan to use the RV.

Several years ago, 1994 and older fifth-wheels had a distinct advantage as they offered slide rooms, and the motorized had few, if any. Today that has changed; the fifth-wheel does offer floor plans with two bedrooms for families or more than one couple traveling. However, fifth-wheels are limited by RVIA in the total amount of square footage, and thus motorhomes can offer more interior space. Keep in mind when we talk about "motorized" we are trying to compare like units with similar floor plans and lengths, as several of the smaller Class B, Class C, and Class A units would not be a like comparison.

Even the largest fifth-wheel models are under the 18,000-pound GVW rating, compared to Class A models that are up to 24,000 pounds GVWR just in the gas models. Granted, part of the weight of a Class A would be the engine and drivetrain; however, both the fifth-wheel and motorhome need substructure components like chassis rails, outriggers, and axles and tires.

Motorhomes offer more interior and exterior storage due to the weight-carrying capacity, usually longer floor-plan designs, and more residential interior styling. Using just a motorhome will reduce the overall length by 20 or more feet. But that leaves you without a vehicle to see the sites, which brings up another point of discussion. Traveling with a motorhome requires a tow vehicle to see the sites. Traveling with a fifth-wheel provides a vehicle to use for that purpose, but the larger trucks needed for towing can be difficult to maneuver in downtown traffic, find parking spots for, and, when not in use for towing, the RV becomes a high-maintenance second vehicle with lower mpg at home.

Another advantage of a motorhome is being able to pull off the road during inclement weather and to stay in your RV without getting out and unlocking doors. It is also convenient to pull over for a quick snack at a rest stop or to use the restroom.

## CLASS C VERSUS CLASS A

Class C motorhomes are popular due to the smaller lengths, providing more convenience maneuvering in and out of tight areas and getting off the beaten path. Some like the short 20- to 22-foot length that will fit in a metered spot and require no towed vehicle for touring. Keep in mind that if you are traveling without a towed vehicle, you will need to unhook from your campsite every morning for sightseeing and reconnect every night as well. With a towed vehicle, you can leave everything at the campground each day.

Usually the Class C model will have a lower MSRP, providing an economical option to enjoy the RV lifestyle. Families traveling with children like the overhead bunk available in some models as a separate sleeping area, rather than folding down the dinette or sofa every night. Others like the "automotive" feel of the cab with a driver and passenger door, lower riding height, and dash instrumentation that is more familiar.

Overall, a Class A motorhome will provide more livable space with longer floor plans, more slide rooms, and much more storage. The GVWR of a Class A chassis will range from 16,000 pounds to over 30,000 pounds, while the Class C maxes out at 14,500 pounds. Therefore, the Class A models are designed more for the full-timer or those spending an extended amount of time on the road. Heavier towing capacities, more water capacity, and more residential styling means less compromise while you're "roughing it."

## CLASS A GAS VERSUS DIESEL

As stated previously, several years ago there was a major difference between gas and diesel models in weight-carrying capacity and engine horsepower/torque.

Today that gap has grown closer with the increased horsepower and weight capacity of the gasoline chassis. The advantage of the Class A gas chassis is the MSRP. You must decide if the diesel advantages are worth the extra price for your RV lifestyle.

Some argue diesel models get better fuel economy. However, improved fuel economy when factored with the higher cost of diesel fuel (as of this writing) never makes up the difference in increased cost of a diesel chassis. More important are ride, handling, and weight-carrying capacity.

One big advantage of the diesel that most potential buyers look at is the increased torque at a lower rpm of the diesel, which simply means the ability to pull more weight and maintain better speeds during challenging road conditions, such as head winds and hills. But there are some other distinct advantages of the diesel chassis, such as the improved ride.

Larger frame rails, bigger tires, air-bag suspension, and other features of the diesel chassis provide a smoother ride and are not affected by wind shear and road conditions as much. The increased weight-carrying capacity usually means larger storage compartments, and a raised rail design provides full pass-through storage underneath, similar to a bus.

Diesel-pusher models, those with the engine in the back, allow RV designers to move the entrance door to the front and provide a larger living area with the step well. This usually translates into more residential-style furniture and cabinetry, larger slide rooms, and upgraded furnishings.

# CHAPTER TWO

# UNDERSTANDING WEIGHT

## Weight Ratings
## How Weight Ratings Affect Buying Decisions
## Weighing Your RV
## Matching Truck to Trailer
## Overload Risks

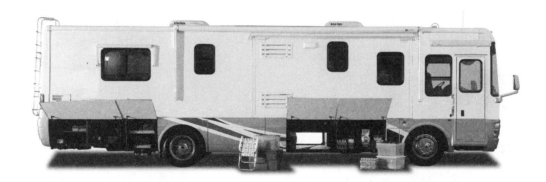

ndividual components of an RV, such as tires, brakes, axles, and even the framework, are designed to withstand only a certain amount of weight. In the case of a motorhome, the engine and transmission also factor into this weight equation. Therefore, weight ratings and limitations are set by the trailer manufacturer and the chassis manufacturer (in the case of a motorhome) to help owners reduce the risk of component failure or diminished longevity due to overloading conditions. Understanding these ratings, and knowing how to properly weigh and load your RV is critical.

## WEIGHT RATINGS

### GROSS VEHICLE WEIGHT RATING—GVWR

Gross vehicle weight rating (GVWR) is the maximum weight at which a fully loaded vehicle may be operated, including fuel, cargo, water, and all other items taken with you. Many factors determine the amount of weight an RV can carry, such as tires, braking capacity, axles, and more. Exceeding the recommended GVWR will affect more than just component longevity; stopping distance will also be affected.

### GROSS AXLE WEIGHT RATING—GAWR

Individual axles also have a maximum weight they can handle due to specific components, such as tires, bearings, and even rims. Often an RV may be under the total GVWR but overloaded on one axle due to excess cargo in the front or back, full water tanks, or heavy appliances.

### GROSS COMBINED WEIGHT RATING—GCWR

The combined weight of your RV at maximum GVWR plus the maximum weight of your tow or towed vehicle cannot exceed the recommended gross combined weight rating (GCWR).

### UNLOADED VEHICLE WEIGHT RATING—UAW

Unloaded vehicle weight rating (UAW) is the weight of the RV as manufactured at the factory with full fuel, engine oil, and coolants. It does not take into account water, propane, and your personal items.

### SLEEPING CAPACITY WEIGHT RATING—SCWR

The sleeping capacity weight rating (SCWR) is the designated number of sleeping positions at a predetermined average of 154 pounds per person (70 kg).

### CARGO CARRYING CAPACITY—CCC

Cargo carrying capacity (CCC) is the amount of cargo you can carry is determined by subtracting the UVW from the GVWR and adding water, propane, and sleeping capacity in the case of a motorhome **(Figure 2.1)**.

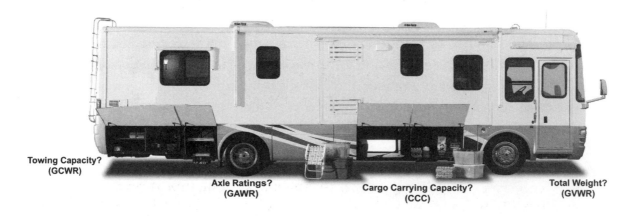

Towing Capacity?
(GCWR)

Axle Ratings?
(GAWR)

Cargo Carrying Capacity?
(CCC)

Total Weight?
(GVWR)

**FIGURE 2.1** Don't leave home without it!

## HOW WEIGHT RATINGS AFFECT BUYING DECISIONS

Let's take a look at GVWR. When shopping for a motorhome, the chassis manufacturer sets the GVWR of a specific chassis, and the RV manufacturers design and build according to those specifications. Some lighter chassis options may have limited carrying capacity and may not be suitable for longer trips, which require more gear, or dry camping, which may require more water.

Going to a heavier chassis usually means a substantial jump in price. Therefore, determine your usage, the amount of items you need to take along, and do the math. However the lighter chassis may suit your needs if you decide not to travel with full water (8.3 lbs/gallon), propane (4.2 lbs/gallon), and only have two people instead of full sleeping capacity (1.54 lbs/person factored into CCC).

The GVWR of a travel trailer will determine the type of vehicle you need to tow that much weight. Trailers vary from the lightweight pull-be-hind type, which can be towed by most trucks and even some automobiles, to the larger fifth- wheel trailers that weigh over 14,000 pounds. More information on this is available in the "Matching Truck to Trailer" section of this chapter.

## WEIGHING YOUR RV

So where do you find the ratings and what your RV or the one you are looking to buy actually weighs? In 1996, RVIA required all RV members to disclose the various weight ratings. In September 2000, the label was modified to provide more information and included the SCWR and the CCC.

As of this printing, a recent NHTSA ruling only requires the vehicle weight as it leaves the factory and the maximum cargo weight. As you can see, this new label requires more calculations by the potential owner. Use the label only as a guide and know the limitations **(Figure 2.2)**.

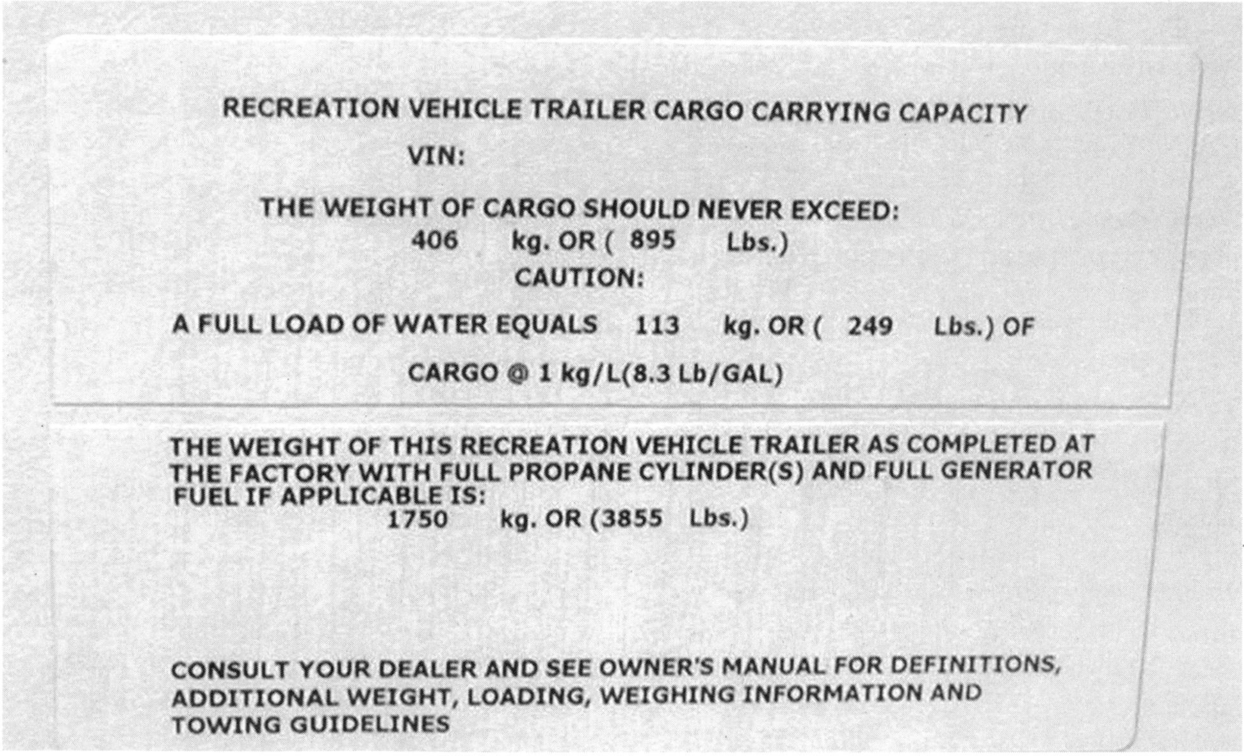

RECREATION VEHICLE TRAILER CARGO CARRYING CAPACITY

VIN:

THE WEIGHT OF CARGO SHOULD NEVER EXCEED:
406   kg. OR ( 895   Lbs.)
CAUTION:

A FULL LOAD OF WATER EQUALS   113   kg. OR ( 249   Lbs.) OF

CARGO @ 1 kg/L(8.3 Lb/GAL)

THE WEIGHT OF THIS RECREATION VEHICLE TRAILER AS COMPLETED AT THE FACTORY WITH FULL PROPANE CYLINDER(S) AND FULL GENERATOR FUEL IF APPLICABLE IS:
1750   kg. OR (3855  Lbs.)

CONSULT YOUR DEALER AND SEE OWNER'S MANUAL FOR DEFINITIONS, ADDITIONAL WEIGHT, LOADING, WEIGHING INFORMATION AND TOWING GUIDELINES

**FIGURE 2.2** Today's weight sticker provides limited information and does not include dealer-installed items.

**FIGURE 2.3** Weighing by individual wheel position is the best way to determine proper overall weight distribution.

RV's are not designed or built for optimum weight distribution. If they were, we'd see all the heavy appliances and cabinetry in the center supported by the frame rails and the aisles or walkways out around the edge. This type of floor plan would obviously not sell very well; therefore, it's not uncommon to see units with a considerable amount of weight on a particular axle, side, or even wheel position).

It's important to weigh your RV by individual wheel position **(Figure 2.3)**. With this information, you know how much capacity you have for specific compartments, water, and towing. The typical weight scale available at larger fueling stations will only provide individual axle weights by platform rather than wheel position. Individual wheel weighing can often be found at RV club rallies or dealers. One organization providing the service is the Recreation Vehicle Safety and Education Foundation (RVSEF). Check their Web site at: www.rvsafety.com for additional weighing information and locations.

If individual wheel-position weighing is not available, axle weights can be obtained using commercial-grade scales such as CAT scales. These scales can be found at most truck stops throughout the country or visit www.catscale.com and click on the location finder. This will help determine individual front- and rear-axle weights as well as the overall gross vehicle weight. Use the worksheets in **Exhibit 2.1** to record your weights (also see Appendix).

Trailer towing weights can also be obtained by placing the front wheels of the tow vehicle on the first platform, the rear wheels on the second, and the trailer wheels on the third.

After packing up your coach for the next great adventure, it's a good idea to have it weighed because you may often underestimate the amount of stuff you put in your rig. If individual position weighing is not available, sectioned platform scales can be used if they are level and do not have steel pillars on the sides. Place only the driver-side wheels on the platforms first, then the passenger

# Motorhome Weight Worksheet

| FRONT AXLE | REAR AXLE | TOWED VEHICLE |
|---|---|---|
| 1. Mfg GAWR _____ | 3. Mfg GAWR _____ | Towing Capacity _____ |
| 2. Actual GAWR _____ | 4. Actual GAWR _____ | Actual Weight _____ |

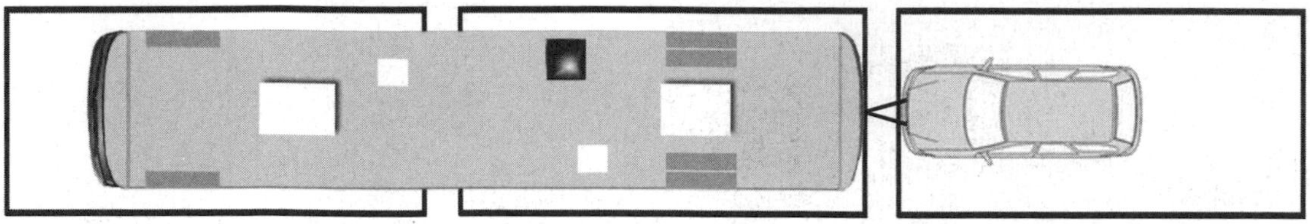

Item 1 minus item 2 = _____      Item 3 minus item 4 = _____

5. Mfg Gross Vehicle Weight Rating _____      6. Actual Weight (2 + 4) _____

# Trailer Weight Worksheet

| TOW VEHICLE FRONT AXLE | TOW VEHICLE REAR AXLE | TRAILER WEIGHT |
|---|---|---|
| 1. Mfg GAWR _____ | 3. Mfg GAWR _____ | 5. Mfg GVWR _____ |
| 2. Actual GAWR _____ | 4. Actual GAWR _____ | Actual Weight _____ |

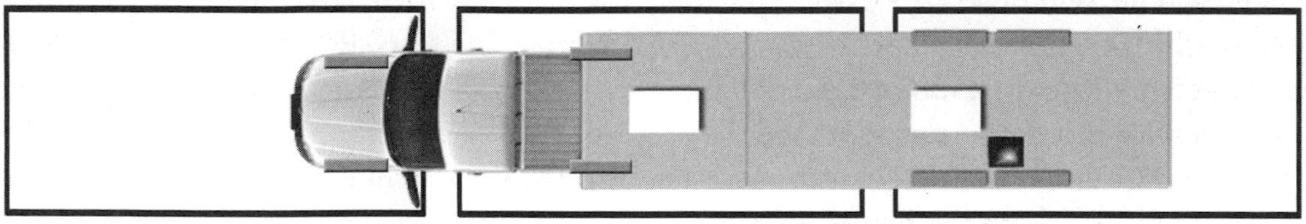

EXHIBIT 2.1  Weight Worksheets

side, which will provide individual weights. Finally, add them up for GAWR and GVWR ratings.

Trailers should be weighed with the tow vehicle hitched to the trailer but off the scale. This is the weight used to determine if the axle or tire load ratings are too heavy. Then unhitch the tow vehicle to determine the weight of the trailer or GVWR. Smaller trailers will have a more balanced weight distribution and not require individual wheel-position weighing; however, larger trailers with multiple slide rooms, larger generators, refrigerators, other appliances, and especially fifth-wheels should be weighed by individual wheel position.

The amount of weight on the hitch is also an important factor that affects the trailer's stability and therefore handling. Hitch weight is measured by positioning the trailer so the hitch support (tow vehicle or tongue jack) is off the scale. Keep in mind, load-distributing hitch-spring bars will prevent an accurate reading.

Weigh the trailer wheels only; subtract that figure from the trailer's gross weight to determine hitch weight.

If a single platform scale is all that is available, you will need to weigh your vehicle in several different positions.

### WEIGHING THE MOTORHOME

To determine the weight of a motorhome, first, get an overall weight with the entire RV on the platform; next, just the front axle, then the back axle, driver side, and finally the passenger side (Figure 2.4).

### WEIGHING THE TOW VEHICLE/TRAILER

First weigh the tow vehicle with the trailer attached, but not on the platform. With the tow vehicle attached, weigh only the trailer on the platform. Next weigh the trailer unhitched from the tow vehicle. Weigh each individual side, and finally weigh just the tow vehicle unhitched from the trailer. The difference in weight from the hitched and unhitched will determine the amount of hitch weight. *It is important your vehicle be level when weighing.*

### MATCHING TRUCK TO TRAILER

If you currently have a vehicle you are planning to use for towing, it is critical you know its towing capacity. Each year Trailer Life publishes a comprehensive towing guide that can be found on their Web site at www.trailerlife.com. Go to the Tech tab. Here you will find a link to several model years and information on both cars and trucks. Match the year, model, and engine type and see what weight-carrying capacity your vehicle can handle (Figure 2.5).

Another weight factor to consider is the amount of weight being placed on the rear axle and GAWR. Usually a pull-behind trailer will only add approximately 10 percent of the final weight to the tow bar; however, fifth-wheel trailers can be more of a problem, especially those with large overhead bunks and a wide-open storage compartment up front (Figure 2.6). Even if your unit is under the GVWR and GAWR ratings initially, it is a good idea to get your entire rig weighed after loading it up for the first road trip. CAT scales have platforms that section your vehicle's front tires, back axle, and trailer to obtain the proper ratings. You may need to shift some personal

It is important that your vehicle be level when weighing:

| | |
|---|---|
| Diesel fuel | 6.6 lbs/gallon |
| Gasoline | 6.0 lbs/gallon |
| Water | 8.3 lbs/gallon |
| Propane | 4.2 lbs/gallon |

**FIGURE 2.4** A platform scale will provide the most accurate axle-weight readings.

**FIGURE 2.5** Trailer Life's Towing Guides

**FIGURE 2.6** Matching the proper towing and weight-carrying capacity is critical.

items either forward or back to adjust the weight.

One more consideration for matching a truck to a fifth-wheel trailer is the turning radius of the RV and the length of the bed. Some short-bed truck models only have a 6-foot, 6-inch bed, which means the hitch is generally mounted in the middle or at around 3 feet, 3 inches. Today's wide-body RVs measure 102.5 inches wide or slightly over 8 feet, 6 inches, which will create a problem during tight turns. Sliding hitches are available for these applications.

## OVERLOAD RISKS

Exceeding the recommended GVWR or GAWR may not have immediate or even noticeable consequences, but eventually you will find diminished reliability and performance. Some noticeable effects could be increased stopping performance, decreased fuel economy, and decreased performance such as acceleration and handling. Exceeding the tire ratings is more critical and covered in detail in the tire section. An overloaded or underinflated tire is dangerous and could fail, immediately putting you in an unsafe situation **(Figure 2.7)**.

**FIGURE 2.7** Overloading an RV can cause premature component failure.

# CHAPTER THREE

# TIRE BASICS

### Read a Good Tire Lately?
### The Importance of Tire Pressure
### Checking Tire Pressure
### Proper Tire Blocking
### Weather Checking
### Tire Storage and Maintenance
### Replacing Tires
### Verifying Proper Tire Size

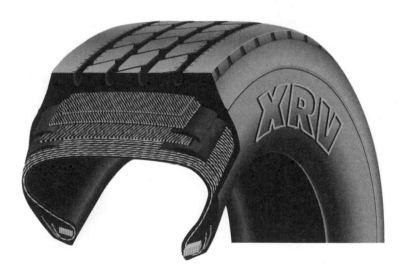

Tires can be one of the most vulnerable components on an RV and yet the most neglected. They are the only contact point between an RV and the road, yet most RV owners spend little time with tire maintenance. In just one month, even a perfectly good tire can lose 1 to 2 pounds of air pressure. We can't just fill the tire to recommended psi and forget about it, although a recent survey indicated almost half of all RVers say they go six months or more before checking the pressure. That could mean a loss of up to 12 psi, which becomes a serious underinflation situation. And keep in mind; it's the air inside that supports your vehicle, not the tire itself (**Figure 3.1**).

**FIGURE 3.1** Proper tire pressure, maintenance, and inspection are critical to enhanced tire performance.

Although new technology and more information on weight and pressure have helped reduce tire failures, it is still a common topic of discussion at campgrounds and RV forums. The purpose of this section is to help educate you on tire ratings, limitations, and suggested maintenance.

## READ A GOOD TIRE LATELY?

Tires have a tremendous amount of information stamped on the sidewall, and knowing what this information means is critical. First, the tire size will provide information about the usage, width, profile, and diameter of the bead.

Here is an example of the common light truck tire, LT235/85R16:

**LT**—stands for light truck; on other applications **P** stands for passenger car, and **ST** is for special trailer.

**235**—is the width of the metric measurement of the tire at the widest point.

**/**—indicates ratio.

**85**—is the aspect ratio, or the height of the tire compared to the width, which in this case is 85 percent.

**R**—indicates radial design.

**16**—is the diameter of the rim in inches.

Larger tires used on motorhomes start with metric-width measurements and don't have usage designations such as 275/80R22.5 LRG **(Figure 3.2)**. The numbers indicate the same information as a passenger tire; however, the LRG stands for load range G. The load range for passenger tires is usually stamped separately on passenger and trailer tires.

## LOAD-CARRYING CAPACITY

The load range or weight-carrying capacity is also stamped on the sidewall, either as a separate listing or as part of the size in larger units. In the past, tire manufacturers listed "ply" ratings, and many RVers looked for the heavier ply ratings or sidewall thickness to reduce the potential for tire failure.

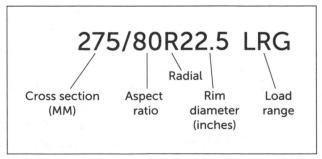

**FIGURE 3.2** A typical tire sidewall provides a wealth of information about size, weight ratings, and more.

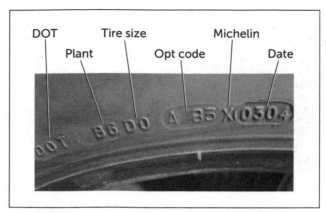

**FIGURE 3.3** Most tire manufacturers recommend replacing a tire that is more than ten years old.

With new technology and materials used in the construction of tires, the ply system is no longer applicable. It's more important to look at the load-carrying capacity.

### HAPPY BIRTHDAY!

The longevity of your tires will be determined not only by weight and pressure but also by factors such as age, weather, and storage condition. That's why, in addition to regular tire maintenance, it's important to have a qualified tire technician inspect your tires on a yearly basis. Most tire manufacturers recommend a tire be replaced after ten years of service, although most RV tires don't last that long.

The age of your tire is stamped on the sidewall as a Department of Transportation (DOT) code. Locate this code starting with DOT and ending with the week and year of manufacture **(Figure 3.3)**.

## THE IMPORTANCE OF TIRE PRESSURE

Maintaining proper tire pressure is the most important factor in prolonging the life of your tires and ultimately reducing tire failure while driving. Underinflation reduces the weight-carrying capacity of your tires, which are probably very close to the maximum capacity already. Underinflation also causes premature wear, excess heat, and uneven tread wear.

Overinflation will decrease the amount of the treads' contact to the road and cause problems with handling, traction, and stopping distance.

### CORRECT TIRE PRESSURE

Most RV owners believe correct tire pressure information can be obtained from the data-plate sticker inside the unit or stamped on the sidewall of the tire. In our cars and trucks, we use those psi ratings, and it seems to work without failure. However, in the case of a car, we usually are not adding substantial weight that would place the tire in an overload condition.

The psi stamped on the tire is the maximum inflation pressure and also the minimum pressure required to carry the maximum load also stamped on the sidewall. To find the correct or optimum tire pressure, you must obtain the weight on each wheel position of your fully loaded vehicle **(Figure 3.4)**.

Once you determine the weight on the wheel position, refer to the tire manufacturer's tire load inflation chart available on its Web site. For example, a 275/80R22.5 LRG with 5,400 pounds on

**FIGURE 3.4** Individual wheel position weights are the best method to obtain proper tire pressures.

the left front, 5,100 on the right front, 8,500 on the left-rear duals, and 9,200 on the right-rear duals, for control of the RV it is critical that the tire pressure be the same across the axle. Therefore you must "overinflate" the right front and right rear dual tires. Checking Michelin's tire chart, notice that these tires must be inflated to 95 psi "cold."

To determine the air pressure on the rear duals, refer to the chart and again take the heaviest position, which is 9,200 pounds, and here see that 85 psi will support up to 9,380 pounds on two dual wheels. It is important that you do not exceed the maximum inflation stamped on the tire **(Table 3.1)**. Additional tables are available in the Appendix, page 223.

## WHEN SHOULD YOU CHECK YOUR TIRES?

Always check your tire pressure before starting out on a trip when they are "cold," meaning you have not driven more than a few miles. It is not

TABLE 3.1 Load Inflation Table (275/80R22.5 LRH—Michelin XZE, XZA3)

| PSI | | 75 | 80 | 85 | 90 | 95 | 100 | 105 | 110 | 115 | 120 |
|---|---|---|---|---|---|---|---|---|---|---|---|
| kPa | | 520 | 550 | 590 | 620 | 660 | 690 | 720 | 760 | 790 | 830 |
| Lbs | Single | 4915 | 5175 | 5435 | 5690 | 5940 | 6190 | 6435 | 6680 | 6920 | 7160 |
| | Dual | 9080 | 9560 | 10030 | 10500 | 10970 | 11430 | 11880 | 12330 | 12780 | 13220 |
| kPa | Single | 2240 | 2340 | 2470 | 2570 | 2710 | 2800 | 2900 | 3030 | 3120 | 3250 |
| | Dual | 4120 | 4320 | 4560 | 4760 | 5000 | 5180 | 5360 | 5600 | 5760 | 6000 |

**Maximum load and pressure on the sidewall**

| Single | 7160 lbs @ 120 PSI |
|---|---|
| Dual | 6610 lbs @ 120 PSI |
| Single | 3250 KG @ 830 kPa |
| Dual | 3000 KG @ 830 kPa |

uncommon for a tire to increase 10 or more psi as the temperature heats up and driving increases. Here are a few other recommendations:

- Use a professional gauge and have it calibrated at a certified tire center.
- Don't eyeball or use the "thump" of a small bat or club.
- Check at least once a month.
- Check before and after storing your rig.

## MAKE IT EASY

The harder it is to check your tires, especially duals, the less likely you will do it. If using valve-stem extensions for inside duals, verify they are the latest technology "cored" stems that will not lose air if cut or sliced.

Older models were simply tube extensions with the valve at the end. A slight cut, or rubbing against a rim or random debris, could cause sudden air loss.

"At-a-glance" pressure-checking systems, available at most truck-repair facilities, display a color such as the "Cat's Eye" system, or others that combine the two valve stems into a common, easily accessible fitting with a direct-reading gauge to visually check pressure during your walkaround.

Several aftermarket companies offer a remote sensor with an easy-to-read panel located on the dash. It may seem expensive initially; however, the replacement of one tire often is more than the price of the sensor, not to mention the cost of a service call or tow.

## SUDDEN LOSS OF PRESSURE

Knowing what to do in case of a tire failure or sudden loss of pressure is critical to maintaining control of your vehicle. When you experience a sudden loss of pressure your instinct is to slam on the brakes and get to the side of the road. This is actually the opposite of what is recommended. As you lose pressure, the momentum of your vehicle will start to shift to that direction instead of moving forward. When you apply braking pressure, you increase that momentum shift and actually make it more difficult to maintain control the vehicle.

You should depress the accelerator—*yes, actually increase speed*—which will help direct the momentum back to the forward position, and then slowly reduce speed when you have control of the vehicle. Michelin has developed an excellent video that all RV owners should watch called *The Critical Factor*. To view this video, download it from their Web site at: www.michelin-rvtires.com and click on the video library.

## PROPER TIRE BLOCKING

Many RV owners like to "block" their tires, which means using wood or predesigned plastic materials to help raise and level the rig. Use extreme caution to ensure the entire tire is supported by the width of the block. In the case of duals, *both* tires should be blocked evenly; if not, the one sidewall could become weak or damaged.

As stated before, this may not be an immediate failure, but sometime later down the road—when most inconvenient—as the material in the sidewall and tread continue to weaken, the tire will eventually fail.

For some correct and incorrect methods of blocking your tires, see **Figure 3.5**.

## WEATHER CHECKING

Unlike passenger car tires that get used almost every day, RV tires are subjected to very harsh conditions, especially sitting for long periods of time with the sun beating down on them. This results in a condition called *weather checking* and can ruin a tire prematurely. During your pretrip inspection, look for tiny cracks in the rubber surface of the sidewall. If the crack is less than $1/32$ inch, the tire is okay to drive. If it's between $1/32$ and $2/32$ inch, it should be inspected by a certified tire center. Anything over $2/32$ inch should be replaced. Michelin has provided a handy weather-checking guide **(Figure 3.6)**.

Here are a few maintenance tips to reduce damage to your tires:

- Keep your tires clean by washing them with a mild detergent soap.
- Do not use harsh chemicals, alcohol-based cleaning products, or abrasive cleaners.
- Avoid prolonged exposure to the sun, heat, cold, or moisture.
- Do not use tire "dressings" that contain petroleum, alcohol, or silicone. This will cause deterioration and accelerated aging.
- If repairing a nail or other type of hole in your tire, *never plug the tire*. Always have a qualified repair facility use the recommended patch.

## TIRE STORAGE AND MAINTENANCE

Most RVers are not using their units year round, and therefore will need to store them for an extended period of time. A little tire maintenance will help prolong the life of your tires.

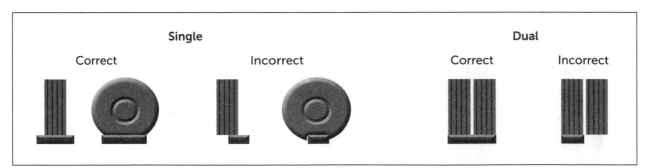

**FIGURE 3.5** Proper tire blocking will extend the life of your tires.

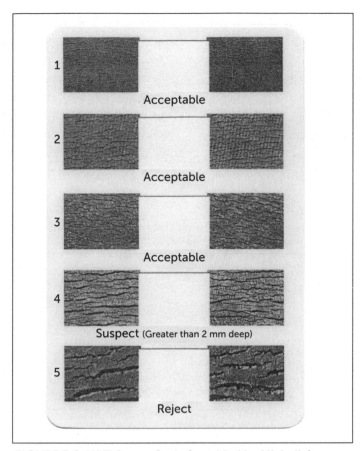

**FIGURE 3.6** MRT Ozone Scale (provided by Michelin)

- Clean your tires with water and soap prior to storage of your unit.
- Check to ensure proper inflation.
- It is recommended that you place a piece of cardboard, plastic, or wood as a barrier between your tires and the surface. **(Figure 3.7 & 3.8)**

Before removing your vehicle from storage check the following:

- Proper tire inflation
- Tire wear and alignment
- Your tires should wear in a smooth, uniform pattern if they are maintained properly and have the correct inflation.

If you experience handling difficulties, a bumpy ride, or uneven wear patterns, have your tires checked for balance and alignment. Most chassis manufacturers recommend you have your vehicle aligned after the initial purchase since items you bring on a trip will increase the weight and ultimately affect the factory-set alignment when the coach is unloaded.

- Tire manufacturers recommend rotating your tires periodically, some at every 6,000-mile interval. Check your chassis manual for recommendations.
- If you carry a spare make sure you include it in the rotation

**FIGURE 3.7** When storing your vehicle, clean the tires with soap and water and place a moisture barrier between the tire and the ground.

**FIGURE 3.8** If stored outside, cover the tires to protect them from UV rays.

**FIGURE 3.9** A penny may be used to measure tread depth, but a depth gauge is recommended

## REPLACING TIRES

All tires sold in North America are required to have a tread-wear indicator to help warn drivers that their tires have reached an unsafe wear condition. The depth of these indicators will vary according to the different tire applications and weight ratings.

The Rubber Manufacturers Association recommends that tires on vehicles of more than 10,000 pounds gross weight be replaced when less than 4/32 inch of tread depth remains (not including tread-wear indicators).

On vehicles less than 10,000 pounds gross weight, front tires should be replaced when worn to the tread-wear indicators, or when 2/16 inch or less of the tread remains. A depth gauge is recommended to verify the amount of tread left on your tire; however, a quick reference can be obtained using a penny **(Figure 3.9)**. Place the penny into the tread groove with Lincoln's head facing down into the groove. If his head is covered, you will have more than the legal amount; if not, it's time to replace.

When it is time to replace your tires, there are several critical factors you need to be aware of. Always match the load range and size with the original tires. If replacing just one tire, it is recommended to match not only these factors but also the tread design and usually the manufacturer or brand to ensure a proper match.

Replacing a tire with a different size can affect the speedometer reading, vehicle clearance, wheelwell clearance, and is especially important in the spacing of dual tires.

## VERIFYING PROPER TIRE SIZE

When purchasing a used unit, you don't always know that the proper tire size was installed by the previous owner. If the unit was overloaded and the tires underinflated, tire failure could have occurred. Without proper tire education, many owners simply blame the tire manufacturer and decide to step up to a larger or heavier tire, which is actually masking the problem.

To verify the correct tires are on a used unit, locate the data plate either inside a motorhome or attached to the front hitch or tongue of a trailer. This data plate will list the Original Equipment Manufacturer (OEM) installed tires sizes. Anything other than OEM sizes must be verified for width, clearance, and the other factors listed previously.

# CHAPTER FOUR

# MOTORHOME CHASSIS

## The History of the RV Chassis
## Class A Chassis—Gas
## Class A Chassis—Diesel
## Gas Versus Diesel
## Class C Chassis
## Vehicle Identification Numbers
## General Maintenance

O ver the years, the ability to choose your own chassis has been limited due to availability and weight ratings. The Class C market was limited to Chevrolet in light/short models and only Ford in the higher GVWR models. The Class A market provided a choice between Chevrolet and Ford but little choice when it came to the diesel models. Each year, *MotorHome* magazine publishes the *Dinghy Guide*, which features the various chassis offerings for the year, including wheelbase length, engine offerings, gross vehicle weight ratings, and towing allowances.

In the past few years, new chassis innovations have provided more of a choice for RVers, including the expansive offerings from Workhorse, Freightliner, and the Sprinter Class C chassis. In 2009 the excitement continued with the first ever Sprinter Class A chassis, new front-engine diesels, rear-engine gas, and hybrids. These recent chassis developments have opened new avenues for RV manufacturers with more power, weight-carrying capacity, and towing ability.

## THE HISTORY OF THE RV CHASSIS

Finding the true origin of the first motorhome chassis is a journey in itself. Many credit Ray Frank with building the first Class A on a Dodge truck chassis and actually calling it a motorhome in 1953. However, there have been numerous "customized" rigs prior to that, most of which were house cars built on an existing truck chassis or a converted bus. In 1958, Frank's son, Ronald, started Frank Motor Homes and by 1962 Dodge was advertising Dodge motorhomes. As Ronald ultimately went out of business, the next motorized RV company to emerge was Travco, which had purchased the body molds from Ronald and partnered with Dodge.

In 1958, Winnebago Industries started manufacturing Aljo travel trailers and introduced a Class A motorhome in 1966, again built on the Dodge chassis.

Over the years there were a few other chassis options, such as the front-wheel-drive GMC built from 1973–1977, the Ford truck platform customized by Newell in 1968, and a diesel pusher introduced a few years later.

Motorhome chassis have evolved substantially from the early days in the mid-sixties when the only choice was the underpowered Dodge. In the early 1970s, Chevrolet came into the market and provided people with another choice until Dodge discontinued production in the mid-seventies. Then Ford entered in the late eighties and the debate began. Ford was the first to offer a fuel-injected engine and overdrive transmission. With the new competition came a push to increase horsepower and weight-carrying capacity.

The reason for this history lesson is to provide information on older models and point out some areas of concern. Due to the limited choice of chassis manufacturers, there was very little consideration for weight and towing ratings. In 1998, the Recreational Vehicle Industry Association (RVIA) required weight labels to inform potential buyers of the carrying and towing capacities of specific units. Prior to that, overloading was a common problem, especially with the introduction of the basement models. Vast storage compartments reaching from front to back tempted owners with little education on weight ratings and carrying capacity to fill them to the brim. For more on these ratings, refer to Chapter 2, "Understanding Weight Ratings."

In the formative years of RVing, you didn't have all the modern conveniences of today. It was a simpler time for RVing, more intended for getting away and not taking it all with us. There were no microwave ovens, large-screen TVs, or solid-surface countertops.

However, when you look at purchasing an older, used RV, you need to be informed before upgrading to today's technology.

As stated earlier, older RVs did not have weight labels other than the GVWR, which is the total amount the unit can weigh after the unit is loaded with people, liquids, and your stuff.

## CLASS A CHASSIS—GAS

It started with the Dodge Chassis and a 318-cubic-inch engine. Then along came Chevrolet, Ford, and even a brief stint by John Deere. Due to the weight limitations of the earlier Class A chassis, several features found on today's models were not available, such as slide-outs, solid-surface countertops, or drivers' doors. Most of the weight issues were caused by the lighter front axle rating and the weight of the drivetrain.

For example, the Chevrolet P-30 chassis, one of the most popular chassis used in the eighties and nineties, had a GVWR of 16,000 pounds, but it only offered a 5,000-pound gross axle weight rating (GAWR) on the front axle, which left little weight-carrying capacity once a driver and passenger were factored in.

Today, Class A chassis are available from the following manufacturers.

## WORKHORSE CUSTOM CHASSIS COMPANY (WCC)

The Workhorse Custom Chassis Company was formed in 1998 after acquiring the Chevrolet P-30 Class A division, and it introduced its first Class A chassis in January of 1999. Since then, it has expanded to offering gasoline-powered chassis ratings of 10,000 to 26,000 GVW and is the only source of GM gasoline engine and power trains in a Class A. In 2005, Navistar, the parent corporation of International Truck and Engine Corporation, purchased Workhorse Custom Chassis Corporation and it offers the following under the WCC name.

### Front Engine Gasoline (W-Series)

The W-Series offers GVW ratings of 20,700 (W20), 22,000 (W22), and 24,000 (W24) pounds, all powered by the GM Vortec 8.1L engine with 340 hp at 4,200 rpm **(Figure 4.1)**. All three chassis options offer an impressive weight-carrying and towing capacity. Even more impressive is the three-year/36,000-mile limited engine warranty, five-year/200,000-mile limited Allison transmission warranty, and three-year/36,000-mile roadside assistance program, all of which are transferrable to second owners.

For shorter applications, a 16,000-pound GVW chassis (W16 and W18) features the GM Vortec 6.0L engine and an 18,000-pound GVW chassis (W18) powered by the GM Vortec 8.1L engine. Both are equipped with a GM 4-speed Hydra-Matic transmission.

**FIGURE 4.1** Workhorse Class A Chassis

FIGURE 4.2 Workhorse UFO Chassis

### Rear Engine Gas—
### Universal Fuel Option (UFO)

The UFO is a 26,000-pound GVW rear-engine chassis that can be outfitted with a GM Vortec 8.1L engine, Cummins ISB 6.7L diesel, or International Maxxforce 7L diesel **(Figure 4.2)**. All three options offer the Allison 6-speed transmission.

### FORD F-53

The Ford F-53 Super Duty® chassis **(Figure 4.3)** features a 362 hp Triton® V10 gasoline engine, 5-speed TorqShift® transmission, and a five-year/60,000-mile powertrain warranty on all GVWR chassis. It is available from 16,000 pounds GVW to 24,000 pounds GVW.

FIGURE 4.3 Ford F-53 Class A Chassis

## CLASS A CHASSIS—DIESEL

### WORKHORSE CUSTOM CHASSIS

#### Front-Engine Diesel (WD)

Currently, WCC offers a 16,000 and 20,000 GVW front-engine diesel Class A chassis featuring an International Maxxforce diesel engine with 200 hp (W16D) and 230 hp (W20D). Refer to "Diesel Versus Gas" in Chapter 1, "Choosing the Right RV," for a comparison of horsepower, torque, and rpm.

#### Universal Fuel Option (UFO)

The UFO is a 26,000-pound GVW rear-engine chassis that can be outfitted with a GM Vortec 8.1L engine, Cummins ISB 6.7L diesel, or International Maxxforce 7L diesel. All three options offer the Allison 6-speed transmission.

### Freightliner Custom Chassis

#### *XC Chassis*

Freightliner's popular XC chassis is available in GVW ratings of 26,850 to 34,000 and offering the powerful Cummins® 5.9L 300 hp diesel up to the 8.9L with 400 hp **(Figure 4.4)**. It also features a tight sixty- degree turning radius and optional independent front suspension (IFS). Several RV manufacturers use the Freightliner XC chassis as a base for their own specifically engineered foundation.

#### *Front-Engine Diesel (FRED)*

Freightliner manufactures a front-engine diesel chassis called the *FRED* that features two Cummins 6.7L engines, one with 300 hp and 620 pound-feet of torque, and the other with 340 hp and 640 pound-feet of torque.

Some manufacturers like the increased carrying capacity of 22,000 and 26,000 pounds GVWR,

**FIGURE 4.4** Freightliner XC Chassis

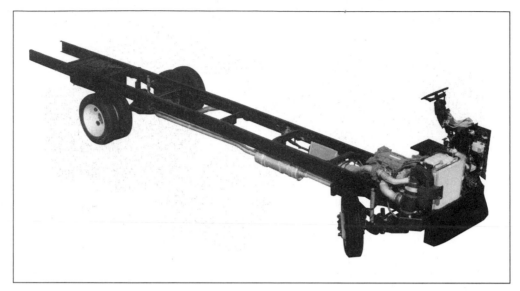

**FIGURE 4.5** Freightliner Front Engine Diesel—"FRED"

and the lowered engine means no protruding engine cover commonly referred to as a "doghouse." Noise levels seldom exceed that of the gasoline engine, while fuel economy is superior **(Figure 4.5)**.

### ecoFRED

Recently, Freightliner introduced the ecoFRED, which combines an internal-combustion diesel engine with an electric motor driven by lithium-ion batteries.

This chassis has been used in its commercial vehicle market for more than ten years. An energy-management system selects the most efficient mode of operation—diesel, electric, or both—for the RV, depending on engine speed and driving conditions.

Hybrid-electric technology constantly recharges ecoFRED's batteries through the operation of its diesel.

Cummins® ISB 6.7L electronic diesel engine provides 300 hp and a full 620 pound-feet of torque engine and through regenerative braking—eliminating the need to plug into an electrical source for recharging

### MC-L Front-Engine Diesel

FCCC also offers a lighter-weight chassis in the MC-L series with 18,000-pound GVWR and the

Cummins 6.7 L 200 hp and 520 pound-feet of torque and an Allison 6-speed transmission.

## SPARTAN CHASSIS, INC.

Some manufacturers are offering their high-line coaches on the Spartan chassis, featuring the Cummins diesel engines ranging from 425 to 600 hp, Allison 6-speed transmission, and fifty-five-degree turning radius.

Several manufacturers use the Spartan chassis as a base for their own specifically engineered foundations.

## SPRINTER CLASS A

As of this writing, Winnebago Industries is the first RV manufacturer using the 11,300 pound GVWR Sprinter chassis built by Daimler World Wide in a Class A application featuring 154 hp. 3 ol, 6-cylinder turbo-diesel engine and 5-speed transmission **(Figure 4.6)**.

Since the cab and dash instrumentation is not provided by the chassis manufacturer—rather the motohome manufacturer—it falls into the Class A category.

**FIGURE 4.6** Sprinter Class A Chassis

## GAS VERSUS DIESEL

For years, the difference between gas and diesel was worlds apart with gas-powered RVs limited to smaller payloads, lighter towing capacity, and even shorter lengths. However the line has blurred with higher GVWR and more horsepower in the gasoline chassis while diesel chassis prices have become more affordable.

What drives an RV up a steep grade and provides acceleration is torque. However, most people look simply at horsepower ratings in the diesel engines such as the 6.7L Cummins with 300 hp and more.

While the gasoline engines generally have been rated by displacement, such as the Vortec 8.1L and Triton V10, both of these engines are providing more horsepower as stated earlier, with the Vortec at 340 hp and the Triton at 362.

Keep in mind, the horsepower rating can only be achieved at the peak rpm, therefore it's a combination of hp, rpm, axle ratio, and transmission. A diesel engine provides peak horsepower at a lower rpm, which is superior for towing and hill climbing.

However, there are several other comparisons of gasoline versus diesel that you should consider, which were covered in Chapter One.

## CLASS C CHASSIS

### FORD

Ford offers two Class C chassis options, the E-350 and E-450 with a 305 hp 6.8L Super Duty V10 SEFI Triton engine with 11,500 pounds GVW, and the E-450 with the same engine in a GVW rating of 14,500 pounds **(Figure 4.7)**.

### CHEVY-WORKHORSE CLASS C

Available in three GVW ratings: 9,600, 12,300, and 14,050, this Class C chassis features the 323 hp Vortec 6.0L V8 and 4-speed overdrive transmission.

### SPRINTER

Daimler World Wide, the parent company of Dodge, Freightliner, and Mercedes Benz, builds the Sprinter chassis, originally available in a Class C and Class B configuration and marketed through all three companies. **(Figure 4.8)**

It is available with a 3.0L Mercedes Benz CDI six-cylinder, 154 hp turbo-diesel engine, 5-speed

**FIGURE 4.7** Ford E-450 Class C Chassis

automatic transmission, and 4-wheel ABS brakes. Daimler World Wide has announced that the Sprinter will no longer be marketed through Dodge, and future owners will be required to get warranty work only from authorized Freightliner Truck service centers.

## VEHICLE IDENTIFICATION NUMBERS

Your RV comes with two distinctively different vehicle identification numbers: the RV manufacturer's serial number and the chassis serial number. These numbers can be found on the data plate located on the inside of the RV, usually on the driver-side wall, or driver's door pillar if so equipped.

The RV manufacturer's serial number is used by dealers and manufacturers to identify built date, which helps to verify specific components and appliances that were installed at the time of build, and the purchase date to verify warranty dates.

The Vehicle Identification Number (VIN) is the legal identification of the chassis and not only provides chassis information but is also used to register the vehicle with the Department of Transportation (DOT).

It is not uncommon to have a discrepancy in the model year of the chassis and the actual RV, as manufacturers will stockpile chassis, and actual model-year-changeover dates seldom match.

Therefore, it is important that your local DOT register your vehicle as the RV model year. If you are having difficulty with this registration, contact your dealer or the RV manufacturer for assistance in getting the proper year.

## GENERAL MAINTENANCE

### ENGINE OIL

The engine of your RV chassis is lubricated with oil that is pumped from the oil pan located un-

**FIGURE 4.8** Sprinter Class C Chassis

derneath the engine, through an oil filter to an external oil cooler usually located in the lower section of the radiator, thus removing engine heat. This cooler oil then returns to the engine through specific routes, lubricating the various moving parts, and then back into the oil pan.

## OIL QUALITY

The American Petroleum Institute (API) designates the quality of oil with standards on each label. The API "Starburst" certified symbol on the front of the container is recommended for all gasoline engines, while the API-CG-4 is best for diesel engines. The CG-4 may appear alone or in combination with other API designations, such as CG-4/SH, CG-4/SJ, SH/CG-4, or SJ/CG-4.

## VISCOSITY

Engine-oil viscosity, or thickness, has an effect on fuel economy with lower viscosity providing the best. However, higher temperature weather conditions require thicker oils for lubrication. Engine damage could occur if not using the recommended viscosity.

## GASOLINE ENGINES

All engine manufacturers provide a viscosity chart in the owner's manual, and most recommend SAE 5W-30 and SAE 10W-30 if the temperature stays above 0°F (−18°C). If temperatures are above 40°F (4°C), most recommend a straight SAE 30 weight.

**NOTE:** Both Workhorse and Ford have removed the SAE 10W-40 recommendation because research laboratories have found reduced fuel economy, inadequate additives, as well as inferior viscosity requirements in test results.

## DIESEL ENGINES

SAE 15W-40 is recommended for operating temperatures above 0°F (−18°C). However, check your owner's manual for temperatures above 32°F (0°C).

## CHECKING OIL LEVELS

It is critical to check your engine oil periodically to reduce the potential for engine damage. Oil levels should be checked warm during fuel stops or when the engine has been running for at least 15 minutes and with the engine shut off, which will allow the oil to drain back into the pan for an accurate reading.

Also, make sure the vehicle is level and the dipstick is properly seated to the tube before removing to read. Oil levels above the full mark or lower by over 1 quart can cause aeration that could make valve lifters collapse and cause major engine damage.

## CHANGING THE OIL

Engine manufacturers have different oil change recommendations. For example, Ford recommends 7,500 miles in their *2010 E-Series Scheduled Maintenance Guide*, while Chevrolet relies on the computer system to let you know when it's time to change oil and filter based on engine revolutions and temperature, not mileage. When the system calculates that oil life has diminished, it will indicate that an oil change is necessary. A CHANGE ENGINE OIL light will come on. If the system fails, they recommend you change oil and filter at 3,000 miles.

It is also recommended to change the oil prior to putting your rig in storage for more than three months, as used oil contains contaminants that have the potential to pit or corrode bearings when exposed for long periods of time. It is also possible for condensation to collect in the oil pan, cylinder heads, and piston/ring area, creating the potential for engine failure.

## OIL CONSUMPTION

Since engine oil lubricates and protects load bearings and internal parts, it is common to experience some oil consumption. Many factors can affect this consumption, such as high-speed driving, high rpm operation, and towing. It is important to periodically check your positive crankcase ventilation (PVC) system because blockage or damage will result in increased oil consumption.

### Measurement of Oil Consumption

New units require a break-in period to ensure all moving parts seat properly, which will require additional oil usage.

Check your owner's manual for specific break in mileage, instructions, and acceptable oil consumption.

## ENGINE COOLING

The cooling system removes excess heat from the engine, utilizing coolant that flows through the engine and ultimately flows through the radiator. It is important to assure proper airflow through the radiator, and most body manufacturers work with the chassis providers to ensure nothing is mounted in front of the condenser that would block airflow.

Therefore, adding auxiliary transmission coolers, air horns, or other aftermarket items are not recommended in this area.

### Gas-Engine Cooling

Gasoline engines are supplied with long-life engine coolant, such as Dex-Cool, with a service interval of five years or 150,000 miles. If adding coolant, it is important to use the same type or an equivalent silicate-free coolant. Non-recommended coolants could cause premature engine, heater core, or radiator corrosion.

### Diesel-Engine Cooling

Most diesel engines are supplied with a lifetime service interval coolant recommended for diesel engines. Once again, only add the existing type or equivalent coolant if needed.

## ENGINE OPERATING TEMPERATURES

Normal operating temperatures are between 190°F to 240°F. Engine temperature will increase as ambient temperatures and load increases. Suspect temperatures of 247°F and up and inspect these. Newer dash instrumentation (2002 and newer) has overheated-warning indicators.

## ENGINE FUELS

Gasohol, a mixture of 10 percent ethanol and 90 percent gasoline, is approved for all gasoline engines without voiding the warranty. However, this fuel source does operate leaner, which can result in drivability conditions such as spark knock, increased and decreased exhaust emission levels, and reduced fuel economy. As of this writing, E-85 fuels are not approved for Class A gasoline engines.

### Diesel Fuels

Weather and temperature play a big factor in the grade of fuel recommended for a diesel engine.

Wax or paraffin present in diesel fuel increases the amount of energy; however in cold weather it can clog the fuel filter and slow the flow of fuel, resulting in decreased performance and even stalling. No. 1 grade diesel fuel has much of the paraffin removed. However, it will result in power and performance loss and, more important, in warm climates may result in stalling, poor starting when the engine is hot, and damage the fuel-injection system.

- No. 2 grade fuel should be used year-round, specifically, brands that "blend" No. 2 to address the climate differences. The challenge comes when traveling from southern states or filling large fuel tanks with unblended fuel, and limited driving, which could result in having the wrong blend or grade in your tank when weather changes.
- Other conditions to consider are moisture content, additives, and quality of fuel. The Certane number is used in rating diesel and is an indication of energy content. The higher the number, the higher the energy content and improved cold-starting performance.
- Moisture in the fuel can affect performance and starting capabilities because water will separate out of the fuel and settle in low areas, sometimes freezing. Additives can help reduce or even prevent freezing.
- It is important to periodically drain moisture from your system by using the drain plug on the water separator.

## SERVICE ENGINE SOON

### Service Engine Soon/Check Engine Light

Most vehicles today have an on-board diagnostic system that will provide a warning light if there is a problem with the engine emissions, oil levels, or other issue requiring service.

If the light is steady, not blinking, and the engine is running okay, a Check Engine light is not a reason to be towed, but get the problem fixed promptly.

If the light is blinking, it indicates a more urgent situation, which might result in damage from continued driving.

There are pages and pages of items that can cause a Check Engine light to come on. Having it checked with a scan tool will narrow down the problem area.

Common symptoms can be a faulty oxygen sensor or exhaust component, fuel system component, and even leaving the gas cap open for an extended period of time.

With the introduction of E-85 (85% ethanol) gasoline, vehicle owners have inadvertently filled non-flex fuel vehicles with E-85 which will cause the Service Engine Soon/Check Engine light to activate. This generally will not cause immediate damage to an engine; however, extended use will. If you have introduced E-85 fuel to your system, you'll notice reduced fuel economy, and it is recommended that you run the tank below a half tank and fill up with a non-ethanol fuel to reduce the ethanol content.

Eventually the light will go off; however, it is recommended that you take the vehicle to a certified technician to verify the code and have it erased from the history.

In areas where emissions tests are done, your coach will fail if the Check Engine light is on, and fuel mileage generally is lower when the Check Engine light is on. Even if your basic warranty has expired, an extended warranty covers emissions-related components. For more information, go to epa.gov.

## FUEL TANKS/STORAGE

Fuel tanks are generally painted on the outside and coated on the inside with oil for rust protection. When storing your RV for an extended period of time, it is recommended to fill the tank with fuel and add a fuel stabilizer to prevent moisture buildup by reducing condensation.

## ENGINE BATTERY

The 12-volt automotive batteries are designed to provide high cold-cranking amps and should be visually inspected periodically. Most have some type of state-of-charge indicator and will provide several years of service with just a little battery education. During storage, it is recommended that a low-amp battery charger be installed to maintain state of charge. See Chapter 10, "The 12-Volt Direct Current System," for details.

## BRAKE FLUID

Chassis manufacturers use specific types of brake fluid. Not everyone uses the common DOT 5 used in the past, but rather DOT 3 instead. When filling the brake-fluid reservoir or adding any fluid to your engine, consult the owner's manual because these different fluids will not mix properly.

Although your owner's manual doesn't specifically list a brake-fluid-change interval, most brake manufacturers recommend changing the brake fluid every two or three years, especially on those units with high usage, extreme heat conditions, and towing.

# CHAPTER FIVE

# DINGHY TOWING

**Weight Ratings**
**Hitch Ratings**
**Hitch Receivers**
**Vehicle Weight**
**Towing Basics**
**Supplemental Braking Systems**
**Towing Tips**

Towing a vehicle has become so easy that most motorhomes rolling down the road today have a towed vehicle (toad) behind them. Towing a dinghy adds convenience, mobility, and versatility to motorhome travel **(Figure 5.1)**. The advantages have been stated earlier: not having to disconnect all the utilities every morning to go sightseeing and the security of a backup vehicle in case of a breakdown.

The disadvantage of towing is adding the cost of a second vehicle, insurance, and maintenance if you must purchase a vehicle specific for towing. However, if you already own a vehicle that is suitable for towing, the additional expense is minimal.

**FIGURE 5.1** The most popular method of towing a "toad" is "four-down."

Many RVers choose the motorhome mode of travel because they prefer not to tow a travel trailer. However, connecting a vehicle to the rear of a motorhome creates a towing situation that requires hitching and unhitching. Reduced maneuverability is a dinghy-towing drawback, particularly when negotiating turns in tight places. Backing up with a dinghy in tow is generally not recommended because it may require unhitching the dinghy and individually driving each vehicle out of the difficulty.

## WEIGHT RATINGS

Before considering whether to tow or not, make sure you have a good understanding of the weight ratings of your motorhome and potential towed vehicle outlined in Chapter 2, "Understanding Weight Ratings." Towing legally and towing safely can be two different things.

### GROSS COMBINED WEIGHT RATING (GCWR)

GCWR is the combined weight set by the chassis manufacturer adding the gross vehicle weight rating (GVWR) with the weight of the towed vehicle. For example, the Workhorse W22 has a GVWR of 22,000 pounds, which is the total the coach can weigh with all fuels, passengers, and cargo, while the GCWR is 26,000 pounds. This means a coach built on this chassis has a towing capacity of 4,000 pounds

The GCW ratings of motorhomes have increased dramatically, just as weight-carrying capacity has increased. It is not uncommon for the average motorhome to have a 5,000-pound towing capacity, something that was limited to expensive diesel-pusher models in the late 1990s. Today's diesel-pusher models offer 10,000-pound and even more towing capacity.

## HITCH RATINGS

Just because a chassis has a higher GCWR, does not always mean the motorhome has that towing capacity. Some manufacturers limit the towing weight due to frame extensions, outrigger capacity, and to ensure adequate performance and braking by installing a hitch only rated for the amount of weight desired.

Class I—Up to 2,000 pounds
Class II—Up to 3,500 pounds
Class III—Up to 5,000 pounds
Class IV—Up to 10,000 pounds

## HITCH RECEIVERS

Check the rating of your hitch receiver to ensure it is rated for the heaviest load you intend to pull. If a receiver is already installed on your unit, the weight limits and class should be stamped on it. Tow bars are designed to ride parallel to the ground; however, the ride height of most motorhomes rarely matches up with that of the dinghy requiring an adjustable drop hitch receiver. Both Blue Ox and Roadmaster recommend a limit of no more than 3 inches above or below the motorhome ride height. **(Figure 5.2)**

## VEHICLE WEIGHT

Knowing what your vehicle weighs is important for safe towing. This can generally be found on the data plate listed as GVWR. However, physically weighing your toad is the best method. Each year, *MotorHome* magazine publishes the popular *Dinghy Towing Guide* **(Figure 5.3)**, which provides a complete list of new towables, their curb

**FIGURE 5.2** Use the correct receiver hitch to match the baseplate with the receiver height.

**FIGURE 5.3** *MotorHome* Magazine's *Dinghy Towing Guide*

weight, speed/distance limitations, and tips for safe towing. A copy can be downloaded at www.motorhomemagazine.com.

## TOWING BASICS

Almost every type of car, truck, and SUV can be towed in some manner, keeping in mind the weight restrictions. The easiest method of towing is on all fours or flat towing. However, not all vehicles can be towed in this manner due to transmission issues. These vehicles require a transmission lube pump, a driveline disconnect, a tow dolly, or a trailer. Always check the vehicle owner's manual before towing.

As with any trailer, the law requires safety cables, lights, and mirrors on both sides of the tow vehicle.

### FLAT TOWING

Towing a vehicle with all four wheels on the ground using a tow bar is the easiest and adds lit-

tle or no hitch weight to the motorhome. An economical four-passenger compact car can double as a second vehicle when not traveling and can also hold additional weight or supplies if the motorhome is full. Most flat-towed dinghies track so well that many motorhome drivers don't even know they are there. Front-wheel-drive vehicles with manual transmissions and four-wheel-drive vehicles with manual transfer cases are the most popular and economical to tow.

Some vehicles require special attention while towing, such as starting the engine every 200 miles to circulate transmission fluid. Others require the ignition switch to be in a position that allows the steering wheel to be unlocked, which also leaves power applied to various electrical circuits. Over the course of a full day of driving, this could lead to a significant battery drain. Check the vehicle owner's manual or the *Dinghy Towing Guide* for specific details **(Figure 5.4)**.

### TOW DOLLY

Some owners of front-wheel-drive vehicles use a tow dolly rather than add an aftermarket pump or disconnect **(Figure 5.5)**. This gets the drive wheels off the ground and "free-wheels" the back set. This setup usually requires finding a separate location for the tow dolly at a campground and requires additional time for connecting and disconnecting.

### TRANSPORTATION TRAILER

A flatbed or enclosed trailer can be used to transport a towed vehicle; however, pay close attention to weight ratings and braking requirements.

### MECHANICAL LINKAGE

Safe towing requires a properly installed mechanical linkage between the motorhome and the

**FIGURE 5.4** Check your owner's manual or the *Dinghy Towing Guide* for towing specifications of your vehicle.

**FIGURE 5.5** A towing dolly supports the front axle of the towed vehicle.

**FIGURE 5.6** Blue Ox Ambassador A-Frame Tow Bar

towed vehicle. Hitch receivers, tow bars, and baseplates must all be in good working condition and designed/rated for the specific application.

Receivers should be bolted (not welded) in place, using at least grade 5 bolts and lock washers, locking nuts, and thread-locking sealer.

## TOW BARS

Tow bars are available in two basic styles: A-frame or self-aligning. A-frame tow bars offered as "solid" or "folding" are the most economical **(Figure 5.6)**. However, they fit a limited number of vehicles and usually require two people to connect to a motorhome: one to position, and the other to drive the vehicle to the exact spot.

Self-aligning tow bars are available in two styles: dinghy mounted and coach mounted. Coach-mounted units are the most popular as there is less chance of damage when not in use, no additional weight is added to the car, and it's usually a one-person connection job **(Figure 5.7a, b, c, d)**.

## BASEPLATES

The baseplate is a critical link in the towing chain since different models and years of towed vehicles require different baseplates and installation procedures **(Figure 5.8)**.

On some vehicles, the bumper covering must be removed, and minor drilling and trimming may be required.

Other models require even more customizing, such as trimming of the air dam, belly pan, and shock-absorber pads. Such requirements are described in the manufacturer's fitment charts and are recommended procedures best handled by trained professionals to reduce unpleasant surprises.

All fifty states require RV-activated rear lights and properly rated safety chains or cables to keep the dinghy from separating from the motorhome if the tow bar or ball fails. Safety chains or cables should be connected securely to the dinghy and crossed under the tow bar, then secured to the hitch receiver. They should be long enough to allow full turning without binding but not drag when slack.

## TRACKING

Some cars and trucks track better than others while being towed, due to different steering geometry. If a vehicle does not track well, have the alignment checked. Some vehicle manufacturers suggest having the front-wheel caster set to the maximum factory-recommended setting. Maintain maximum air pressure in the tires to help reduce tread wear.

In the few cases in which the towed vehicle's

**FIGURE 5.7a** Blue Ox Acclaim—Dinghy Mounted Self-Aligning Tow Bar

**FIGURE 5.7b** Roadmaster "StowMaster"—Self Aligning Dinghy Mount Towbar

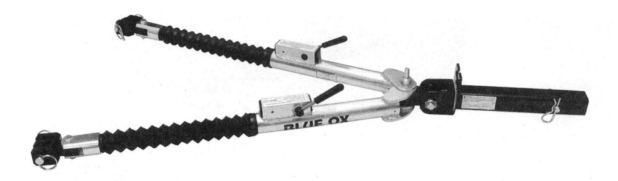

**FIGURE 5.7c** Blue Ox Alladin—Self-Aligning Motorhome Mounted Tow Bar

**FIGURE 5.7d** Roadmaster Sterling—Self-Aligning Motorhome Mount Tow Bar

front wheels have a tendency to reverse steer (crank all the way in the wrong direction) in driveways, it may be necessary to use a stretch cord to anchor the steering wheel to a point behind the driver's seat so the wheel cannot make a full revolution. This is not ideal because it accelerates tire wear, but it will prevent an annoying lockup situation in driveways and uneven terrain.

While maneuvering the motorhome, avoid sharp turns at slow speeds. Motorhomes have long rear overhangs, and sharp turns cause rapid lateral movement of the hitch ball that tends to drag the towed vehicle sideways.

Backing up a towed vehicle or tow dolly is not recommended because the towed vehicle will not steer in the same intended direction as the mo-

**FIGURE 5.8** Proper baseplate installation is critical to safe towing.

torhome, and the front wheels could suddenly turn in another direction and cause damage to the vehicle. You may be able to back up in a straight direction for a few feet in tight situations.

## SUPPLEMENTAL BRAKING SYSTEMS

With the additional weight of a towed vehicle to the back of a motorhome, it is important to consider the braking capacity of your motorhome. Most chassis manufacturers specify that loads in excess of 1,500 pounds should have supplemental brakes and a safety breakaway system. Several states have supplemental brakes listed on their road use laws (see Appendix); however, most are vague on the classification of towed trailer or towed car **(Figure 5.9)**. Recently RV owners visiting Canada have been given tickets for the lack of supplemental brakes in towed vehicles. Whether it's the law or the chassis

manufacturer's recommendation, supplemental brakes should fall under the "legal versus safe" towing concern.

There are several systems on the market today that all have a similar purpose: to activate the towed vehicles onboard braking system at the time the motorhome brakes are applied. To better understand the various systems, we need to look at how your vehicle's braking system works under normal conditions.

Brake pads are activated, or pushed against the wheels' rotor by hydraulic fluid that starts with depression of the brake pedal, through the master cylinder, and boosted to provide pressure to individual wheels, and ultimately the pads and rotor.

This all happens with the engine running and an assist from a powered vehicle. However, during towing, the vehicle is not powered and thus operates in the same manner as a "dead-pedal" situation. Federal law mandates that vehicles must be able to stop without power assistance in case

**FIGURE 5.9** Supplemental brakes are not only a good idea, they are required by law in several states.

of a power failure, so supplemental brakes are engineered to work within the dead-pedal limitations.

There are four basic types of auxiliary braking systems: (1) surge or mechanical, (2) hydraulic, (3) air, and (4) vacuum.

### SURGE OR MECHANICAL BRAKES

The towed vehicle's brakes are activated when the momentum of that vehicle pushes against a specially designed hitch during deceleration. This mechanical system requires no wiring other than an indicator light for the driver. A series of pulleys inside the surge brake pull the pedal and ac-

tivate all four brakes. This system assures that the towed vehicle will never have to stop more than its own weight.

A new type of supplemental braking system has been introduced by Blue Ox and Roadmaster. The Blue Ox Patriot **(Figure 5.10)** uses an electric cylinder inside the brake unit and an onboard battery for power. This eliminates the need for air pumps, storage tanks, wires, or hoses. It also applies proportionately smooth braking rather than the all-on or all-off method. A wireless remote for inside the RV provides information and allows the owner to activate the brakes manually.

The Even Brake by Roadmaster **(Figure 5.11)** is a portable, proportional towed vehicle braking system. It automatically increases or decreases brak-

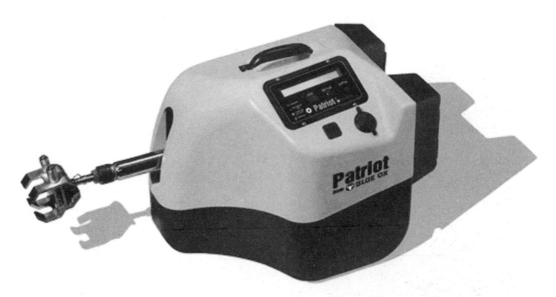

**FIGURE 5.10** The Patriot is an electric surge supplemental braking system from Blue Ox.

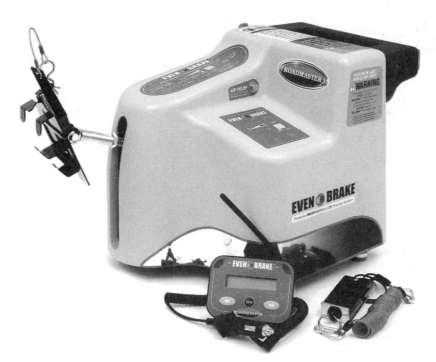

**FIGURE 5.11** The Even Brake by Roadmaster

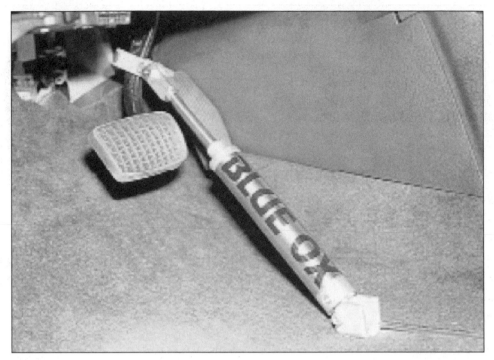

**FIGURE 5.12** Air-Assisted Supplementary Braking System

ing pressure in direct proportion to the motorhome

The unit is positioned between the driver seat and the brake pedal, operates utilizing an onboard air cylinder, and plugs into the towed vehicles 12-volt power outlet.

## HYDRAULIC BRAKES

Hydraulic brakes also operate on the surge or inertia of the towed vehicle on the back of the coach. The difference here is that instead of a mechanical cable running back to the brake pedal, it actually comes with a master cylinder of its own and taps into the brake lines of the towed vehicle. When the towed vehicle surges forward, the master cylinder pushes brake fluid directly into the front-brake calipers, thus applying the towed vehicle's brakes.

Based on this explanation, you can tell that this system will also work on any coach and any towed vehicle with normal hydraulically actuated brakes.

## AIR BRAKES

Air systems will either get air from an air source on the coach or will provide their own air supply. Either way, they use that air to actuate an air cylinder; which either pushes or pulls an unassisted brake pedal down **(Figure 5.12)**. These air cylinders can either be permanently installed, removable, or part of a removable box that sits in front of the driver's seat.

## VACUUM BRAKES

There are several vacuum-assisted supplemental brakes on the market today. Some models require tapping into a vacuum source on a gas-powered coach to supply vacuum to the towed vehicle's master cylinder. While you are towing, your towed vehicle actually has a "live" pedal or, what could be called an *assisted* pedal. Other brakes actually contain a vacuum pump that supplies the vacuum

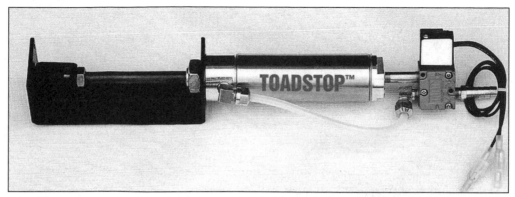

**FIGURE 5.13** Vacuum-Operated Supplemental Braking System

needed in the master cylinder. The brakes are ac-tuated electronically, and the pedal is pulled down by use of a cable or pushed using a vacuum cylin-der **(Figure 5.13)**. These units come as self-contained units and also as individual components for those who would like a permanent installation.

See the Appendix for individual state laws on towing weights, supplemental brake require-ments, and towing checklists.

## TOWING TIPS

Follow these steps for a problem-free towing experience:

1. Hook up on a flat, smooth surface.
2. If you have a coupler-style tow bar, check the fit of the coupler on the ball. Adjust the coupler if necessary.
3. Hook up the tow bar.
4. Set up the towed vehicle's steering and transmission to tow.
5. Check your parking brake to ensure it is disengaged.
6. Latch the legs on a self-aligning tow bar.
7. Cross the safety cables underneath the tow-bar and attach.
8. Attach the electrical cable.
9. Check the function of all lights on both vehicles.
10. Locate your spare key, and lock the towed vehicle's doors.
11. Drive with care and remember your vehicle will be about 25 feet longer while towing.

Each time you stop, check the tow bar, base-plate, and cables to make sure they are still prop-erly attached. Check the tires of the towed vehicle to make sure they are not going flat. If you are using a dolly or trailer, check the wheels to make sure they are not hot to the touch. If the wheels are hot, it may indicate a brake or bearing prob-lem. Each day, before you start, check the lights to make sure they are working properly. Between trips, clean the tow bar and cables to keep them in good shape. Also, clean and lubricate the tow bar as recommended by the manufacturers.

# BEFORE YOU TOW

- Make sure your equipment is rated for the dinghy's weight and that you are not exceeding your motorhome's gross combination weight rating (GCWR).

- Confirm hitch height is correct

- Confirm all hitch bolts and tow-bar and baseplate fasteners are securely tightened.

- Confirm all hitch and wiring connections are engaged and secure; all safety chains or cables are attached; and all locking pins are properly installed.

- Connect brake system and breakaway device.

- Check motorhome and dinghy for proper function of taillights, brakelights, and turn signals.

- Check tire pressure of all tires on motorhome and dinghy—including spare tires.

- Make sure the dinghy is set up for towing: steering unlocked; hand brake off; gear selector in the position specified by manufacturer; ignition in proper position; lube-pump switch; driveshaft coupler; 4WD transfer case and hubs (if applicable) in proper position.

# AS YOU GO

- Observe the speed limit for towing in each state or province you traverse.

- Maintain adequate stopping distance from the vehicle in front of you. A minimum five-second interval is recommended.

- Avoid towing in snowy or icy conditions.

- Pay particular attention to traffic merging onto the freeway and be prepared to take evasive action to avoid "daydreamers."

- Plan ahead—most flat-towed dinghies can't be backed more than a few feet, so it's necessary to focus on easy ingress and egress. Most tow-bar manufacturers will not warrant damage caused by backing. Dollies tend to jackknife quickly. It's better to disconnect the dinghy and drive to a safe place to reconnect.

- Avoid having to make tight turns; they put a lot of pressure on tow bars.

- Towing in deep sand or gravel may cause the dinghy's front wheels to turn to one side. If this happens, you must manually recenter them before continuing.

- Walk around the coach and dinghy to inspect all connections, check tire pressure (or use a monitoring system) and look for signs of trouble every time you stop.

# CHAPTER SIX

# TOW VEHICLES

**Towing Guides**
**Selecting Your Vehicle Type**
**Maximum Tow Rating**
**Other Considerations**
**Used Vehicles**

In the first chapter, we covered matching your truck to a trailer, which aimed at providing important weight information when shopping for a trailer. Weight ratings and towing capability can limit the size of the trailer you are able to safely tow. Keep in mind, there is a big difference between the amount of weight you can tow and the amount you can "safely" tow. Too often we see mismatched combinations with too much weight on the back of a truck, or a light-duty truck pulling a 10,000-pound trailer. Doing your homework and understanding weight ratings is important when properly matching a truck that will perform and handle properly with the trailer of your choice. It's not uncommon to get incorrect advice when shopping for a truck and trailer just to make a sale. It takes a little work to find the ratings, as they generally are not posted on the vehicle. You must do the legwork.

## TOWING GUIDES

Most motor-vehicle manufacturers offer a considerable amount of specific information on vehicle types and how they should be equipped in the form of trailer-towing guides **(Figure 6.1)**. However, selecting a suitable used vehicle becomes more challenging as older-model guides are harder to find. Most manufacturers list current model-year guides on their Web sites, possibly going back one to two years. Also, it's not easy to find a used vehicle that already is equipped with a specialized towing package. Some can be retrofitted with aftermarket options, but some required a larger braking system, specialized transmission, and internal transmission-cooling unit, which cannot be retrofitted.

*Trailer Life's Towing Guide* contains ratings designed to solve that problem—ratings for passenger cars, light- and heavy-duty trucks, vans, and sport-utility vehicles, beginning with the most recent model year and dating back several years. You can e-mail info@trailerlife.com and request late-model guides as well. *Trailer Life's Towing Guide*, combined with the information provided in this chapter, provides you the ability to make an intelligent, accurate tow-vehicle choice **(Figure 6.2)**.

Tow ratings for all vehicle manufacturers are listed in alphabetical order and are organized by model type and configuration. Under each vehicle brand, you will find three headings: Vehicle, Engine, and Tow Limit (pounds). The Vehicle heading describes the vehicle model and/or configuration and indicates whether the vehicle is 2-wheel drive (2WD, front or rear), 4-wheel drive (4WD), or all-wheel drive (AWD). The Engine heading shows the engine size expressed in liters, followed by the configuration (I = In-line, V = V engine as in V-6 or V-8) and the number of cylinders. Under Tow Limit, you will find the manufacturer's stated maximum tow capacity for that vehicle. In many instances, you may note a letter(s) and/or symbol(s) after the model or tow rating, which indi-

**FIGURE 6.1** Manufacturers' towing guides offer detailed information regarding weight and towing capacity.

**FIGURE 6.2** *Trailer Life's Towing Guide* is available at www.trailerlife.com.

cates a footnote listing specific requirements for that rating, such as a particular gear ratio.

## SELECTING YOUR VEHICLE TYPE

In Chapter 1, "Choosing the Right RV," we discussed evaluating your needs for camping and limitations of tow vehicles, such as the number of people you can take, car versus truck, and economics. We will approach this section in a different direction: you don't currently have a vehicle cable of towing and you have decided on the trailer you want.

Just a few years ago, the choices were very limited because few truck manufacturers offered much capacity in the light and medium-duty line. Once you hit 10,000 pounds, it put you into the heavy-duty category and heavy-duty pricing. To-

day's selections are numerous and can be overwhelming **(Figure 6.3)**.

Once again, you will need to understand the weight ratings and how they apply to your towing situation. Please refer to Chapter 2, "Understanding Weight Ratings."

## MAXIMUM TOW RATING

Maximum tow rating is the manufacturer's weight limit for towed loads. For conventional trailers, this normally includes a hitch-weight limit as well; for fifth-wheels, the pin weight is applied to the truck's GVWR and its rear-axle GAWR.

The first step is to find your trailer's UVW rating and CCC **(Figure 6.4)**. This will tell you what the trailer weighs empty, and the maximum it should weigh with all cargo, water, and propane. These weight ratings are required by RVIA code

**FIGURE 6.3** Towing capacities have increased dramatically in recent years.

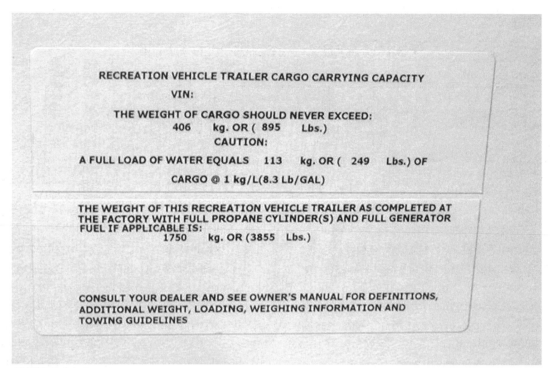

**FIGURE 6.4** The RVIA weight sticker provides cargo-carrying capacity (CCC) information.

and are usually listed on the weight sticker located inside the RV. Keep in mind that optional equipment installed by a dealer or aftermarket items are not included on the manufacturer's weight sticker and must be included.

The best way to determine what your trailer weighs is to fill it with all the items you intend to take along and weigh it at a fuel service station. CAT scales are located at major truck stops all over the country **(Figure 6.5)**. Visit www.catscale.com to find the closest one in your area. These scales are sectioned with platforms allowing you to weigh individual axles with the truck axle on the first, back axle on the second, and trailer axle on the third. This will help identify how much weight is on each axle and provides an overall weight, which allows you to compare GAW and GCW ratings.

To a lesser extent, tow-vehicle weight is variable as well. Brochures and tow guides frequently list how much a truck weighs, but this number generally applies to the most basic model in that configuration, without any options. In some cases, distinctions are made by engine, transmission,

drive system (2WD or 4WD/AWD) and, in other cases, by cab or bed styles. If the dealer does not have a vehicle equipped as you want that is available to weigh, or cannot provide option weights, you can form rough estimates.

Bigger engines add weight; diesels more so because they come with additional accessories; 700 pounds more than the standard gas engine is common. Add up to 175 pounds for an optional transmission, about 400 pounds for 4WD, and a bit less than 300 pounds for longer beds. Then add other options such as luxury-trim levels, because all those electric motors add up. The towing package and hitch could go another 100 pounds, and even larger wheels, two-tone paint, and exterior trim can have an effect.

## THE NUMBERS ARE DECEIVING

The listed towing capacity of any given truck may not be the "realistic" towing capacity; you have to do the math. Yes, MATH. Here is an example:

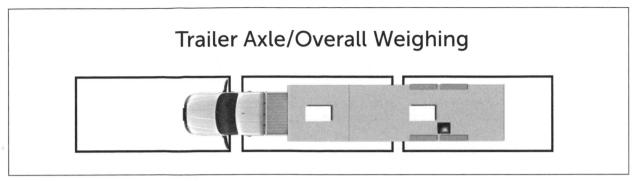

## Trailer Axle/Overall Weighing

**FIGURE 6.5** Finding the overall weight of a used trailer can be done at a CAT scale,

Manufacturers calculate towing capacity by subtracting the actual weight of an unloaded vehicle from the GCWR. In other words, a vehicle that has a GCWR of 23,000 pounds would have subtracted the unloaded weight of the truck, for this example—6,000 pounds. That calculates to a towing capacity of 17,000 pounds. However, those numbers do not include cargo, occupants, and fuel in the tank, which makes it hard to tow.That same truck has a GVWR of 9,900 pounds, and if you put 3,900 pounds of people, fuel, and cargo in the truck and subtracted that from the 23,000 GCWR it would leave you a towing capacity of only 13,100.

Most owners don't carry the maximum weight capacity in a tow vehicle, so it's important to know what your tow vehicle weighs going down the road with all occupants and cargo. Calculate for heaviest usage, when you will carry the most occupants, and don't forget to include the portable generator and firewood in the truck bed. This is the number that should be subtracted from the GCW **(see Exhibit 6.1)**.

It's important to factor in the weight of all components such as the trailer hitch, extra propane tank, and tools. Since we have already decided on the trailer and are looking for the proper tow vehicle, it's probably not feasible to actually weigh the tow vehicle fully loaded, so it's important to understand that the listed towing capacity in the guides is for an unloaded vehicle, and what you put inside must be calculated into the formula. **(see Exhibit 6.2)**

### ENGINE/TRANSMISSION/AXLE RATIO

In the past, selecting the proper axle ratio, transmission, and even engine type/size was critical to proper performance and maximum efficiency. Today's modern technology takes most of the guesswork out of the equation by offering over-

---

Here are some realistic numbers:

| | |
|---|---|
| **Unloaded truck** | 6,000 pounds |
| **Four occupants** | 150 to 600 pounds |
| **Gas/22 gallons** | 6 to 132 pounds |
| **Cargo** | 300 pounds |
| **Total** | 6,932 pounds |
| **Realistic Towing Capacity** | 23,000 GCWR—6,932 pounds = 15,068 pounds |

**EXHIBIT 6.1** Realistic Weights

Here are weights you may need to consider:

| | |
|---|---|
| Gasoline | 6.0 pounds/gallon |
| Diesel | 6.3 pounds/gallon |
| Occupants | 154 pounds (airline calculation standards— adjust accordingly!) |
| Water | 8.3 pounds/gallon |

**EXHIBIT 6.2** Weights to Consider

drive transmissions, towing activation buttons, and computerized shift-point adjustments. However, it is important to understand axle ratios when looking at older vehicles.

The axle ratio is the relationship between driveshaft revolutions and wheel revolutions. For example, in a vehicle with a 3.50:1 axle ratio, the driveshaft revolves 3.5 times for each revolution of the wheels.

Typically axle ratios for vehicles without a trailer are higher, such as 3.08:1. This keeps engine rpm low for better fuel economy. The choice of axle ratio for a tow vehicle is a compromise between fuel economy in solo driving and performance while driving.

Numerically high ratios are better for power and worse for mileage, and low ratios are just the opposite. Fortunately the new overdrive transmissions adjust to weight, grade, and driving characteristics providing better performance.

## OTHER CONSIDERATIONS

### TOWING PACKAGE

Manufacturers of tow vehicles offer special trailer-towing equipment packages that are generally re-quired to obtain the maximum towing rating. If a tow package is available, it's generally more economical to purchase the package rather than trying to install aftermarket items. Some of the components are visible, such as the hitch and wiring harness, but heavy-duty towing packages usually include upgraded wiring; transmission cooler; trailer-brake wiring; and heavy-duty items, such as an alternator, battery, and power steering. These items generally cannot be installed later; therefore, it's a good idea to review the towing package available and compare those items to other vehicles you are considering.

### BED LENGTH

When looking at the tow ratings, usually the bed length reduces the towing capacity because the longer bed actually weighs more. However, it's a slight decrease and the longer bed can be beneficial when towing a fifth-wheel trailer **(Figure 6.6)**.

### SINGLE/DUAL WHEELS

Most people believe a rear "dually" can out-tow single-wheeled vehicles, but that is not always the case. Other weight factors will limit the towing capacity, but a dually usually provides a higher GAW rating on the back axle, provides more stability, and is better suited for fifth-wheel trailers and the heavier pin weight.

## EQUIPMENT AVAILABILITY

Before purchasing any tow vehicle, review the towing equipment you will require and the compatibility with that vehicle. Is there a fifth-wheel hitch available or do you need an expensive aftermarket "adapter"?

Some require special-order parts for the hitch ball and receiver. Read the manufacturer's trailer towing guide and look for any limitations the vehicle may have in towing capacity and or state emission restrictions.

## USED VEHICLES

Due to some of the confusion and misinformation that RV owners have received over the years, many RV dealers have added a used tow-vehicle division. This provides an educated buying decision and a much more enjoyable RV experience.

If you're in the market for a used vehicle, check the manufacturer's ratings provided in *Trailer Life's Towing Guide* to give you an idea of the engine sizes and axle ratios suitable for various trailer weights, along with the types of special equipment recommended or required by the manufacturer, and check the vehicles you're considering for similar equipment. Also, a thorough mechanical evaluation of a used vehicle by a reliable mechanic can be helpful to eliminate headaches later down the road.

**FIGURE 6.6** The shorter bed of the F-350 extended cab makes it difficult to corner a fifth-wheel with a conventional hitch.

# CHAPTER SEVEN

# Safe Towing

**Hitch Systems**
**Hitch Ratings**
**Conventional Hitch Hardware**
**Proper Weight-Distributing Hitch Adjustment**
**Sway Control**
**Freeway Hop**
**Trailer-Wiring Connectors**
**Fifth-Wheel Towing**

**M**atching the proper tow vehicle with an RV is the first step in safe towing. Understanding your weight ratings, braking capacity, and the dynamics of towing a vehicle are all important factors in safe towing and an enjoyable towing experience. Another factor is proper installation and initial setup of equipment by a qualified technician. Many RV enthusiasts have spent years running down the road "fighting" poor towing characteristics without realizing there is something that can be done to improve the journey.

**FIGURE 7.1** Travel trailers are subject to sway, but proper installation and adjustment can smooth out the ride.

## HITCH SYSTEMS

Hitch systems are engineered to connect a tow vehicle and trailer in a manner that will result in a safe and appropriate towing combination **(Figure 7.1)**. In order for the hitch system to perform well, the correct components must be selected for the job, the equipment must be properly installed, and it must be maintained so it can continue to perform as designed.

For conventional trailers, there are two different hitch types: weight carrying and weight distributing. Trailers are available in two types; conventional travel trailers and fifth-wheel trailers.

Depending on the type of tow vehicle as well as the trailer, stability on the road can vary widely due to different weight distribution characteristics. However, improvements can be made, even in the worst case situation which is discussed later in this chapter. **(Figure 7.2)**.

- A weight-carrying hitch **(Figure 7.3)** is designed to support a full A-frame load on the ball mount (or ball if a separate ball mount is not used). Under this condition, the rear of the tow vehicle bears the entire weight of the A-frame at the point of hitch attachment. If the hitch weight is substan-

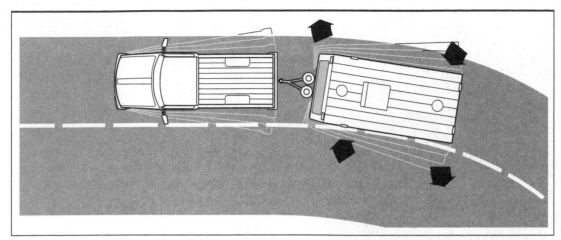

FIGURE 7.2 Lateral movement of a travel trailer exerts steering influence on the tow vehicle.

**FIGURE 7.3** A Weight-Carrying Hitch

tial, the rear of the tow vehicle will be forced downward. As the rear of the tow vehicle is loaded, the front of the vehicle will rise, unloading the front axle. This can result in light steering, decreased front-brake effectiveness, and poor handling. This is one reason weight-carrying hitches are rated only for lightweight towing. Sway-control devices are sometimes used in conjunction with weight-carrying hitches, depending upon the trailer towed.

- A weight-distributing hitch includes spring bars that attach between the ball mount and the trailer frame to distribute the hitch weight evenly to the front and rear axles of the tow vehicle, as well as to the trailer axles **(Figure 7.4)**. Used properly, a weight-distributing hitch sustains the tow vehicle and the trailer at level atti-

tudes after the full weight of the A-frame has been imposed on the ball mount. Sway-control devices are commonly used with weight-distributing hitches.

A fifth-wheel hitch consists of a platform that is installed in the bed of a truck above the rear axle **(Figure 7.5)**.

The uppermost part of the hitch is the saddle, which carries the weight of the pin box (the coupling system that is attached to the trailer). This is, in essence, a weight-carrying unit because the full hitch weight of the trailer is borne by the rear of the tow vehicle without being distributed fore and aft by hitch components. However, because the hitch point is centered almost directly above or just forward of the rear axle, there is none of the leverage on the rear of the tow vehicle that a conventional trailer imposes. With the hitch point so far forward, a portion of the hitch weight is distributed to the front axle so the tow vehicle maintains a more level attitude than it would if the same amount of weight were loaded on a conventional hitch **(Figure 7.6)**.

Because of the location of the hitch, fifth-wheel trailers can only be towed by flatbed or pickup trucks with open cargo boxes. Sway-control devices are not necessary, and in fact cannot be employed in conjunction with fifth-wheel hitch systems **(Figure 7.7)**.

**FIGURE 7.4** A Weight-Distributing Hitch

**FIGURE 7.5** A Fifth-Wheel Hitch

## HITCH RATINGS

Conventional hitches are rated by the manufacturer according to the maximum amount of weight they are engineered to handle. The weight rating refers to the total weight of the trailer, including all fluids and cargo ready to roll down the road. Hitch ratings are established by the Trailer Hitch Manufacturers Association and available in the following classifications:

Class I:   up to 2,000 pounds and 200-pound tongue weight

Class II:   up to 3,500 pounds and 350-pound tongue weight

Class III: up to 5,000 pounds and 500-pound tongue weight

Class IV: up to 10,000 pounds and 1,000 to 1,400-pound tongue weight

Class V:   anything over 10,000 pounds and 1,000 to 1,200-pound tongue weight

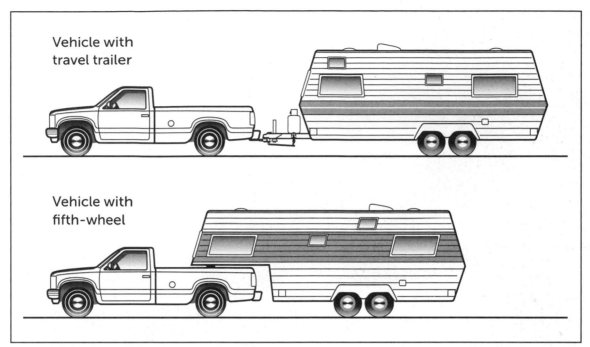

Vehicle with
travel trailer

Vehicle with
fifth-wheel

**FIGURE 7.6** Travel trailers are subject to sway, which can be controlled, while fifth-wheel trailers cannot be controlled.

## CONVENTIONAL HITCH HARDWARE

### RECEIVERS

A conventional hitch platform is secured beneath the rear of the tow vehicle. The rearmost part of the platform is the receiver—a section of reinforced square-steel tubing into which the shank of a ball mount is inserted.

### SHANKS

For lightweight load-carrying service, there are ball-mounted shanks made of square-steel tubing. Heavy towing, on the other hand, requires a solid shank. In both cases, the shank has a hole through it that lines up with holes on opposite sides of the receiver.

When the hole in the shank is lined up with that in the receiver, a hitch pin is inserted and held in place by a clip or lock. Seasoned RVers of-

ten refer to this as the "stinger." Walk behind an unhooked RV or tow vehicle with a ball and shank protruding out and soon you will understand why the name is appropriate.

### BALL MOUNTS

A ball mount is attached to the end of a shank. Some ball mounts are adjustable to accommodate varying coupler heights and to permit fine-tuning of the hitch to optimize performance. After the ball mount has been properly adjusted, it need never be readjusted unless it is to be used with a different tow vehicle or trailer. When setting up an adjustable ball mount, level the trailer on a level surface. Measure from the inside of the coupler to the ground to determine the starting ball height. Set the ball so that it is approximately 1 to 1½ inches higher than the measured fixture. This is your starting point. Adjustments may be needed after the spring bars are attached. If you plan on using a welded ball mount, make sure a certified shop does the welding. Adjustable ball mounts

**FIGURE 7.7** Use the appropriate ball size for the trailer hitch.

that bolt together, however, provide flexibility for unseen circumstances.

## THE BALL

A ball of appropriate size and rating is installed on a ball mount. Balls are available in sizes from $1^7/8$ inches to $2^5/16$ inches, with a variety of risers to elevate the ball above the mount **(Figure 7.7)**. Balls are rated for loads ranging from 2,000 to 10,000 pounds, but raised balls usually have lower ratings. It is critical that the ball rating be equal to or greater than the GVWR of the trailer.

To be safe, three or four threads of the ball shank should be showing past the nut and lock washer when properly tightened. Balls should be greased with a thin layer of ball grease (available at most RV-supply stores).

## SAFETY CHAINS

Safety chains are not only a vital part of safe towing, but also required by law in most of the United States and Canada. Chains should be connected in such as way as they run from their A-frame connection to the hitch receiver in pre-engineered loops. Adjust the chains for slight free play to allow for cornering without binding, yet taut enough to keep them from dragging on the ground. Properly hooked up, safety chains should cross beneath the coupler so that if the trailer were to come uncoupled, the A-frame would be supported by the chains. Make sure the chains are positioned inside the V formed by the spring bar and that they are rated higher than the GVWR of the trailer.

## SPRING BARS

Spring bars are used with weight-distributing hitches to spread the hitch weight among the axles of both the trailer and tow vehicle. Spring bars are rated in various weight capacities and the correct ones must be employed to allow the load-distributing system to function properly. The rule of thumb is to utilize spring bars that are rated slightly higher (up to 250 pounds) than the trailer's actual hitch weight. If spring bars of insufficient capacity are used, the rear of the tow vehicle will sag under the weight of the A-frame, or the spring bars will need to be over tensioned to maintain a level tow vehicle. If spring bars of excessive capacity are used, the ride quality could be harsh.

When the spring bars are attached between the ball mount and the trailer frame, tension adjustment is made by selecting the appropriate links of the spring-bar chains. This permits fine-tuning of the system for the proper amount of weight transfer ( **Figure 7.8)**.

## PROPER WEIGHT-DISTRIBUTING HITCH ADJUSTMENT

If a weight-distributing hitch is installed, proper adjustment is important for successful operation. Proper adjustment means that the trailer is level and that the tow vehicle remains in the same attitude as before hitching. For example, if the tow vehicle was canted up at the rear before hitching (typical of pickup trucks), it should remain at that angle after hitching. The concept of a properly operated load-distributing hitch is that it

**FIGURE 7.8** Correct adjustment of spring-bar tension is based on proper measurements at the front and rear of the tow.

should distribute hitch weight to all axles of the tow vehicle and trailer **(Figure 7.9)**.

To make sure this happens, follow these steps:

1. Begin with the tow vehicle and trailer parked on level ground. Block the trailer wheels. Unhitch the trailer and use the tongue jack to adjust the trailer. Measure the distance between the trailer frame and ground at the front and rear corners, and adjust until the frame is level.

   Note the following measurements:

   a. Distance from the ground to the top of the inside coupler socket.

   b. Distance from the ground to the lower corner of the bumper at all four corners of the tow vehicle. You can also use the distance

from the bottom of the wheel wells to the ground as a reference point.

2. Hitch the trailer and measure the ball height from the ground. Depending upon the hitch weight and the type of tow vehicle, the ball height will need to be adjusted so that it is slightly higher than the distance from the ground to the inside of the top of the coupler.

   Use the following as a guide:

   a. For trucks with extra-heavy-duty springs, set the ball height equal to the coupler height.

   b. For pickups with standard springs, raise the ball height about $1/32$ inches for each 100 pounds of hitch weight.

   c. For passenger cars, raise the ball height about $1/16$ inch for each 100 pounds of hitch weight. After the rest of the hitching process has been accomplished, it may be necessary to fine-tune the system by moving the adjustable ball mount up or down to achieve a near-perfect ball height.

3. Remeasure front and rear reference points. If the rear of the vehicle has dropped 1 inch and the front has only dropped $1/4$ inch, add more tension to the spring bars, which will raise the rear and lower the front. Continue adjusting until measurements are approximately the same.

If the spring bars cannot be adjusted tight enough to achieve similar or identical vehicle-height measurements, stiffer spring bars may be needed. The spring bars should be rated for at least the amount of the hitch weight of the trailer, plus about 200 pounds if the tow vehicle is softly sprung.

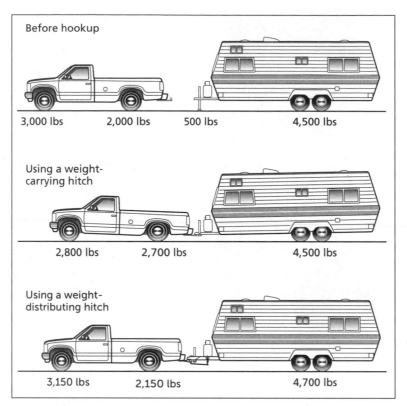

**Before hookup**

3,000 lbs · 2,000 lbs · 500 lbs · 4,500 lbs

**Using a weight-carrying hitch**

2,800 lbs · 2,700 lbs · 4,500 lbs

**Using a weight-distributing hitch**

3,150 lbs · 2,150 lbs · 4,700 lbs

**Figure 7.9** A weight-distributing hitch distributes weight to all axles of the tow vehicle and the trailer.

## SWAY CONTROL

### WEIGHT AND BALANCE

Trailers are available in two types: conventional travel trailers and fifth-wheel trailers. The conventional trailer is much more vulnerable to destabilizing forces such as sway, technically known as yaw. Sway is a fishtailing action of the trailer caused by external forces that set the trailer's mass into a lateral motion with the trailer's wheels serving as the axis or pivot point **(Figure 7.10)**.

All conventionally hitched travel trailers will sway slightly in response to crosswinds or the shear of a passing truck. The good ones will need little correction by the driver and will quickly restabilize. Only poorly balanced or poorly designed trailers will continue to sway after the force that caused the instability has ceased. In fact, the sway motion of a poorly balanced trailer may increase until control is lost.

Weighing your tow vehicle and trailer is critical to proper balance and weight distribution. It's not uncommon for an RV to weigh more on one side than the other, as manufacturers design a floor plan that will sell versus one that is properly balanced. To compound the matter, large storage compartments tempt owners to fill them to the brim, which will also cause weight and balance issues.

**NOTE:** Refer to Chapter 2, "Understanding Weight Ratings," for proper weighing procedures.

Use a platformed scale that will allow you to weigh the front axle of the tow vehicle, the back axle, and the trailer independently. Once you obtain the fully loaded tow vehicle and trailer weight, unhook the trailer and weigh the tow vehicle with the front axle on one platform and the back axle

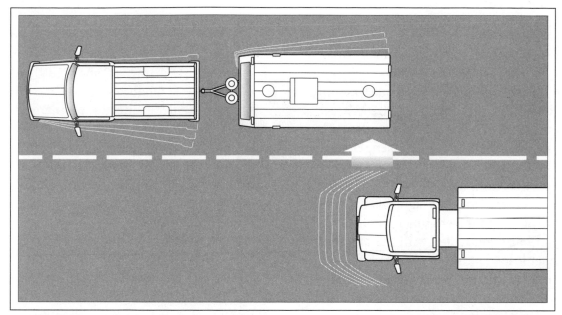

**FIGURE 7.10** The bow wave of a truck overtaking from the rear may require defensive steering.

on another. Subtract the weight of the back axle unhooked from the back-axle weight hooked to the trailer and you will get the hitch weight of your rig. This figure is important because we discuss hitch weights and handling characteristics next. It's also a good idea to weigh the vehicle from side to side to see if adjustments are needed here as well.

There are several ways to evaluate the potential of a travel trailer to sway and to correct the problem if it occurs.

## STABILITY CHECKUP

A trailer's inherent stability is part of its design, based on the amount of weight in front of the axles versus the amount of weight behind. A weight-forward bias results in hitch weight and is necessary for control. Trailers with insufficient hitch weight have two deficiencies:

1. The weight mass behind the axles(s) is too high; when set in motion it acts as a pendulum, and sway oscillations tend to increase until control is lost.
2. The distance between the hitch ball and the trailer axles is insufficient to give the tow vehicle steering leverage over the trailer.

Elementary physics helps explain why distance between the hitch ball and axles is important. We all know that we can use a board (lever) positioned on a rock (fulcrum) to move another rock that is too heavy for us to lift without assistance. The lever gives us a mechanical advantage (leverage) on the rock. Likewise, trailers that have considerably more length in front of their axle(s) than in the rear give tow vehicles a mechanical advantage: the tow vehicle has a long lever with which to steer the trailer. This balance question is dealt in terms of pounds of hitch weight.

Simply stated, trailers with a high proportion of hitch weight to gross weight usually have more of their length ahead of the axles and they handle better. The generally accepted industry standard is that hitch weight should be approximately 10 percent of gross weight. In fact, that is a bare minimum, and some trailers with 10 percent hitch weight don't handle well. Hitch weights of 12 percent or higher (up to the weight limit of the hitch being used) assure proper handling.

In marginal hitch-weight situations, the owner's ability to handle an unstable trailer will depend on the inherent stability of the tow vehicle, which is another variable. A truck or van with a long wheelbase, relatively short rear overhang, and stiff springs will at least partially make up for a trailer's lack of inherent stability. But if the trailer is towed by a softly sprung truck, van, or passenger car, the trailer's shortcomings will be more obvious.

A brief driving test on a section of straight road with no other traffic in sight will give you an assessment of your trailer's inherent stability. The trial should be conducted with the tow vehicle and trailer loaded normally for travel. Make sure the refrigerator door is secured and that the contents of cabinets will not be dislodged. If you have a friction-type sway-control device, set the adjusting lever so the device is not operational. A sway-control device is a valuable asset and should be employed, but for the purposes of this test should be disconnected so it does not camouflage inherent trailer instability.

For this trial, trailer brakes should be working effectively, and the manual control lever on the brake controller should be within easy reach of the driver. If your brake controller does not have a lever that allows you to actuate the trailer brakes independently of tow-vehicle brakes, it's important that you change to a controller that does. Independent use of trailer brakes is the single most effective countermeasure to reduce or eliminate trailer sway.

Begin the test at about 20 miles per hour, and crank the steering wheel sharply to the left, simulating an attempt to avoid an obstacle in the road. Note the reaction of the trailer. Repeat the experiment while increasing speed, but take care not to overdo it. Practice actuating the trailer brakes independently of the tow-vehicle brakes so you can do it almost instinctively. As speeds increase, the trailer will sway more dramatically. With each trial, note the severity of trailer sway and how many oscillations occur before the trailer destabilizes. Again, take care not to exceed the limits of your tow vehicle and trailer.

The most pronounced sway oscillations should be the ones produced by your sharp steering input; subsequent oscillations should diminish rapidly. If the second and third sway oscillations are equally as severe or worse than the first, the trailer is unstable (or marginally stable at best) and needs correction. Don't be lulled into complacency by the fact that the trailer handles much better when your sway-control device is in use because an emergency maneuver may overcome the effect of the sway-control unit and result in an accident.

## EVALUATING THE TRAILER AND HITCH

If you experience a sway problem during your test, there are adjustments that can be made. If your hitch-weight percentage is down around 10 percent or less, moving heavier items in your trailer should help. Trailers with 15 to 20 percent hitch weight provide the best handling situations, but it's important that the weight does not exceed the rating of the hitch and the GAW rating.

Weight "culprits" are heavy items placed at the back of the trailer such as spare tires and storage pods. Move these items to the front of the RV or even inside the truck bed if possible. Another possibility is the battery bank; if carried in the rear, it could be relocated to the trailer A-frame.

The freshwater tank should not be located behind the trailer axles, although this does occur in some cases.

Water weighs 8.3 pounds/gallon; therefore a 50-gallon tank would add 415 pounds to the back of the unit and drastically affect handling. You can find a different tank and relocate it forward under a dinette seat, or travel with the tank empty and fill it once you get close to or at the designated camping area so you only travel a short distance with a handling issue. Ideally, the water tank should be located over the axles so it does not affect hitch weight. Be sure to dump the holding tanks before leaving; there is no need to carry waste water all over the country!

**FIGURE 7.11** Most seasoned RVers prefer a friction-sway-control device for the best possible handling.

## SWAY-CONTROL DEVICES

Assuming hitch weight is raised to at least 12 percent, using an effective sway control should give the trailer reasonably good road manners. The two most common types of mechanical sway-control devices are friction-type **(Figure 7.11 )** and dual cam-type.

Because of the way friction-sway-control units operate and the forces they impose on the trailer A-frame, they are not recommended for use on trailers with surge brakes or on trailer A-frames with less than .080-inch-wall thickness.

Friction-sway-control mechanisms consist of a bracket that attaches to the trailer frame with either brackets or a small socket and ball, a friction assembly with a friction plate that is adjusted by turning a screw-in handle, and a slide bar with a small ball socket on the front end. For increased control, two units can be installed, one on each side of the trailer A-frame.

In operation, the slide bar slips through the friction assembly, which is tightened until it acts as a brake on the slide bar, permitting the bar to slide in and out only under the influence of great force. The socket end of the slide bar fits over a small ball located to one side of, and to the rear of, the hitch ball on the ball mount. This sets up a triangle between the trailer frame, the sway control, and the hitch system.

The sway-control unit acts as a variable-length side of the triangle. Its length is permitted to change when turning corners, yet the braking action of the friction assembly and slide bar resists unwanted pivoting motion of the trailer and tow vehicle while traveling.

A dual-cam sway control is recommended only for trailers with fairly heavy hitch weights (usually larger trailers in the 28- to 32-foot range). It is a bit more complex than a friction-type unit, with more hardware involved. Once installed, however, no ad-

**FIGURE 7.12** The Pullrite hitch repositions the pivoting hitch point forward, similar to a fifth-wheel setup.

justment is needed. For even greater control, it can be used along with a friction-type unit.

With the dual-cam sway-control system, vertical movement of the tow vehicle and trailer is permitted, but trailer sway is dampened by torsion action of the cam arms because they resist lateral movement.

The proper adjustment of the friction cams of the dual-cam system is very important for the best stability.

## THE PULLRITE HITCH

The Pullrite hitch is an unconventional product that repositions the pivoting hitch point forward under the tow vehicle to a location immediately behind the back axle **(Figure 7.12)**. Moving the hitch point forward effectively delivers handling characteristics similar to that of a fifth-wheel hitch. The trailer no longer pivots on the hitch ball, so it's necessary to visualize the trailer A-frame having been extended about 5 feet underneath the tow vehicle to the pivot point.

The Pullrite has a dramatic effect on towing stability. Even a basically unstable trailer is cured of its bad road manners. On the road, directional control of the tow vehicle is not significantly affected by the steering forces of a marginally stable trailer. It utilizes a long draw bar and a radius bar, adding about 60 additional pounds to the rear axle.

The draw bar extends 11 inches behind the vehicle's bumper when the bar is straight to the rear. It can be swung out of the way when the hitch is not in use and locked in a stored position.

While making turns, the Pullrite causes the trailer to follow the tow vehicle farther toward the inside of the turn, which requires some practice to keep the trailer from running over obstacles.

## THE HENSLEY ARROW

Another effective stabilizing trailer hitch is the Hensley Arrow **(Figure 7.13)**. The Arrow allows movement on the ball in every direction except side to side. Side-to-side movement is forced to go through the linkage system, which is one directional. From the trailer side, the linkage is solid. Pivoting by the linkage must be initiated through the tow vehicle. The system's design is inherently stable. However, when the driver wants to turn, the linkage permits a normal turn.

The Hensley system consists of many components but is suitable for owner installation. Once installed, hitching is simplified since all components stay with the trailer when the tow vehicle is unhitched. Rehitching involves backing the tow-vehicle hitch receiver onto the hitch-bar shank, which requires a little practice.

## FREEWAY HOP

A bouncing, jerking motion, commonly known as freeway hop, occurs in some trailer rigs enough to become uncomfortable. The problem is difficult to solve, even though it has existed for years. It's caused by poor highway design—unfortunate spacing of seams in the concrete (typically 15-foot sections)—so they set up a rhythmic bounce that reverberates throughout the tow vehicle and trailer **(Figure 7.14)**.

There are procedures to try and remedy this:

- Change the distance between the tow vehicle and trailer axles by extending the

**FIGURE 7.13** The Hensley Arrow® mechanically locks sway out and creates an inherently stable relationship between the trailer and the tow vehicle.

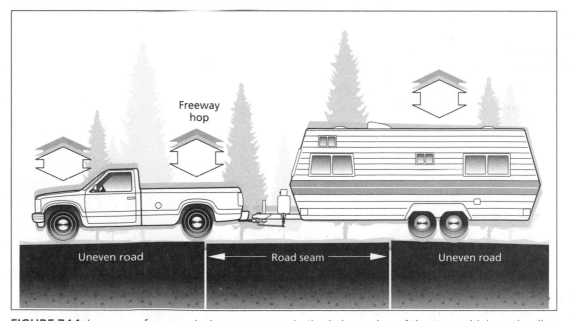

**FIGURE 7.14** Improper freeway design can cause rhythmic bouncing of the tow vehicle and trailer.

ball 3 to 4 inches with a longer hitch bar. However, this increased distance could also affect the trailer stability and sway control.

- Use a combination of 1,000-pound hitch-spring bars and good shocks.
- Change to better shocks on your tow vehicle.
- Add shocks to your trailer if not supplied and check with the manufacturer to see if they offer an upgrade kit.

## TRAILER-WIRING CONNECTORS

The trailer receives power from the tow vehicle for exterior trailer lights, brakes, and battery-charging capabilities. Traditional wire connectors were flat 4-wire connectors that ran 12-volt DC power for ground (white), running lamps (brown), right turn signal (green), and the left-turn signal (yellow), while the brake lights utilized the turn-signal bulbs. These are generally found on smaller trailers without the need for 12-volt DC battery-charging capabilities or electric brakes.

Larger vehicles will be supplied with a 6-way connector providing the basic exterior light function described earlier with two pins for electric brakes and a 12-volt "hot" lead.

Most RVs use a 7- or 9-flat-pin Bargman or Pollak plug and receptacle (**Figures 7.15** and **7.16**). The 9-pin plugs are used only when a trailer is equipped with a refrigerator that is operated on 12-volt DC power while traveling. To simplify things, color codes have been standardized by the RV industry.

It is important to compare the 12-volt DC requirements and configuration of your RV electrical connection with the connection of your tow vehicle. An adapter may be required to avoid "splicing" into the vehicle's electrical wiring.

Troubleshooting an electrical connection can be accomplished with a simple test light. With the trailer plug disconnected, have an assistant operate each function/circuit, one at a time from the tow vehicle, and probe each terminal to verify power.

**7-Pin Connector**
(Socket Interior)
1. White, ground
2. Blue, elect. brake
3. Green, tail
4. Black, batt. charge
5. Red, stop/left-turn
6. Brown, stop/right-turn
7. Yellow, aux. circuit

**9-Pin Connector**
(Socket Interior)
1. White, ground
2. Blue, elect. brake
3. Green, tail
4. Black, batt. charge
5. Red, stop/left-turn
6. Brown, stop/right-turn
7. Yellow, aux. circuit
8. Gray, aux. circuit
9. Orange, refrigerator

**FIGURE 7.15** Diagrams for trailer connectors are essential in verifying correct wiring hookup.

**FIGURE 7.16** A traditional 7-flat-pin receptacle provides power from the tow vehicle on larger RVs.

If a terminal does not light during the function, the problem is in the tow vehicle wiring; if it does light, move to the trailer wiring. Check for continuity and especially a ground connection.

## FIFTH-WHEEL TOWING

There are several different brands and weight capacities of fifth-wheel hitches on the market, but only two basic types: fixed and tilting-head models. The fixed head is held level with the sides of the bed of the truck and can only pivot in a back-and-forth direction. The tilting-head model pivots in a back-and-forth direction and side-to-side motion, allowing the fifth-wheel to be easily connected on ground that is not level.

Fifth-wheel hitches also come in several weight capacities, from 15,000 pounds to more than 30,000 pounds. Never use a hitch that is rated lower than the GVW rating of your RV. It is important to match your trailer GVW rating to the hitch rating and even wise to calculate an additional 10 percent.

There are four basic fifth-wheel hitches: (1) floor mount; (2) crossbar or side rails, (3) gooseneck, and (4) the air hitch.

### STANDARD FLOOR MOUNT

As the name indicates, the standard floor-mount hitch mounts to the bed of the truck bolted to the truck frame for rigidity. The horseshoe-shaped flat top accepts a king pin mounted to the trailer's overhang. Hooking up is easy: Back the tow vehicle aligned to the center of the trailer until it locks into place. This design allows the trailer to corner or pivot at 90 degrees without scratching or damaging the truck bed or side rails. Spring-loaded levers release the locking mechanism in the plate, and locking pins prevent the lever from becoming dislodged.

An advantage of this design is the limited space it requires, while the plate can be removed and the truck becomes useful for other applications.

### CROSSBAR/SIDE RAIL

The crossbar/side rail design has several of the same components as the standard floor mount, such as the horseshoe baseplate, locking mechanism, locking lever, and pins **(Figure 7.17)**. The difference is in the mounting design, where a steel rail is mounted on each side of the truck bed and the crossbar containing the baseplate is connected. The high-profile design is popular with short-bed truck owners as it raises the hitch point above the fenders.

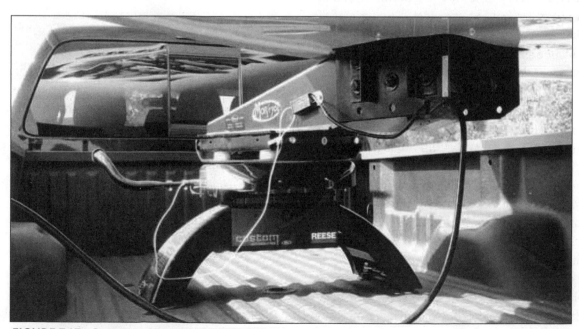

**FIGURE 7.17** Crossbar-Mounted Fifth-Wheel Hitch

**FIGURE 7.18** Fifth-Wheel Air Hitch

### GOOSENECK

With a hitch ball mounted to the truck bed and a conventional A-frame receiver to the trailer, the gooseneck design is a complete opposite of the previous hitches. Some companies offer a pop-up or hidden design that provides a flat floor in the bed for use when not towing the trailer.

### AIR HITCH

Designed to smooth out road vibration and improve the truck-to-trailer flexibility, several hitches utilize air-bladder-type bags to support the weight of the kingpin **(Figure 7.18)**. Ride and stability can be adjusted by the amount of air pressure similar to your vehicle's tires. Since there are several designs and manufacturers to choose from, it's important to understand the design requirements and limitations of your truck and to match them to the appropriate style of hitch.

Short-bed pickups have become very popular; however they do pose a challenge for towing a fifth-wheel, especially during sharp turns. Several hitches are available that will adjust or slide to accommodate the turning radius and prevent the trailer from hitting the back of the cab or the side rails. Some operate by manually pulling a lever and sliding the hitch, while others automatically adjust the movement and return to the normal position after the turn. Adjustments can be up to 22 inches of travel for some models, which could provide a turn as tight as 90 degrees. Trailer manufacturers have also introduced new designs engineered to accommodate the sharp turns as well.

### HITCH INSTALLATION

A fifth-wheel hitch should only be installed by a qualified technician. Most experts recommend installing the hitch 2 inches in front of the rear axle line for heavier loads and in-line with the axle for standard loads. Never locate the hitch pin behind the axle line, as this will adversely affect handling. Due to truck-bed limitations and manufacturers' recommendations, proper location may be confusing or challenging. This is why it is important to consult a professional installer. If your vehicle has a plastic bed liner it must be removed or cut out to accommodate the bed rails. This will allow the bed rails to be mounted flush against the bed and allows installation of recommended spacers between the bed and bed rails.

## MAINTENANCE

There is a tremendous amount of pressure between the pin and the hitch saddle. To minimize the wear and prevent binding between the pin, lubrication is recommended. Before lubricating, remove the old grease. Use a plastic lube plate or automotive-type chassis grease to lube the plate and white lithium spray on other moving parts. Before each use, pull all levers, pins, or other moving parts to ensure proper operation.

Undoubtedly the most important maintenance is proper tire inflation. Low tire pressure can cause extreme heat and lead to tire failure. Proper weight distribution and tire pressure are keys to longevity and a comfortable ride. Refer to Chapter 3, "Tire Basics," for more details.

## PROPER HITCHING/UNHITCHING

Driving away with your fifth-wheel landing gear down or dropping the unit on the pickup bed is not only embarrassing but expensive! A systematic approach to hitching and unhitching will reduce the chance of having such a problem.

### HITCHING

Follow these guidelines for proper hitching:

1. Set the proper hitch height by raising or lowering the trailer.
2. Open the locking bar on the hitch and back the tow vehicle under the trailer until the hitch connects to the kingpin.
3. Secure the locking bar.
4. Put the tow vehicle in forward gear with your foot on the brake to provide a slight forward movement to ensure the mechanism is locked, then place the vehicle in park.
5. Connect all electrical cords and breakaway cables; check all operating lights.
6. Raise the landing gear and remove any chocks.

### UNHITCHING

Follow these steps for proper unhitching:

1. Chock the trailer wheels to prevent movement.
2. Lower the landing gear.
3. Disconnect all electrical cords and breakaway cables.
4. Put the tow vehicle in reverse with your foot on the brake, providing a slight movement back that will take the pressure off the locking bar, put the vehicle back into park, and apply the parking brake.
5. Disconnect the locking bar.
6. Slowly drive forward, visually checking the locking mechanism, cords, and cables to ensure they are all disconnected and the tow vehicle drives away clear.
7. Adjust the trailer height as needed.

### BEDSAVER/PINLOCK

Accidentally dropping a fifth-wheel trailer onto your truck bed can be not only expensive but dangerous as well. It happens more often than one might think. Most states require safety chains while towing any type of trailer other than a fifth-wheel.

What happens if your fifth-wheel trailer comes unhooked while towing?

Blue Ox has developed a hassle-free safety de-vice called the *Bedsaver* which is easy to install and requires no drilling or modification **(Figures 7.18 and 7.19)**. Hooking and unhocking is done in the normal function, and the device will catch the pin and hold it safe and secure.

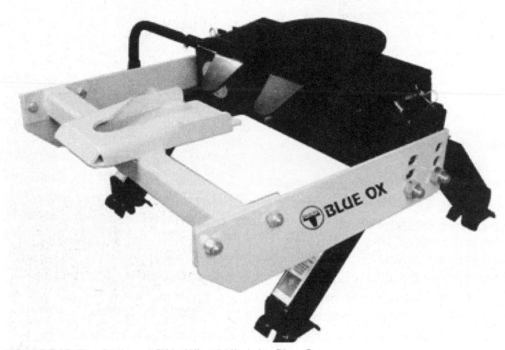

FIGURE 7.18 The Bedsaver Fifth-Wheel Hitch by Blue Ox

FIGURE 7.19 Accidentally dropping a fifth-wheel trailer can be expensive!

# CHAPTER EIGHT

# The Basics of RVing

**Freshwater Tanks**
**The Waste-Water System**
**The Electrical System**
**RV Appliances**
**Air-Conditioning Systems**
**Basic RVing Equipment**

To thoroughly understand the basics and enjoy all the features and benefits of your RV, it is imperative that you read the owner's manual and all accompanying manuals provided by individual appliance manufacturers, the original equipment manufacturers (OEMs). This may seem like a daunting task as the piles of manuals, papers, and diagrams are generally sitting in a drawer or binder. This handbook is designed to supplement the owner's manual since we would never have the time to cover every make, model, and option of every RV.

**FIGURE 8.1** Freshwater tanks can be located underneath a dinette, a bed, or in the "basement."

RVs vary widely in size and complexity, with the smaller trailers being relatively simple and the 40+-footers offering all the amenities of home, and then some. Over all, most RV systems operate in a similar manner, and this chapter, aimed at the novice, will define the basic components and how they are used, and provide some troubleshooting tips.

## FRESHWATER TANKS

Water can be supplied to an RV one of two ways, from an outside hose providing pressurized water through a city-water-fill connection, or from an onboard freshwater tank and pump. The fresh-

water system operates much like that in a house; water flows automatically when a faucet is turned on or the toilet flushed.

When using the city-water connection, pressure is provided by the outside source, and water is routed through piping to all faucets and the toilet, bypassing the onboard water pump. The onboard system starts with a freshwater tank located inside the RV, usually under the bed, a dinette seat, or in the compartments of basement RVs **(Figure 8.1)**. A 12-volt DC demand pump provides pressure when the faucet is opened. When the switch (usually located in the kitchen and another in the bathroom) is turned on, the pump automatically cycles on and off as needed to pressurize the system to 20 to 40 psi. The onboard tank

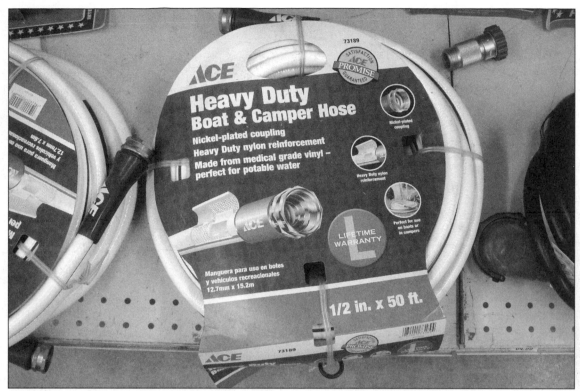

**FIGURE 8.2** Always use an FDA-approved water hose for safe drinking water.

is filled through an inlet on the side of the coach, commonly referred to as the *gravity fill*. Some RVs offer a valve that will divert city-water pressure to the onboard tank, which allows you to fill the tank before you leave the campground.

When connecting a hose to the city-water hookup, make sure you are using a hose that is made with FDA-approved materials for safe drinking water **(Figure 8.2)**. Run the faucet briefly to fill the hose before connecting to the RV. This will reduce the amount of air entering the system.

When the water tank is being filled, the hose is inserted in the gravity fill, or the city-bypass valve is engaged, and water enters the tank from the top. Air inside the tank will escape through a vent, generally located next to the gravity fill. If the vent is obstructed, or the line kinked, the tank will fill very slowly, or water will come back out of the gravity fill **(Figure 8.3)**. Here it is important to identify all drain valves and shut them off prior to filling. Otherwise, they will let you know where they are by draining on the ground. Re-

fer to your owner's manual regarding location and how to close them.

When the RV is new, and after taking it out of storage, you will need to purge the air in the lines. To do this, turn on the pump and open all faucets one at a time, hot and cold, allowing water to flow until air is purged. Purge air from the cold-water lines each time you reconnect to a campground source.

Water pressure at a campground or from a residential source may exceed the capacity of your plumbing, especially the fittings. Your RV system is generally rated at 40 to 50 psi, and it is not uncommon to see pressures of 100 psi in campgrounds. Therefore, it's a good idea to use a pressure regulator that controls the amount of pressure coming into the system **(Figure 8.4)**. Some RVs come with a simple pressure regulator built into the city-water valve; however, a heavy-duty aftermarket regulator is still recommended.

Many RVers carry an auxiliary water filter that is connected outside, downstream of the pressure

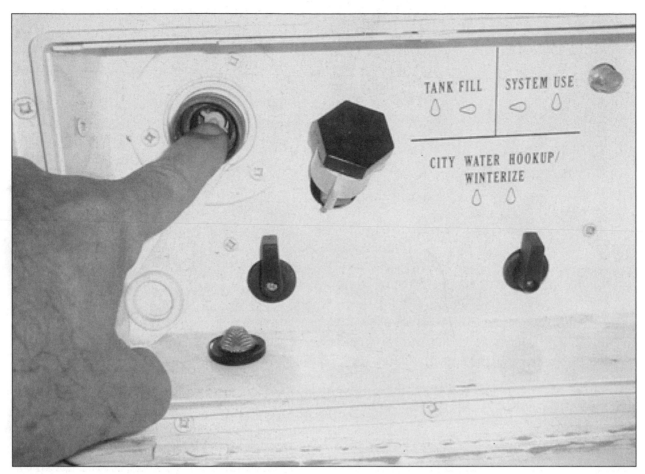

**FIGURE 8.3** A clogged or obstructed vent will make filling the freshwater tank difficult.

regulator, to filter sediment and odor. A typical under-the-counter residential filter will work and most home improvement stores carry a variety of models and several different filters.

## WATER PUMP

The demand pump is powered by the 12-volt DC supply and requires very little maintenance. There are a variety of electric pumps on the market, so make it a point to become familiar with the one installed on your RV **(Figure 8.5)**. Most pumps use some type of rubber diaphragm, while others use a rotary-impeller system. The diaphragm pump operates more quietly and will not be damaged if it accidently runs dry. If the water pump runs but

fails to deliver water, the cause is most often a restriction in the suction or inlet side of the pump. Check all water lines for pinching or kinks and tightness of connections that would allow air to be drawn in. If water is reaching the pump, check for debris in the inlet/outlet valves, which can be done by simply removing the lines on each side. Some manufacturers install a screen or in-line filter, which should also be checked.

To quiet a noisy water pump, check the platform to which the pump is mounted. Most pumps have rubber mounts to dampen the vibration; however, installing the pump on a strip of carpet or padding will further the noise reduction. It may be necessary to build a small wooden box to get the pump off the floor of the compartment or RV as well. Also check the inlet/outlet lines. During start

**FIGURE 8.4** Always use a water-pressure regulator to protect your freshwater plumbing.

and stop, there is added vibration and they may be "thumping" against the floor or wall. Some manufacturers use a soft plastic line for the inlet/outlet hose instead of the rigid plastic used throughout the coach. This will reduce the vibration and thumping effect. For more in-depth troubleshooting and repair, refer to the service guide.

Most RV manufacturers provide a standard water pump that offers adequate pressure and noise resistance. However, there are upgrades that provide higher pressure, less cycling, and whisper-quiet operation, such as Shurflo's Whisper King. Another upgrade is an accumulator tank, which has an internal bladder that prevents air from being dissolved into the water. It is usually installed close to the outlet side of the pump and can be mounted in virtually any position. The

air bladder is compressed when the pump charges the water system and returns pressure to the water system when a valve or faucet is opened. This provides a smoother flow of water and reduces the number of times the water pump must cycle to deliver the same volume of water.

**LEAKS**

Cracks or leaks are not uncommon in RV water systems due to the rigorous usage, road vibration, and temperature fluctuations. It is a good idea to carry a repair kit designed for your type of system. Most manufacturers have gone to the plastic PEX (cross-linked polyethylene) lines that can be spliced without the need for a plumbing expert and "sweating" pipes. PEX offers superb expandability if frozen (although not guaranteed), keeps water warmer and cooler, and creates no plastic taste or odor. Some manufacturers use a color-coded line for hot and cold to help identify them. Although this type of line usually requires a special clamping method for fittings during initial installation, a new compression fitting is available at plumbing-supply stores and home improvement centers that makes it easy to splice and repair the line. These compression connectors can be used on copper, PVC, and PEX and are a must for any toolbox **(Figure 8.6)**. Another must is Rescue Tape, a silicone tape that will fuse to itself and holds pressure up to 500 psi, and can work in wet conditions. This can be used to temporarily hold a valve or fitting in place, a crack in a water line, or many more repairs.

Visit them at www.rescuetape.com.

## HOT-WATER TANK

Since RV water heaters are generally available in 6- to 12-gallon capacities, long, hot showers are relegated to the campground bathroom. However, today's quick-recovery systems provide hot water in less than an hour. Atwood and Suburban are the two major suppliers and both their hot-water tanks require occasional maintenance for optimum performance.

The water in most hot-water tanks is heated via a propane-fired burner, although some may use 120-volt AC power as a heat source as well. Both fuel sources can be used for quicker recovery.

Certain Suburban water heaters are protected by an anode rod that also serves as the drain plug. Replacement of the rod is recommended when the consumption of the material is greater than 75 percent. The anode rod is a sacrificial rod that pro-

**FIGURE 8.5** An onboard demand pump provides pressurized water throughout the RV.

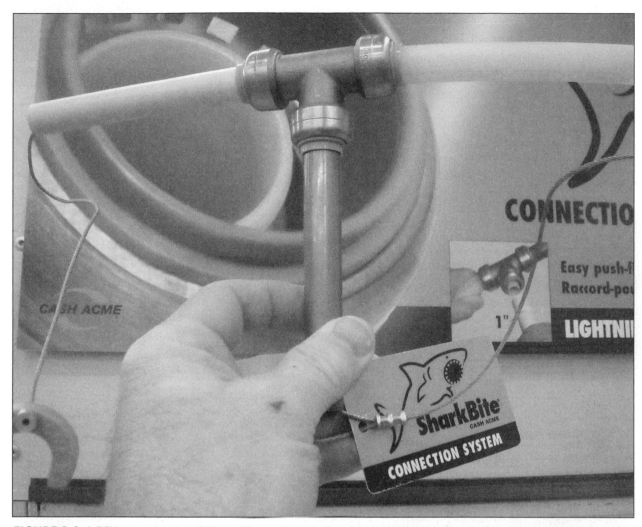

**FIGURE 8.6** A PEX compression fitting offers quick repairs of cracked lines.

vides cathodic protection for the tank. This is important: Failure to do so can lead to premature tank wear. Atwood models feature a stainless-steel tank and do not utilize the anode technology.

It is important to drain and flush your water-heater tank periodically to clean out accumulation of dirt and scale. To clean the tank, turn off the main water supply, drain the tank by removing the drain plug, open the relief valve, and drain the tank. Clean out any buildup of scale at the drain, then turn on the water supply and flush the system for about 5 minutes. Close the drain or replace the drain plug.

### WINTERIZING THE FRESHWATER SYSTEM

Winterizing the RV's water system is necessary to protect all components from freezing. There are two ways to accomplish this job:

1. Drain all water from the system and use compressed air to blow out any remaining water that may lie in low spots within the system.
2. Fill the system with a potable nontoxic antifreeze until all water is removed from the system.

In each case, the hot-water tank must be drained. When a nontoxic winterizing fluid is used, it is best to install a winterizing (bypass) kit or valve that allows the water system to bypass the hot-water tank so that expensive antifreeze is not needed to fill the tank.

### WINTERIZING USING COMPRESSED AIR

To winterize the freshwater system using compressed air, follow these steps **(Figure 8.7)**:

1. Open all drains in the system, including the hot-water tank.
2. Insert a commercial air fitting designed for the city-water hookup.
3. Operate the 12-volt DC water pump with the faucet open until dry.
4. Connect the air fitting to the city-water hookup and close all the drains except the one for the hot water.
5. Check the pressure of the compressor to ensure it is on a low setting (under 100 psi) and blow air until all the water is removed from the hot-water tank.
6. Close the bypass valves to the water heater, open the faucet farthest from the water pump, and blow air through until only air comes out the faucet.
7. Open the next farthest faucet, close the first one, and blow air until the water is gone. Continue this procedure for all faucets, including the shower and exterior shower.
8. Open the toilet valve and allow air to purge this as well.
9. Close all faucets.
10. Add RV antifreeze to any sink. There could be water in the p-trap of the plumbing.
    **CAUTION:** Use nontoxic RV antifreeze only!

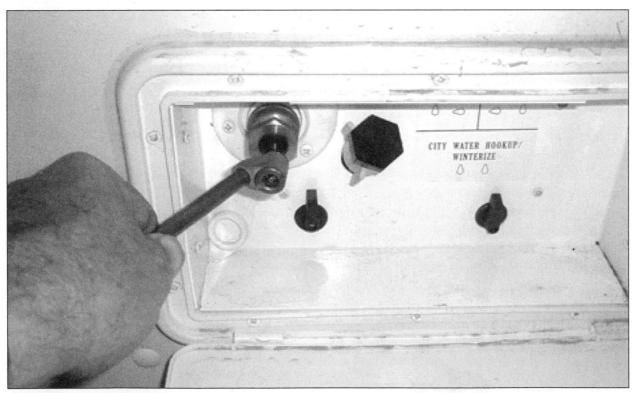

**FIGURE 8.7** This aftermarket air valve can be purchased at Camping World or other RV parts and accessory stores.

## WINTERIZING USING NONTOXIC ANTIFREEZE

Some RV owners do not have access to an air compressor, especially while traveling down the road. Others like the flexibility of having the antifreeze in-line and a small amount in the freshwater tank to use the toilet. There are two ways to add antifreeze to your system **(Figure 8.8)**.

1. Pour a few gallons in the freshwater tank that has been drained of water. Operate the water pump and open the faucet farthest from the pump until the pink-colored RV antifreeze is visible. Operate each faucet in the same manner until

the antifreeze is in every line.

2. This method uses an antifreeze fill line on the inlet side of the pump and a valve that allows you to draw antifreeze directly from the bottle, through the pump, and throughout the RV.

After storage, turn on the hot-water-bypass valve, install the drain plug, and flush any antifreeze from the system. Even though it is odorless and tasteless, some RVers like to sanitize the system.

## WATER-SYSTEM SANITATION

Bad taste and strange odors coming from your water system could be the signs of contamination or just stale water. In either case, it's a good idea to sanitize the system.

1. Drain the water tank completely, then refill halfway with clean, fresh water.
2. Mix ¼ cup of household bleach for every 15 gallons of tank capacity in a container with a gallon or two of clean water.
3. Pour this mixture in the freshwater tank.
4. Top off the tank with fresh water, and drive the RV around the block to mix the solution.
5. Pump water through each faucet until the distinct smell of bleach is present.
6. Make sure the hot-water tank has been purged of any old water by opening hot faucets.
7. Let the bleach/water solution stand for several hours.
8. Drain the entire system.

**FIGURE 8.8** If winterizing with antifreeze, only use a nontoxic RV antifreeze that is safe for copper, brass, and all types of plastic.

The bleach smell will eventually dissipate, but you may wish to use ½ cup baking soda with a gallon of water and run it through the system for faster results, pumping it through the system as described and letting it sit. Drain the system and refill with clean, fresh water.

## THE WASTE-WATER SYSTEM

In a residential setting, all waste water drains to a common pipe and out to the local sanitary system. In an RV there are two systems, the gray-water system, which captures drain water from the shower and sinks, and the blackwater system for sewage. However, it's not always that black and white (or black and gray) as some manufacturers will "mix" systems. In theory, the gray-water tank will capture water from the shower and all sinks. The blackwater system will capture sewage; however, due to tank capacity, compartment limitations, and routing issues, some manufacturers will route/dump waste water from the kitchen or bathroom sink. The shower will generally produce the largest amount of water drainage and can fill a gray-water tank fast. The point of this discussion is you need to identify where the waste water goes, how much capacity you have, and to understand how long you can use certain facilities before the need to empty or to dump. Taking a shower and seeing the floor pan fill up with water due to a full gray-water tank is very frustrating. It's important to know what drains where, what your holding-tank capacity is, and use your monitor panel.

The waste system is dumped using a 4-inch hose provided by the RV manufacturer. The dump valve(s) for the holding tanks are generally combined into a single outlet located on the driver side, or road side, of the unit. By RVIA code, the gray-water tank outlet must be at least 1¼ inches in diameter and the blackwater outlet 3 inches. Dumping must be done only at an approved dump location, such as a campground, approved rest stop, or certified dump station.

When dumping, always wear protective rubber gloves; the disposable kind is preferred by most RVers. Remove the dump-valve cap and connect the sewer hose. Several aftermarket hoses make it easier to connect to a wide variety of dump-station connections. Some have easy-to-use handles, locking rings so the hose does not slip out, and a cap to keep the hose from dripping during storage. Camping World also carries a complete line of adapters and an add-on flushing system that uses water pressure to thoroughly clean the tanks. Whatever type you choose, make sure the hose is securely connected to the dump source and that it will stay in place.

Dump the blackwater tank first by opening the valve and letting it dump **(Figure 8.9)**. Close the valve and run fresh water through the system by flushing the toilet several times. Many RV manufacturers offer a blackwater flush system that sprays fresh water around the tank to loosen everything up and help clean the tank. Simply connect a garden hose to the connection and turn it on. This is also available as an aftermarket item and is a great option to install. Next, dump the gray-water tank. This water is from the shower and sink and will clean the waste of the blackwater tank. Only dump your tanks when they are three-quarters full, and never leave the valve open at a campground because sewer odor will come back up through the hose into the RV.

After both tanks have been drained, and fresh water has been run through them, disconnect the hose and raise it as you walk to the sewage dump to drain all moisture from the hose. It is a good idea to have specific equipment dedicated to the sewage-dump procedure. This means don't use your garden hose or drinking hose to wash out the dump hose, have disposable gloves readily available in the compartment, and use disposable

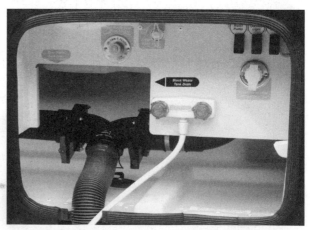

**FIGURE 8.9** Empty the blackwater tank first, then the gray water.

towels. Any tools should be kept in the compartment and sanitized after every dump and not used for any other repair.

## MAINTENANCE

There is little maintenance that is required of a waste-water system, but there are some precautionary actions you may wish to take. One of the most nagging issues with waste-water systems is inaccurate monitor-panel readings. Generally, probes are inserted into the side of waste tank and as the liquid inside rises, it creates an "arc" and lights up the appropriate level indicator. Scale, deposits, and even paper clinging to the side of the tank, can cause a faulty reading. Using the blackwater flush system will help clean the side of the tank and possibly eliminate the problem. Some RVers like to add a powdered water-softening compound to the system by mixing 2 cups of powder to 1 gallon of hot water and dumping it down the toilet and even the shower drain. The soft water reduces scale and hard-water buildup. Remember, always use a toilet paper that is RV approved or made for septic tanks since they will break down faster.

Monitor panels can also be adjusted for sensitivity by removing the panel and slightly moving the "pot" (a small slot or inverted knob) with a small screwdriver. Check your owner's manual for specific locations and technical adjustments.

Another option is to replace it with a Sensa-Tank liquid-level monitor system, with no probes, seals, or conventional meters that can fail **(Figure 8.10)**. The detector cells are installed outside the tank with no drilling or seals and produce a micro-electrical field that detects levels through nonmetallic material from the outside of the tank, completely unaffected by anything inside the tank.

Unlike home sewage that drains into a large underground septic system or city sewer, the waste in RV holding tanks remains in close proximity to the living quarters. To eliminate offensive odors,

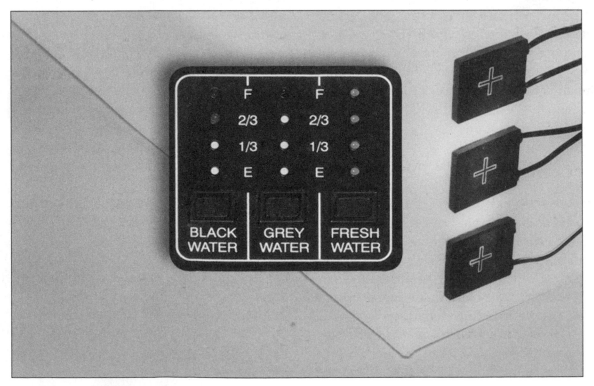

**FIGURE 8.10** The No-Drill "Sensatank" Liquid-Level Monitor System

chemicals must be used in the blackwater tank. Normally the tank is charged with a dose of toilet chemicals after dumping. But during hot summer days, additional chemicals may be necessary. Products are also available to freshen gray-water tanks and there is even a six-month product for use during storage.

Many municipalities require that biodegradable chemicals, devoid of formaldehyde, be used. Therefore, a wide variety of environmentally safe chemicals are now available.

For tank odors, always keep the valves closed while camping. Occasionally cleaning the tank with a bleach-and-water solution will also help reduce odors. A plugged vent will drive tank odors back inside the RV. Check to make sure the vent cap on the roof of the RV is open. P-traps under sinks are designed to hold a small amount of water and act as a buffer or stop for odors coming back up through the piping. Normal driving movement can splash or drive the water out of the trap, so it is a good idea to run some water down the drain of all sinks once you set up camp.

Do not use household detergents or cleaning compounds when cleaning holding tanks. These may contain chemicals that could damage the drain system or termination valves; cleaners that contain petroleum distillates can damage toilet seals and termination valves.

## THE ELECTRICAL SYSTEM

Unlike our homes, two separate electrical systems are used in our RVs: 12-volt DC supplied by onboard batteries or a converter, and 120-volt AC supplied by a campground source or generator.

The 12-volt DC (house) system is self-sufficient, allowing the RV to function without outside power. In cases where 120-volt AC power is available, a power cord is used to make the connection between the RV and an outside power source. Both systems are covered in more detail in the 12-volt DC and 120-volt AC sections that follow.

## BASIC COMPONENTS OF ELECTRICAL SYSTEMS

For the most part, the electrical systems in every RV are very similar, just more complex when more sophisticated appliances and gadgets are found on board. There are several basic components of the electrical systems.

### The 12-Volt DC System

- One or more deep-cycle battery(s) that provide power for interior lights, water pump, monitoring system, and ignition modules for RV appliances that run off propane **(Figure 8.11)**.
- One or more automotive battery(s) used for starting the engine of a tow vehicle or motorhome. This battery/charging system can also provide charging power to the house battery(s)

### The 120-Volt AC System

- A shoreline cord connects to an outside campground source to provide 15-, 30-, and/or 50-amp service, depending on the type of RV and electrical need.
- Power-distribution center/converter receives power and supplies 120-volt power through circuit breakers to appliances while converter supplies 12-volt DC power.
- AC generator, either onboard or portable, can provide power to the power-distribution center.

It is important to understand the electrical needs of your RV when dealing with 15-amp to 30-amp service and the need for adapters, extension cords, and load shedding. Please refer to Chapter 9, "The 120-Volt Alternating Current System."

**FIGURE 8.11** Deep-cycle batteries are used for powering interior components such as lights and appliance-ignition modules.

## RV APPLIANCES

Tiffin Industries coined one of the best sayings for RV comfort: "Roughin' It Smoothly." How appropriate as some RVs have more luxury amenities than the nicest home on the block when we were young. Microwave oven, satellite dish, GPS, and LCD TVs—all of the modern conveniences are at your fingertips and easy to use as well.

### FURNACES

Most RV manufacturers today use a forced-air furnace that blows heat from a mixture of fresh air drawn from the outside and propane burned in a sealed chamber and delivered through ductwork. Air circulation is important because a block-age in return air can cause the unit to overheat or underperform.

The intake/exhaust vent located on the outside also needs to be clear of obstructions. Spiders, mice, and other rodents love to build nests and webs and can render a furnace useless. Periodically check these vents for obstructions. Most furnace manufacturers do not recommend installing an aftermarket screen due to airflow restrictions.

If your furnace is working but not blowing hot air, it could be your furnace is in lock-out mode or the limit switch needs to be reset. Check your owner's manual for specifics. It could also mean your house batteries are under 10.5 volts, which would activate the blower but not the spark module, resulting in air but no heat.

## GAS RANGES

Gas ranges in RVs are quite similar to standard household units, with the exception of models that do not have pilot lights and must be manually lighted. Ranges don't require any maintenance other than cleaning to ensure spills are not caked around the lit flame to catch on fire.

Most modern range tops come with a high-output (9,000 Btu) front burner set in the middle and two medium-output (6,500 Btu) burners at the back. Older four-burner units can be upgraded easily and inexpensively.

While the range produces relatively little carbon monoxide during normal cooking, amounts can increase if the oven is improperly used to heat the interior of the vehicle for several hours. Never use the range for a heat source!

## REFRIGERATORS

One of the most important appliances in an RV is the refrigerator **(Figure 8.12)**. Virtually all refrigerators can be operated on propane or 120-volt AC power, while some will also operate on 12-volt DC. Refrigerators in RVs operate totally differently than our residential models as they use an absorption system, or the use of heat to create cool. Although RV refrigerators are very reliable for the most part, we subject them to some pretty grueling punishment. We expect them to operate on a variety of different power sources and run them down the road at 65 to 75 miles per hour over potholes, bumps, and around curves, not to mention the constant startup, shut-down, and intermittent use of most RV lifestyles.

Over the years, a handful of brands have come and gone, but for the most part, Norcold and Dometic are the major brands. In smaller units, you will see the compact single-door models, moving up to the double-door versions and all the way to the large side-by-side and four-door luxury models.

## How Refrigerators Work

There are no moving parts in an absorption refrigerator **(Figure 8.13)**. The cooling process is based on laws of chemistry and physics rather than mechanics. Water, ammonia, hydrogen gas, and sodium chromate are combined under pressure in what's commonly known as the generator or boiler.

Each of these elements plays an important role in the process of cooling or in the preservation of the equipment. The water, ammonia, and hydrogen gas are directly involved in the cooling process, but the function of the sodium chromate is to prevent the heat from corroding the pipes.

As an electrical heating element or gas burner brings the solution to a boil, liquid percolates up the pump tube. The ammonia is distilled out of the solution and continues to rise up the tube as a gas.

A short way up the tube, the water and ammonia gas part company and the water returns to the reservoir by these pipes. During the water's return, it is recombined with the ammonia at the far end of its voyage.

Meanwhile, the ammonia gas continues upward until it reaches the condenser, where it dissipates its heat and returns to a liquid form. As the drops of pure liquid ammonia fall, they trickle into the evaporator or freezing unit where they combine with hydrogen gas.

This chemical marriage causes very vigorous evaporation, which results in cooling. Because this rapid evaporation process takes place in the freezer unit, that's where most of the cooling occurs, as the heat is absorbed from the unit.

As a result of the evaporation process, the liquid ammonia again becomes a gas and travels to a secondary evaporator in the refrigerator unit where it absorbs more heat. Then the gas enters a return pipe on its way back to rejoin the water and start the process again.

**FIGURE 8.12** Most RV refrigerators operate on 120-volt AC and propane.

### Mode of Refrigerator Operation

Most models are equipped with an automatic switching feature. In the automatic mode, the control system will select the best method of operation and power selection, either 120-volt or LP. Since AC power has priority over gas, it will operate on 120-volt power when it's available from the shoreline power, generator, or from an inverter. If 120-volt power is not available, the system will automatically shift to the LP mode. And in the case of a three-way system, it will switch to 12-volt DC operation.

To operate in the LP mode only, move the switch to the LP or Gas setting. The system will activate the Gas indicator lamp, then the ignition system will attempt to light the burner for a period of approximately 45 seconds. If unsuccessful, the Check indicator lamp will illuminate and the Gas-mode light will turn off. To restart Gas operation, you need to press the main power On/Off button

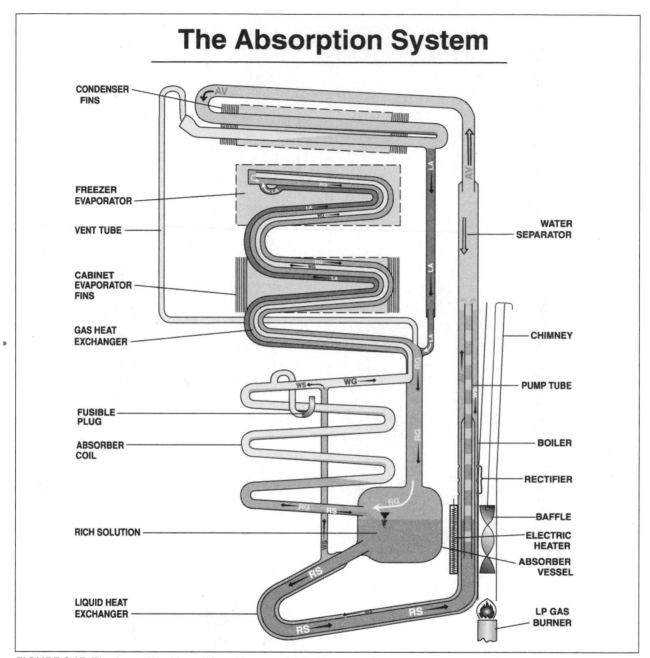

## The Absorption System

CONDENSER FINS

FREEZER EVAPORATOR

VENT TUBE

CABINET EVAPORATOR FINS

GAS HEAT EXCHANGER

FUSIBLE PLUG

ABSORBER COIL

RICH SOLUTION

LIQUID HEAT EXCHANGER

WATER SEPARATOR

CHIMNEY

PUMP TUBE

BOILER

RECTIFIER

BAFFLE

ELECTRIC HEATER

ABSORBER VESSEL

LP GAS BURNER

**FIGURE 8.13** The Inner Workings of an Absorption Refrigerator System

to the Off position and then back to Gas again. It will then attempt a new 45-second sequence.

As with any LP appliance, if the refrigerator has not been in use for an extended period of time, or if the LP-gas supply has just been refilled, air may have been trapped in the lines, requiring you to purge the air.

This means that you will have to perform the restart sequence three to four times or more until the air is removed from the lines.

If the refrigerator does not start after several attempts, first check the propane supply and make sure all the manual shut-off valves are open. Perform a quick check at the stove to make sure there is adequate LP pressure coming into the RV.

For the refrigerator to operate on any mode, DC voltage must be supplied to the terminals at the rear of the refrigerator and must be connected directly to the house battery. The operational range is 10.5 to 15 volts DC.

### Leveling Your Refrigerator

Since the absorption modes work off gravity, fluid running through the coils must complete the cy-

**FIGURE 8.14** Place the bubble level in the freezer compartment to ensure proper leveling.

cle. If the RV is too off-level, the fluid in the generator will pool on one side and leave part of the chamber dry, which will cause the heating element to cook the sodium chromate. It gets hard and brittle and can flake and float around until it finds a place to lodge in the pump tube. Eventually this would result in refrigerator failure.

Since the absorption design relies on gravity to circulate the solution within the system, it is important to level the RV properly. Norcold and Dometic both specify a "comfortably leveled coach" is acceptable. However, using the round-bubble level provided by the manufacturer is the safest method to determine proper leveling. Place the bubble level on the base of the freezer compartment and if the bubble is at least halfway inside the ring, it is good **(Figure 8.14)**.

### Troubleshooting a Refrigerator

Let's look at insufficient cooling **(Figure 8.15)**. Some models have a thermister attached to the interior cooling fins to detect interior temperature. Moving this higher on the fins will lower the temperature. One problem could be the wrong temperature setting; a simple adjustment on the thermostat to a higher setting will fix that. Another cause may be restricted air circulation over

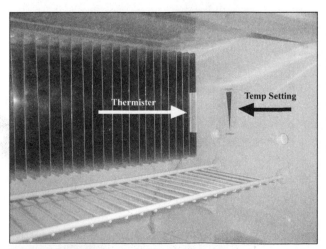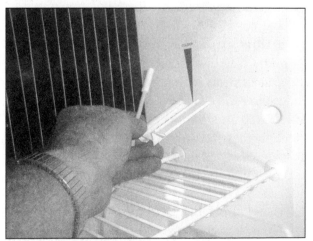

**FIGURE 8.15** Some models utilize a thermister or temperature sensor clipped to the cooling fins.

the cooling unit due to obstructions. Check for fallen insulation, dirt, or debris buildup, or even a bird's nest.

Next, check for voltage drop or a break in the electrical circuit by checking fuses, switch wiring, and proper voltage coming into the RV. A more detailed troubleshooting guide for both Norcold and Dometic is available in the appendix.

## Tips and Tricks for Better Refrigerator Operation

Precool the refrigerator by starting it the night before a trip. This should be done with no food in the compartments. Wait until the refrigerator is thoroughly cold before placing food inside. Precool food in your home refrigerator rather than trying to cool warm food with your RV refrigerator. Proper refrigeration requires free air circulation within the compartments.

Don't overload the refrigerator and don't cover the shelves with paper or large containers that block airflow. To reduce frost buildup, cover stored liquids and moist foods, and don't leave the door open too long. Always wipe moisture off the outside of containers before putting them in the refrigerator. This will help prevent frost buildup, which consumes cooling power.

Periodically clean out the burner unit. LP-gas has a garlic or rotten-egg odor that becomes especially strong as the cylinders or tanks run low. This scent attracts spiders, which will build nests in the burner. Clean out the refrigerator's roof-exhaust vent. Birds' nests, leaves, twigs, or other debris can lodge there, choking the refrigerator's efficiency. A spider-web brush works very well for this.

You may need to install a fan in the compartment behind the refrigerator to speed the removal of hot air. This will significantly enhance the performance of your refrigerator. These fans can be operated in the 12-volt DC mode, and should be mounted above the coil rather than on the floor for superior airflow.

## AIR-CONDITIONING SYSTEMS

Once considered a luxury item, air conditioners have certainly become a popular item because most RVers travel during warm-weather seasons or to warmer regions of the country to escape the cold weather.

For the most part, RV air conditioners are similar to 120-volt AC window-mounted units used in homes. Operation is controlled by either a wall-mounted thermostat or by using two knobs that control on/off, fan-only, and AC operation on high and low fan speeds located on the front of the air-conditioning unit.

Few problems occur with this type of AC unit, but there are a few maintenance suggestions and tips for operation that you should be familiar with. The air conditioner should never be used when voltage drops below 105, which may be indicated by low fan speeds and the compressor cycling on and off. Low voltage at a campsite hookup can be tested with a multimeter. Refer to Chapter 9, "The 120-Volt Alternating-Current (AC) System."

Always make sure the air conditioner is turned off before connecting the RV power cord to an outside source of power or when starting the generator to prevent an electrical surge.

When the outside temperature drops to below 75°F, the air-conditioner thermostat should be set to a midpoint between "warmer" and "cooler" to prevent ice buildup on the evaporator coil. If ice-up occurs, it is necessary to turn off the air conditioner to allow the coil to defrost before resuming normal operation. Consult your owner's manual for recommended defrost procedures.

To help maintain a clean air conditioner, the roof-top unit should be kept covered in the off-season to prevent dirt, debris, and small animals from getting inside. Once a year, remove the cover and, using a compressor, blow the dust, bugs, leaves, and other debris out of the unit.

Remove and clean the filter inside the RV by washing or replacing the original pad (**Figure 8.16**). A dirty filter will block airflow and reduce

**FIGURE 8.16** Clean or replace the air-conditioning filter periodically to provide optimum airflow.

the cooling ability. Check your owner's manual for the proper filter location of your air-conditioner filter as some ducted models may have a remote location.

## BASIC RVING EQUIPMENT

Before the maiden voyage, it's important to have specific equipment for utilities, hookups, leveling, and for inhabiting the coach. Make a list of the test equipment, tools, and connectors needed as detailed in each chapter of this handbook.

A spare tire and equipment to change a flat should be inspected prior to taking off down the road as several larger RVs do not come with a spare. This may seem odd, but some manufacturers believe seasoned RVers will actually call

for roadside assistance rather than trying to lift a 30,000-pound vehicle and changing a 200-pound tire and rim. Make sure you know what to do in case of an emergency **(See Exhibit 8.1)**.

Several companies offer roadside assistance, such as Good Sam Emergency Road Service (ERS). Staffed with the largest dispatch network in the industry, the Good Sam ERS program offers twenty-four-hour customer service assistance with trained technicians that can often help troubleshoot the problem immediately.

For the most technical information and troubleshooting assistance, pick up a copy of Trailer Life's *RV Repair & Maintenance Manual* written by Bob Livingston. This manual has been the ultimate reference book for RV owners and technicians for more than two decades.

Visit www.trailerlife.com for more details.

**EXHIBIT 8.1** Recommended Basic Tools and Parts Kit

- Combination English (SAE) wrenches, (both open and box end) 3/8 to 1 inch
- Combination metric wrenches, (both open and box end) 6mm to 24mm
- Several common sizes each of flat-blade and Phillips screwdrivers
- A 3/8-inch-drive SAE ratchet set with sockets from 3/8 inch to 3/4-inch
- A 3/8-inch-drive metric ratchet set with sockets from 6mm to 19mm
- A 1/2-inch-drive SAE ratchet set with sockets from 1/2-inch to 1 inch
- A 1/2-inch-drive metric ratchet set with sockets from 10mm to 24mm
- A set of Torx (star-shaped) bits
- Needlenose and regular pliers, c-channel or "slip-joint" pliers, and channel lock pliers
- A 1-pound hammer
- A pocket knife, razor knife, or other cutting/scraping device
- Spark-plug socket, check the appropriate size of your engine and generator as well
- A good set of high-quality, long, heavy-duty jumper cables
- A set of Allen wrenches
- "Certified" tire-pressure gauge
- An electrical test light assortment such as circuit tester, multimeter, and voltage tester (See Chapter 10)
- A flashlight with batteries
- Rescue Tape
- Silicone
- Spray lubricant—check your owner's manual for specific types recommended for slide-room seals, leveling jacks, awning, windows, and doors
- Hose-repair kit with extra washers
- Various hose clamps—automotive "screw-tight" style
- Spare fuses (check the size and type of automotive and 12-volt used in the power center)
- Extra engine fluids such as motor oil, transmission fluid, brake fluid, antifreeze, etc Check your owner's manual for additional "specialty" fluids that may be required such as hydraulic fluid or synthetics
- Duct tape

This is a basic kit. As your technical skill level increases, your tool kit will get larger as well. Keep in mind, the more tools you bring, the more weight you add to the RV.

# CHAPTER NINE

# The 120-Volt Alternating-Current (AC) System

## Units of Measurement
## How Electricity Is Supplied
## Electrical Safety
## Electrical System Diagnosis

During the course of a day, your home is heated and/or cooled, your water is kept hot, television entertains you, and the Internet keeps you connected all without much thought about how or where that electricity comes from. You take it for granted since there is little you can do outside of checking a breaker or calling an electrician.

In your RV, it's much more complex. However, RV owners can do some basic troubleshooting by understanding the fundamentals of the RV electrical system. Also, a problem could be something simple that appears complex or just a simple switch, but even if it's a major problem, knowing what's wrong and how the system works will help when dealing with a repair facility.

**FIGURE 9.1** All the modern conveniences of home require the 120-volt-AC power of home as well.

Unlike most homes, your RV utilizes two sources of electricity: 120-volt AC, which we are familiar with in a residential setting, and 12-volt DC through the use of batteries and converted power, which was covered in Chapter 8. It is important to identify which appliances and systems operate on 120-volt AC and which are 12-volt-DC powered—and which utilize both **(Figure 9.1).**

## UNITS OF MEASUREMENT

When you work with electricity, an understanding of the basic terminology is important. However, sometimes the technical description doesn't tell us how it applies to our RV challenges. The following are some common electrical definitions and what they mean in RV terms.

### VOLTAGE

*Voltage* is the amount of electrical force pushing the electrons through the circuit. In principle, it is the same as pounds per square inch in a water system.

**RV Translation:**
An external electrical source such as an outlet at the campground or garage should provide 120 volts, but it is important to check the source to verify you are within 117 to 120 volts. It is important to know that if the voltage coming from your campground source is low voltage (under 110 volts) it could cause damage.

### AMPERES (AMPS)

*Amps* are units of electrical flow, or volume. This is analogous to gallons per minute of water. Often, small currents such as those that run clocks are rated in milliamps. One milliamp is 1/1000 of an amp.

**RV Translation:**
Your electrical source will be rated for a specific amperage: 15 amps in residential, 30- or 50-amp service in campgrounds.

Knowing what your requirements are will be important to monitoring the system and not blowing a fuse.

## OHMS

An *ohm* is a measure of resistance to flow, or restriction. Think of it relative to the size of the pipe or how far the faucet has been opened.

**RV Translation:**
Checking the ohms reading of components will help diagnose faulty equipment. Other than that, there's not much the average RVer needs to know about ohms.

## WATTS

A *watt* is a measure of electrical power, or work. One watt equals 1 volt × 1 amp or, said another way, volts multiplied by amps equal watts. Larger amounts of power are measured in kilowatts (1,000 watts).

**RV Translation:**
This becomes important when looking at the proper size generator or inverter. You must list the continuous power rating in watts of all the appliances you intend to operate to determine the appropriate size.

## ALTERNATING AND DIRECT CURRENT

Most of us are familiar with the terms 120-volt AC and 12-volt DC; however, we may not be familiar with alternating current (AC) and direct current (DC) terminology.

Direct current is constant; the electrons flow steadily in one direction. With alternating current, the electrons rapidly and constantly reverse direction. The frequency with which they reverse direction is measured in cycles per second, or Hertz (Hz).

The standard frequency for alternating current in the United States is 60 Hz. Oftentimes this is referred to as 110-volt AC, but it actually is 117 to 120-volt 60-Hz AC.

## HOW ELECTRICITY IS SUPPLIED

Electricity is supplied by one of three sources: an outside campground source commonly referred to as "shoreline power," an auxiliary AC generator, or from an inverted 12-volt DC source in smaller applications.

Power is brought into the coach by means of a cord commonly called the "shoreline" cord to a distribution panel, the heart of the 120-volt AC system **(Figure 9.2)**. Direct circuits inside this panel are protected with circuit breakers for permanent appliances such as air conditioners, microwave ovens, and wall outlets. Most RVs include an electrical converter that converts 120-volt AC into 12-volt DC to power interior lights and ignition modules for appliances that run off propane, such as the water heater, furnace, stove top, and refrigerator.

If an onboard generator is available, the power cord is plugged into a separate outlet or receptacle,

**FIGURE 9.2** 120-volt AC power can be supplied by plugging in the "Shoreline Cord" into a campground source.

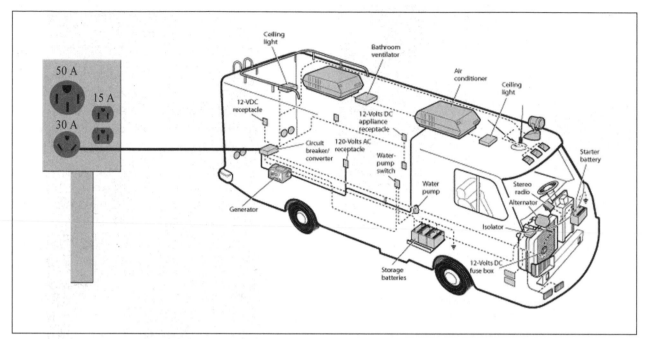

**FIGURE 9.3** 120-Volt AC System for Motorhomes and Trailers

usually in the electrical service compartment. Newer models feature an automatic switchover device that detects the generator input and switches electrical sources without the need to physically plug the shoreline cord into a generator source.

When the source of 120-volt AC is present, the AC system provides power to appliances similar to your home, while the converter supplies power for the 12-volt DC systems, usually protected by automotive-style fuses.

The converter may also provide a charge to the house batteries. An increasing number of RVs are also offering inverters that will change 12-volt DC power from the house batteries into 120-volt AC power for select appliances. A smaller 300-watt inverter is usually an option for powering a TV and VCR/DVD player but not much more. The large 2,000-watt inverters can power more appliances **(Figure 9.3)**. Refer to the inverter section of this chapter for information on battery capacity and amp-hour calculations.

With 30-amp service, there are three incoming wires from the source, two for power transmission and a ground for safety. With 50-amp service, a third power-transmission wire is added.

All appliances and wall outlets in the RV should have three connections **(Figure 9.4)**:

(1) *Line*—commonly referred to as "hot," usually a black wire
(2) *Neutral*—known as "common," usually a white wire
(3) Ground—usually a green wire

It is important to be aware of potential overloads **(Figure 9.5)**. For example, if the receptacle in

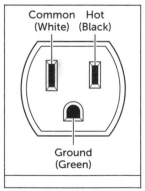

**FIGURE 9.4** Correct polarity of the RV 120-volt AC system can be checked at any wall outlet with a test light, multimeter, or polarity check device.

FIGURE 9.5 Correct polarity of the campground 120-volt AC system can be checked using a simple circuit tester. **Note:** make sure you test the actual outlet you will be using!

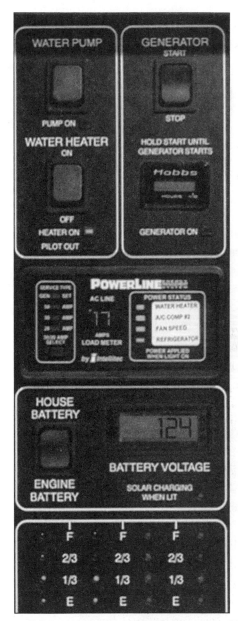

Figure 9.6 An energy-management system (EMS) automatically controls key components to reduce overload.

a campground and the shoreline cord are rated at 30 amps, it's possible to turn on enough appliances to exceed that rating. If an RV has two roof air conditioners, most manufacturers wire the coaches so only one can be operated from the campground source; the other must be operated from an onboard generator. This is designed to prevent an owner from operating both AC units and then turning on an appliance such as the microwave and going over 30 amps, which would overload the circuit.

A list of appliances frequently used in RVs and their typical power requirements is shown in **Exhibit 9.1.** Keep in mind, appliances differ and power ratings will vary. For exact ratings, refer to the ID plate on the appliance (see Appendix).

## ENERGY-MANAGEMENT SYSTEMS

Several companies are offering an energy-management system (EMS) that temporarily shuts down key components to avoid an overload situation in the case of a 15- or 30-amp service **(Figure 9.6)**. For example, if the roof air conditioner is running the refrigerator and television, you might be only at 24 amps. However, if you turn on the microwave oven, it would certainly go over the 30-amp service. The EMS will sense the overload condition and shed

the back AC compressor. If it still senses an overload condition it will shut down the fan, then the water heater, and finally the refrigerator. The theory is you only need the extra power for a short period of time, (2 to 3 minutes in a microwave) and shutting down noncritical appliances for that time would not affect cooling capabilities in your RV. It takes the place of doing it the old-fashioned way of running around shutting appliances off

**EXHIBIT 9.1** Common RV Appliances and Their Power Requirements

| Appliance | Wattage | 5 mins | 15 mins | 30 mins | 1 hour | 2 hours |
|---|---|---|---|---|---|---|
| Color TV, 13 inch | 50 | .33 | 1 | 2 | 4 | 8 |
| Color TV, 19 inch | 100 | .66 | 2 | 4 | 8 | 16 |
| Color TV, LCD, 32 inch | 125 | .75 | 2.25 | 5 | 10 | 20 |
| DVD player | 50 | .33 | 1 | 2 | 4 | 8 |
| Blender | 300 | 2 | 6 | 12 | | |
| Power drill | 500 | 3.3 | 10 | 20 | | |
| Coffee maker | 1,000 | 6.6 | 20 | 40 | 80 | 160 |
| Refrigerator, 3 cu. ft. | 150 | | | 2 | 4 | 8 |
| Refrigerator, 20 cu. ft. | 750 | | | 21 | 42 | 84 |
| Toaster | 1,000 | 6.6 | 20 | | | |
| Microwave | 1,500 | 10 | 30 | 60 | 120 | 240 |
| Air conditioner | 1,500 | 10 | 30 | 60 | 120 | 240 |
| Cell phone charger | 15 | 10 | 20 | 40 | 80 | 16 |
| Electric ceramic heater | 1,500 | 10 | 30 | 60 | 120 | 240 |
| Lamp | 100 | .66 | 2 | 4 | 8 | 16 |

## ELECTRICAL SAFETY

Electrical hazards are silent and invisible. The two prevalent dangers are fire and shock. Fires may be caused by short circuits and overloads if the system is not set up and used correctly. Shock is caused when electricity finds an easy path through a person to ground.

## SHORT CIRCUITS AND SHOCK HAZARDS

A short circuit occurs when a "hot" wire comes in contact with a ground (return) connection. This can happen when wires come loose and touch something or insulation is rubbed through. When a short occurs, the safety device (circuit breaker or fuse) should prevent any problems.

Shock and electrocution aren't a danger with 12-volt DC systems, but 120-volt AC systems can knock you for a loop.

To protect yourself from shock, disconnect the power source before working on any electrical device.

## SHORELINE POWER

Before you plug your rig in, be sure all major loads are shut off. Check the electrical outlet, plug, and wire for damage and fraying. The insulation on all wires should be intact and unbroken. Cover any exposed spots with electrical tape, and replace any wiring if the conductors are damaged. Also check the power cord's metal contacts for signs of tarnish or melting of the molded end. Periodically clean the terminals with a fine sandpaper or steel wool **(Figure 9.7)**. Plugging into a campground source with the power on creates a spark or arc that will eventually damage the plug and can cause serious electrical issues inside the coach. Always turn the power off before connecting and disconnecting .Check the campground source for proper polarity, voltage, and even the frequency if possible.

## POLARITY

It's important to verify if the campground source is wired correctly or there isn't a short somewhere

**FIGURE 9.7** Periodically check the power cord connection for signs of damage or tarnished connectors.

Figure 9.8 A voltage tester such as this digital model will verify correct voltage from the campground source.

along the "ganged" line of units. To check polarity, simply use a circuit tester found in the electrical section of most hardware or home improvement stores. Remember, turn the campground switch off before plugging in your tester. Some owners like to use a digital multimeter for testing purposes as well **(Figure 9.8)**. Make sure you are familiar with its operation and settings. If the outlet does not check out okay, do not plug into it or try to fix it yourself. Move to another spot and alert the manager.

## VOLTAGE

Your electrical source should provide between 117- to 120-volt AC power. It is not uncommon to find older campgrounds with less than adequate power, which will cause damage to electrical components and equipment. An analog voltage tester will show the proper range of operation using a scale and can be found in most hardware and home improvement stores. Multimeters will also verify voltage.

Most campground sources will have a variety of outlets ranging from a typical 120-volt 15-amp residential style to 50-amp service. It is important to check the outlet you will actually be plugging into. Most test devices are designed for the residential-style outlet, but you will need a 15-amp to 30- or 50-amp adapter to test the proper outlet.

## POWER CORDS AND ADAPTERS

The typical residential-style outlet will generally only have a 15-amp circuit and is commonly used for smaller trailers and truck campers. A 30-amp service is used in larger trailers and motorhomes to power one roof air conditioner and other appliances inside the coach. However larger units with two roof air conditioners and more power needs will have a 50-amp service. A 50/30-amp adapter will be needed when using a campground that only has 30-amp service, and a 30/15-amp adapter will be needed if you are plugging in a 30-amp cord into your garage or for storage purposes.

Although this is a common practice, you must be aware of the power your RV draws and the limitations you have from the outlet. This is critical when connecting to a 15-amp residential outlet such as a garage due to the power draw of an air-conditioning unit, refrigerator, and other components. Also, keep in mind the residential outlet is usually not a dedicated circuit and could be connected to other outlets in the garage or storage unit that have other things plugged in as well.

The power cord of your RV is rated for the service you require, but many RVers need to "stretch" or add an extension cord to the power supply **(Figure 9.9)**. It is critical to match your power needs here as well as most heavy-duty extension cords are only rated for 15 amps. Using one of these to extend a 30-amp service will created limitations. It is also not recommended to use an extension cord longer than 25 feet.

## GROUND FAULT
## CIRCUIT INTERRUPTER (GFCI)

Another safety device in the 120-volt AC system is a ground fault circuit interrupter (GFCI) outlet

(**Figures 9.10 and 9.11**), which will monitor the variance in current between the hot and ground wires in the outlet. These are located in areas close to a water source, such as the kitchen, bathroom, and outdoor outlets. If a short circuit is drawing current to ground, such as through a human body, the levels of current in the two wires will differ. Sensing this, the GFCI will shut down the outlet.

Usually a GFCI outlet can be identified by the small test(T) and reset(R) button; however, manufacturers are not only using one main test/reset outlet and connecting flat-panel outlets in-line to save money. All these outlets are connected and

FIGURE 9.10 Ground Fault Circuit Interrupters are generally installed near a water source and should be tested periodically.

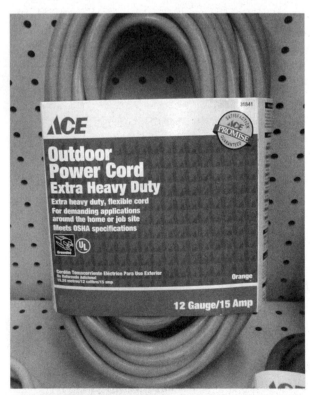

FIGURE 9.9 Even "heavy-duty" power cords are only rated at 15 amps. A 30-amp service could cause a dangerous overload situation.

FIGURE 9.11 Not all GFCI outlets have the "test/reset" button but are connected to one main outlet inside the RV.

controlled by the main test/reset outlet, so you may have a nonworking or "dead" outlet outside due to fact that the test/reset button popped. Using your circuit tester, verify which outlets are connected to the GFCI outlet by pushing the test button while plugged into 120-volt power and testing the outlets inside and outside. Outlets not connected will be "live" while others will be "dead."

To be sure the GFCI is working properly, press the test button. When you do this, the reset button should pop out and the outlet will go dead. You can also use a GFCI certified circuit tester to test each outlet. These should be tested yearly.

## SURGE PROTECTORS

Both lightning and man-made electrical noise can induce extremely short-duration high-voltage spikes on the AC power line, which may then enter an RV via the power cord. The damage caused by low-level spikes is often cumulative in nature, so affected appliances fail for no apparent reason. Larger spikes (such as those caused by a nearby lightning strike) may cause immediate failure.

A variety of surge suppressors are available for protection against spikes **(Figure 9.12)**. These devices typically include a circuit that momentarily conducts current whenever the voltage rises to an abnormal level, thereby short-circuiting (or "clamping") the spike. Basic plug-in models will shut down the power when a spike occurs and require manual reset. The more sophisticated surge protectors automatically shut off the power if abnormal voltage (under/over) is present, such as below 103 volts and above 132 volts or an open circuit, and generally feature an automatic reset. These can be portable, plug-in style, or hard wired, and have capabilities to detect reverse polarity and dangerous current on ground wires.

## ELECTRICAL FIRST AID

To assist someone who has received a severe shock, shut off the power source first if the person is still

**FIGURE 9.12** A surge protector can help protect against electrical spikes and appliance damage.

near or connected to the electrical source; then check for breathing and pulse. Call for help and begin CPR if needed and if you know how.

If an electrical fire occurs, first disconnect the power source by switching off the circuit breakers, unplugging the power cord, shutting off the AC generator, or disconnecting/switching off the batteries. Be careful because the wiring may become very hot. Then aim a fire extinguisher rated for a Class C fire at the base of the flames. Read the instructions on your fire extinguisher now; don't wait until there's a fire. Never use water on an electrical fire while the electricity is on. After the electricity is unplugged, the fire is no longer electrical in nature and water may be used, unless there is a Class B fuel source like flammable liquids involved.

## ELECTRICAL SYSTEM DIAGNOSIS

An organized and logical approach to diagnosis is essential to repair an electrical problem quickly and cost effectively. Since today's RVs are loaded with complicated electrical devices and appliances, the potential for problems increases, and the hit-

or-miss approach of swapping out parts until it works is very costly.

The first step is to verify that proper 120-volt AC power is coming into the control center and to the affected component. Second, determine if the system that is not working is affected in all modes of operation. In other words, is it really an electrical problem or is the component malfunctioning? For example, if the refrigerator is not cooling, does it operate in the propane mode? Since electricity is invisible, this must be done with special testers to check circuits and components.

## USING TEST EQUIPMENT

You can spend a long time chasing an electrical gremlin without the proper test equipment and knowing how to use it **(Figure 9.13)**. A simple circuit tester will help determine not only the proper polarity but also verify power to an outlet. A voltage monitor will verify proper voltage from the campground source and throughout the RV.

## MULTIMETERS

A multimeter performs a variety of functions and is essential for electrical troubleshooting. Today's digital multimeters are inexpensive and easy to use, even for the novice. Multimeters are sold with instructions explaining how to perform a variety of tests, such as continuity and voltage, and can be used for both 120-volt AC, and 12-volt DC testing.

## CHECKING AC VOLTAGE

To check for proper AC voltage follow these steps:

1. Connect probes to multimeter as instructed by the manufacturer. Most require that the probes be inserted into the multimeter first. Set the range selector to the position that includes 120-volt AC. Most likely this value will be higher than 120.
2. Hook the RV electrical cord to campground power, start the generator, or

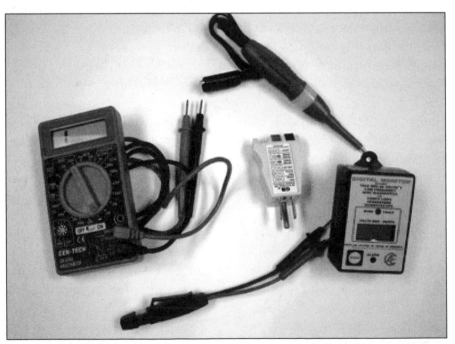

**Figure 9.13** The proper test equipment is essential for monitoring and troubleshooting an electrical system.

activate the power inverter, depending on the source you wish to test.

3. Insert the red probe into the larger, vertical wall-socket slot and the black probe into the other. Read the voltage.

4. Voltage range should be between 110 and 127 with no load on the system. Voltage will rarely exceed 120 in campgrounds; however, AC generators may produce upward of 130 volts and drop when a load is added.

If voltage falls below 100 volts AC, motor-driven appliances will be damaged and 12-volt DC converters may cease to function. Most newer AC appliances are protected against low-voltage conditions. Voltage monitored at wall sockets should be the same as that of appliances and accessories.

### Checking Continuity

The ability to check for resistance to current flow is important in diagnosing electrical problems, or in simple terms, looking for a short circuit. If the flow of current is impeded by broken, corroded, shorted, or poorly soldered or connected wires, resistance occurs.

To check for resistance:

1. Connect the multimeter probes in appropriate slots. Set selector switch to the appropriate position to check continuity.

2. Touch the probes together: The ohms scale or digital screen should read zero (0). Zero means that there is no resistance while holding the two probe tips together; current is moving freely.

3. To check resistance in a wire, touch one probe to one end of the wire and the second probe to the other end. The meter should read zero. If it does not, resistance may be caused by wire damage, corrosion, or poor connections.

4. Check for resistance in a solder joint or solderless connection; touch the probes to both sides of the connection and read the scale. Zero means the connection is good; any other position of the needle or other reading of the digital meter means the solder joint is cold or corroded and/or the connection is bad or badly crimped.

5. To check the resistance in a fuse, touch the probes to the metal ends or tabs of the fuse and read the scale. Again, zero means the fuse is good.

6. Bulbs can be checked by probing the contact and case; zero indicates a good bulb.

Loose wiring, bad connection, and poor ground are common electrical problems due to the harsh conditions we put our RV through. Traveling down the bumpy roads of America, temperature fluctuations of more than 60°F in one day, and leaving the RV sitting for months on end without use all contribute to some challenging situations for electrical components.

### INTERMITTENT ELECTRICAL PROBLEMS

The toughest type of electrical problem to diagnose is an intermittent one. Intermittent opens or shorts are usually caused by something rubbing or a component that changes resistance when it heats up. Corroded and loose connections are also frequently the cause of such problems.

Observe when the problem occurs, and try to discover how to duplicate the problem. For example, does it only happen when going around a corner or over a rough railroad crossing? Sometimes wiggling the wiring harness or tapping your hand on a fixture will locate the problem. Once you can duplicate the problem, follow these test procedures.

### IDENTIFY THE PROBLEM

Operate the problem circuit in all modes. What doesn't work properly? Is it a complete or partial failure? Which systems does it affect? When does it occur?

Determine which components in the circuit, if any, still work. For example, if you find that only one device in the circuit is out, you have eliminated the fuse, switch, and main wiring harness as potential sources of the problem.

Obtain the wiring diagrams for the specific vehicle you are working on, when possible. Over the years, many manufacturers have either gone out of business or been bought by other companies, and wiring diagrams are difficult to find. First check with the manufacturer, then with a dealer that may have carried the product when it was new, as several change brands over time. Another source would be to check with an emergency road service provider such as Good Sam ERS because its technical department usually retains wiring diagrams to assist travelers in case of emergency.

Familiarize yourself with the current flow in the circuit by tracing the path in the wiring diagram. Determine where the circuit receives current, what the circuit protection is, which switches and/or relays control current flow, and how the components operate. Many times what is considered an electrical failure is simply a switch or breaker shutoff somewhere downstream of the nonoperating component. The GFCI outlet is a good example. If the test button on the bathroom outlet is tripped, all the outlets in-line, such as the kitchen and outside compartment, will not work. However, since the outlet in the living room or bedroom works, we assume the outlet is bad.

Another example is refrigerators that feature a high-humidity switch that has three positions: on, off, and storage. If the switch is in the storage position, the refrigerator will not work; however, if you are not familiar with this switch, it seems as though the refrigerator is defective.

Check all fuses and circuit breakers and/or fuses. Some appliances have a separate fuse or reset located in the appliance compartment. If the circuit-protection devices are blown, look for a short circuit; if they are intact, look for an open circuit. Don't assume the circuit breaker is good and power is being supplied just because the breaker is not tripped. Verify power to the appliance by using a circuit tester at the appliance plug-in or a multimeter at the power connection directly to the appliance.

### CONVERTERS

Most RVs are equipped with power converters designed to transform 120-volt AC to 12-volt DC that can be used to operate DC appliances in the RV and charge batteries. There are two types of converters: dual output (linear) and single output.

Dual-output converters were popular because of the inexpensive cost but have not been used since the late 1990s. These units featured two output circuits, one for operating the RV appliances and a second one to charge the batteries. With this type of converter, battery charging was usually not very effective because the amount of power required by appliances is subtracted from the output available for battery charging **(Figure 9.14)**.

A single-output converter is more efficient since the battery is always on line, and the voltage is filtered so that ripples and surges are minimal **(Figure 9.15)**. Newer units use high-frequency switching or solid-state electronics.

### AC RIPPLE

All power converters will have a detectable AC waveform riding on the DC output—no exceptions. RV electrical systems continue to evolve and become more complex, and this has driven the need for cleaner power. Old transformer-based converters like the linear units have a fair amount of AC ripple—in fact, a lack of AC ripple can actually help a technician diagnose certain prob-

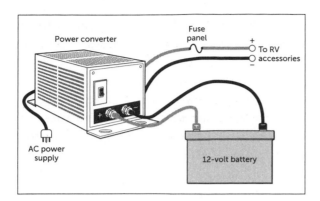

**FIGURE 9.14** Power output of dual-outlet or "linear" converters is split, limiting battery-recharge capabilities.

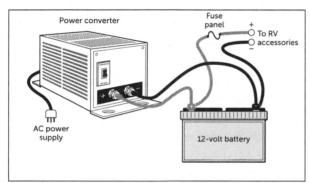

**FIGURE 9.15** The battery is always on line in a single-output converter system.

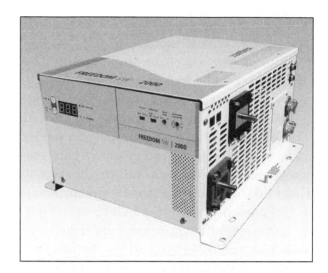

**FIGURE 9.16** Larger inverters provide 120-Volt AC power for appliances from the 12-Volt DC "House" batteries.

lems. Ferro-resonant converters actually rely on the filtering characteristics of the batteries for proper operation and output. The switch-mode or electronic converters provide very clean DC power and have very little ripple—normally in the ½-volt AC range—but no more than 700 mv (.700 volts AC) at full-rated output.

## INVERTERS

Inverters change 12-volt DC battery power to 120-volt AC power to operate appliances without plugging into shoreline power or running the gen-erator **(Figure 9.16)**.

Sizes range from small 100-watt units that are generally located near the TV and only run the TV

and DVD player to large wired-in units rated up to 5,500. The larger units also contain a multi-stage battery charger for proper battery maintenance. This is covered in Chapter 10, "The 12-Volt Direct-Current System."

Over the years, technology advancements, solar panels, battery capacity, and inverters themselves have made this a popular option and not just for "dry camping."

Many RVers like the quick and quiet power an inverter offers when taking a break at rest stops or parking lots versus starting the generator just to watch a little TV. When attending certain events, units are often camped in open fields with no access to electricity, and regulations prohibit the use of generators after specified evening hours.

The length of time the inverter can supply power depends on the number/wattage requirements of appliances and the battery capacity. Most inverter manufacturers have a calculator that will estimate how long a battery/appliance combination will operate together. Simply enter the voltage of your battery, the total amp-hours of the battery bank (available on the calculator), the combined watt value of the appliances you plan to run (listed on the inverter-manufacturer Web site), and click the calculate button to see how many hours your system should run. You can also refer to Exhibit 9.1, page 106 for average consumption of typical appliances. Keep in mind this is based on fully charged batteries.

To determine the size of inverter required, it is necessary to determine which appliances you will need to supply and the battery capacity you have available. Refer to the manufacturer's data plate for usage and calculate the wattage requirements.

Most early inverters produced a square wave output—essentially a voltage that was either switched "full on" or "full off" at any particular instant. As technology advanced, more-delicate electronic equipment required a modified-sine waveform to improve voltage regulations under varying loads.

When viewed through an oscilloscope, a modified-sine wave will have a choppy squared-off wave; however, for most of us, that's too much information. What does that mean for the average RV owner?

Today, inverters are available in modified-sine and true-sine outputs. The modified-sine models will handle the majority of household appliances and electronic components without any distortion or interference.

The problem only occurs when sensitive equipment is installed, such as plasma TVs or owner-installed technology that requires improved clarity of the electronic signal. There's nothing more frustrating than purchasing a high-quality plasma TV and having a distortion line "floating" on screen

Inverters that produce a true-sine waveform are now becoming more commonplace, and costs have dropped for some models to the point where they rival their modified sine-wave counterparts.

The quality of the power produced is actually better than most residences receive and will safely operate any AC appliance as long as the inverter's power ratings aren't exceeded.

### Inverter Installation

Although the small plug-in inverters can be installed or removed in an instant, the larger models often require considerable planning. Larger inverters require large battery banks, which means that the RV's existing batteries may need to be upgraded. This may involve fabricating a well-ventilated battery compartment capable of supporting up to several hundred pounds of additional battery weight.

Furthermore, an inverter supplying 2,500 watts of AC power will draw at least 200 amps of DC current from the batteries. This means the inverter should be installed as close to the batteries as possible to minimize voltage drop, even if very thick power cables, such as 000 gauge, are used. Many can be mounted horizontally or vertically, making aftermarket installation easier. More on the inverter's 12-volt DC functions, such as battery-charging capabilities and requirements are listed in Chapter 10, "The 12-Volt Direct Current (DC) System."

# CHAPTER TEN

# The 12-Volt Direct-Current (DC) System

### Automotive Batteries
### The Charging System
### The Battery Isolator
### Deep-Cycle "House" Batteries
### Accurate Battery Monitoring
### Battery Testing/Inspection
### 12-Volt-System Troubleshooting

n an RV, there are two separate 12-volt DC systems: an automotive engine battery and a deep-cycle battery- supplied house system. In a motorhome, the engine battery supplies power for the exterior lights and other automotive features such as starting the engine. A trailer utilizes the tow vehicle's electrical system through the trailer-wiring connector to operate these features. The house system operates such accessories as the furnace, water heater, and interior lights.

## AUTOMOTIVE BATTERIES

The starting battery or automotive-engine battery is designed to provide high amperage discharges for short periods, as required by the starter motor. These batteries have thin plates suspended in electrolyte, sulfuric acid combined with water, gel, or glass mat, depending on the design. They are rated in cold-cranking amps (CCA), which is the maximum load a fully charged battery can deliver for 30 seconds at 0°F while maintaining at least 7.2 volts (**Figure 10.1**). Most of the newer starting batteries are maintenance free.

Little maintenance is required for the automotive-engine-battery system, but it is recommended that you periodically check the cables and connections to ensure they are tight and the terminals clean. If you see corrosion on the terminals, remove the cables and clean both the terminal and the connection with a wire brush. You can use baking soda and water or a battery-cleaning product if needed.

It is recommended that the negative battery-cable terminal be disconnected first to reduce the potential for a spark or short. It is also recommended to disconnect the negative-cable terminal when storing your unit for an extended period of time to minimize the discharge of your battery. While connected, the ECM, radio presets, and clocks can all drain the battery.

Because your engine and sometimes the transmission are electronically controlled for shift points and engine performance, disconnecting the battery will reset these settings and may require some additional time for this reset. This will also happen if you allow the engine battery to be drained too low during storage.

Some units will require a "relearning" procedure for the engine and transmission, which could include idling at a certain rpm for a specified amount of time, turning the AC on, activating the park brake, and driving a certain amount of time. Check your chassis owner's manual for specifics. If your engine battery tests okay but is not performing well, it could be due to one of the following conditions:

- An accessory left on
- Slow average driving speeds for short periods of time
- The vehicle's electrical load exceeds the alternator's capacity, particularly when aftermarket items are installed, such as CB radios, window defoggers, and plug-in inverters powering electronic devices
- Defects in the charging system, such as electrical shorts, slipping belts, or faulty voltage regulator
- Loose or corroded battery terminals
- Sulfation
- Conditions of high ambient temperature: the temperature of electrolyte may become excessive, causing boiling and loss of levels

**FIGURE 10.1** Automotive engine batteries are designed to provide cold-cranking amps (CCA).

## THE CHARGING SYSTEM

The function of the charging system is to provide electrical power to the engine electrical systems and accessories, and to restore power lost from the battery (**Figure 10.2**).

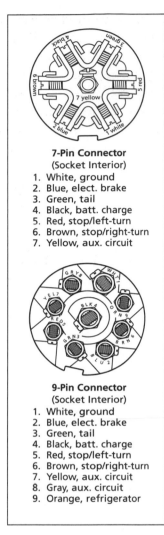

**7-Pin Connector**
(Socket Interior)
1. White, ground
2. Blue, elect. brake
3. Green, tail
4. Black, batt. charge
5. Red, stop/left-turn
6. Brown, stop/right-turn
7. Yellow, aux. circuit

**9-Pin Connector**
(Socket Interior)
1. White, ground
2. Blue, elect. brake
3. Green, tail
4. Black, batt. charge
5. Red, stop/left-turn
6. Brown, stop/right-turn
7. Yellow, aux. circuit
8. Gray, aux. circuit
9. Orange, refrigerator

**FIGURE 10.2** The no. 4 pin provides a charge from the tow vehicle's charging system.

The primary component of the system is the generator, more commonly referred to as the alternator. The voltage regulator controls the output of the generator according to the voltage level of your battery.

The generator/alternator can also provide a charge to your house batteries through the use of an isolator. To check the voltage level of this charge, use the following procedures:

- With the engine off, use a multimeter to check the voltage of a house battery. While connected, have someone start

the engine and within a few seconds, the multimeter should increase to 14 to 14.8 volts.

- Trailers generally utilize the charging system of the tow vehicle via the no. 4 or black socket of a 7-pin and 9-pin connector.
- If the vehicle's lights are excessively bright and bulbs burn out frequently, the voltage regulator may be faulty. Connect a multimeter once again to verify levels. Low-voltage output will cause inadequate battery charging.
- High voltage (above 14.8 volts) indicates a need for regulator replacement. If the voltage is too low, the alternator, wiring, or connections could be defective. Consult a qualified technician for voltage regulator replacement.

## THE BATTERY ISOLATOR

Because RVs have battery-powered appliances that must be operated while the vehicle is parked, a battery isolator is necessary to make sure only the house batteries are used for RV appliances. A battery isolator is a solid-state device used to isolate the house batteries from the chassis battery(s). The isolator disconnects the house batteries from the chassis's electrical system when the engine is shut off. This prevents the chassis battery from losing charge through the use of the RVs electrical components. Once the vehicle has started, the isolator will reconnect the house batteries back into the charging system to recharge the house batteries.

## DEEP-CYCLE "HOUSE" BATTERIES

Deep-cycle batteries are designed for low-amperage discharges to operate accessories, such as the furnace, lights, and ignition modules, or for appliances that operate on propane (**Figure 10.3**).

**FIGURE 10.3** Typical 12-Volt DC House-Battery Setup

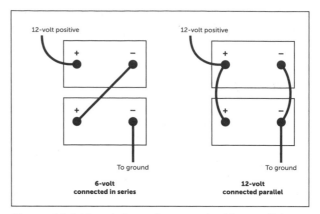

**Figure 10.4** 12-volt batteries are wired in parallel and 6-volt batteries are wired in series.

These batteries are available in three configurations:

1. Conventional flooded-electrolyte
2. Gelled electrolyte (gel cell)
3. Absorbed glass mat (AGM)

Flooded-electrolyte batteries utilize the technology that has been around for decades in which acid and water form electrolyte surrounding positive and negative lead plates. These batteries are most common in new RVs because they provide good reserve capacity at an economical price. This type of battery must be serviced periodically by adding distilled water.

Gel-type batteries utilize a gel to immobilize the electrolyte and calcium on the plates, reducing the battery's tendency to give off gas (the gas is recombined internally).

Absorbed glass mat (AGM) batteries are a type of gel battery in which the electrolyte is absorbed by fine glass mats, and this battery also recombines gases during charging. Both gel and AGM batteries are sealed, eliminating corrosion problems.

There are two types of deep-cycle batteries used in RVs: 6-volt batteries used in pairs and hooked in series to create 12 volts, and 12-volt batteries hooked in parallel **(Figure 10.4)**. Keep in mind, all RV appliances that operate on DC power require 12-volt DC.

## 6-VOLT BATTERIES

Commonly used in the golf and marine industry, 6-volt DC batteries require two batteries connected in series to create 12 volts **(Figure 10.5)**. Many manufacturers like the substantial reserve capacity as well as the resistance to deterioration caused by cycling or repeated depletion and recharge.

A 6-volt battery configuration is hooked in series by connecting the positive post from one battery to the negative post of the second battery. This creates 12 volts DC with an open positive and negative post connected to the RV system. Larger units will utilize two sets (four) of 6-volt batteries, with each set consisting of two batteries hooked in se-

**FIGURE 10.5** A Typical 6-Volt House Setup

ries. For more battery capacity, additional sets (two) of batteries hooked in series can be added.

## 12-VOLT BATTERIES

The 12-volt, deep-cycle battery is more readily available at retail operations such as automotive-parts stores and fuel stations. They are wired parallel, that is, positive to positive and negative to negative. The 12-volt DC batteries are commonly used on smaller RVs, especially trailers, since only one battery is required for power. A 6-volt system would require two batteries wired in series, which increases the cost and requires a larger compartment.

## HOW IT WORKS

As described earlier, both systems provide 12-volt DC power. The positive cable coming off the battery bank connects to the distribution center inside the RV.

This panel has a bank of 120-volt AC circuit breakers and 12-volt DC fuses that provide power to the individual appliances. Some manufacturers use more-sophisticated push-button or reset fuses that may be located in a separate location from the distribution center (Figure 10.6).

The ground wire from the battery bank is generally connected to the chassis, which, in turn, provides a ground source for appliances through a connective network of steel outriggers, risers, and steel framework inside the RV. This is an area of concern in troubleshooting because rust and corrosion can cause intermittent problems. Several manufacturers are now adding welded ground bars extending from the chassis at critical locations to provide a solid grounding point for appliances and lights that may be away from the chassis.

## BATTERY RATINGS

Reserve capacity is the amount of time the battery can sustain a discharge at a specific level. Reserve-capacity ratings are based on how long the battery will sustain a 25-amp load at 80°F before voltage drops to 10.5. Typically an RV will only use approximately 10 amps, except for high-line units. Battery-reserve capacity lasts longer at lower discharge rates.

There are several sizes of batteries available, with the most common being group 24 and group 27. The group 27 is rated at 160 minutes reserve capacity using the previously discussed rating system. The battery may have the old-style ampere-

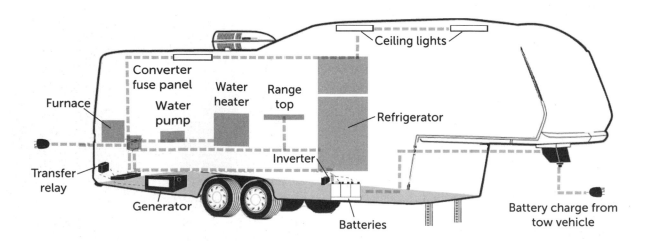

FIGURE 10.6 A typical 12-Volt DC "house" system of a fifth-wheel trailer.

hour rating stamped on the data plate, which is another measurement of a battery's reserve capacity. It is the amount of current that can be drawn from a battery for 20 hours before voltage drops to 10.5.

The 10.5 voltage level is used for these ratings because most 12-volt appliances will not operate below this level. The 20-hour rating is with optimum conditions and the maximum capacity of the battery. Due to less-than-ideal charging practices and system losses, it's best to subtract about 20 percent from this rating for actual usage.

Here's an example:

A group 27 battery is rated to sustain a 5-amp load for 19 hours. For those that want to do the math, that's 95 amp-hours (19 × 5) minus 20 percent, or 19 hours (19 × .20) for the practical purpose of calculating your 12-volt DC needs in a given period of time. Group 24 is rated for 16 hours at a 5-amp draw. This would be with no 120-volt AC power available and would be double for larger units with two batteries wired in parallel.

The typical 6-volt battery is rated at 7.45 to 8 hours depending on battery size at 25 amp-hours; therefore, the 5-amp comparison would be 37 to 40 hours at peak performance. With two batteries wired in a series, that equates to 74 to 80 hours.

By determining the amount of time you will be dry-camping, knowing which appliances you will be running off battery power, and understanding the consumption rate, you will be able to calculate what and how many batteries you will need. However, it is not an exact science, as many factors will affect how long your batteries will last such as:

- A new battery will not provide its full-rated capacity because it must "work-up" by taking 50 to 100 cycles to reach maximum capacity.
- Temperature affects battery capacity. Operating below 80°F reduces battery capacity. At 0°F the battery will only be able to deliver 50 percent of its rated

capacity. At temperatures above 80°F batteries will provide more than rated capacity but will reduce life.

- Proper charging, or more importantly, improper charging and maintenance will diminish your battery capacity.

## PROPER BATTERY CHARGING

You must put the power you have used from your battery back immediately.

Proper charging is important to obtain the maximum performance from deep-cycle batteries because undercharging and overcharging can diminish the life of batteries and are the two most common causes of battery failure. Too often RV owners experience dead or weak batteries and require battery replacement well before the expected life cycle.

To achieve a proper battery charge, it's important to understand the inner workings of a deep-cycle battery. Lead acid batteries have compartments known as cells, three for a 6-volt and six for a 12-volt system. Each cell contains a positive and negative plate with a separator and immersed in electrolyte. **(Figure 10.7)**

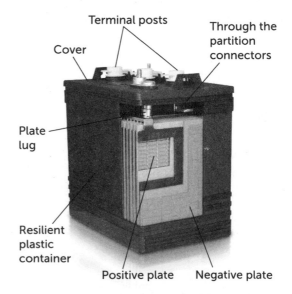

**FIGURE 10.7** Components of a Lead-Acid, Wet-Cell Battery

Lead sulfate forms on the negative plates during the normal process of battery discharge. Batteries become sulfated when the sulfate remains on the plates too long and hardens; this begins within a month, if the battery is left in a discharged state.

The hard coating acts as a varnish, restricting the electrolyte's ability to penetrate the plates. Battery capacity is reduced as sulfation increases.

Most RVs have some type of battery-charging system incorporated into the design, such as a built-in converter that transforms 120-volt AC power to 12-volt DC power for battery charging and to supply the needs of 12-volt DC appliances **(Figure 10.8)**.

However, the onboard converter/ chargers are not always the most efficient method of charging as they are required to provide power for the 12-volt DC lights and appliances, and some lower-line units will only provide 4 to 7 amps of battery-charging capacity.

Most battery manufacturers recommend a multistage charge because manually adjusting charge rates is virtually impossible to correctly charge a battery **(Figure 10.9)**. The latest generation of smart chargers or inverters with a multi-stage charge is the most effective. These units provide automatic, multistage charging:

**FIGURE 10.9** A multistage charger provide bulk, acceptance, float, and equalizing stages.

**FIGURE 10.8** The latest generation of inverters provide a multistage charge for proper battery charging.

### Bulk-Charge Stage

The bulk-charge state provides constant current, up to its maximum rating, for maximum recharging. Smart chargers enter this phase as soon as the charger is activated (AC power via hookup or generator). The charger delivers this high rate of input until the acceptance charge voltage limit is reached. At the bulk rate, the battery is held to a voltage where the battery electrolyte just begins to bubble or boil and give off gas (gassing point). If the charging stops short of this point, sulfate is left on the battery plates and the battery begins to deteriorate.

The gassing point will vary with battery temperature. At 77°F, the gassing point of a 12-volt battery is about 14.0 volts.

Gel cell and AGM batteries can accept a higher current rate of charge (amps), but higher voltage charging can be damaging. They typically require a lower bulk-charge voltage and a higher float voltage than wet-cell batteries.

## Absorption-Charge Stage (Acceptance Charge)

This stage immediately follows the bulk charge. During this stage, the battery voltage is maintained at a specific absorption level to complete the charge without overheating or overcharging the batteries. The battery accepts its final charge current, the last of the sulfate on the battery plates is removed, and the battery is completely charged. Average time for the acceptance charge is 1 hour for flooded-cell 12-volt batteries, 3 hours for gel cells, and 1 hour for AGM batteries.

## Float-Charge Stage

The last stage is the float charge. The float charge holds the battery voltage at a lower, preset level for long-term battery maintenance. During the float stage, the full output current of the battery charger is available to operate any DC appliances. The float stage continues until the charger is disconnected from AC power.

## Equalizing Stage

This is a separate charge for flooded-cell batteries only. This is a controlled overcharge cycle in which the charger will hold at voltages up to around 16.3, with small current flow. After a preset period of time, the voltage gradually tapers back to a float charge. This equalization process is recommended by all manufacturers of deep-cycle batteries to be done monthly or every other month, depending on the brand of battery.

There are several advantages to equalizing RV batteries. It removes all residual sulfate coating from the battery plates. It also brings all the cells in the battery to the same state of charge and capacity and mixes the electrolyte by the vigorous bubbling action of the high voltage.

**CAUTION:** Do not equalize gel-cell or AGM batteries.

## BATTERY DEPLETION/OVERCHARGING

Batteries should not be depleted beyond 80 percent (10.5 volts under a 5-amp load). However, we've all left a light on in a storage compartment for an extended period of time and "flattened" our batteries. This causes stratification, a separation of the acid and water. When this happens, the recharge current should be limited to the capacity divided by 20, which would be 5.25 amps in the case of a group 27 105-amp battery, until at least 20 percent of the battery's capacity is restored. That would be about 4 hours of 5-amp charging before heavier charging could begin. This allows the acid to recombine properly with the electrolyte medium by creating lower heat levels.

This creates a challenge when batteries are drained while camping and the only method of charging available is a nonadjustable converter/charger or the engine alternator. Both systems provide too much voltage and will not recondition the batteries properly. Many seasoned RVers carry a portable 5-amp charger that can also be used as a 2.5-amp charger during storage.

The latest in aftermarket chargers is the CTEK battery charger, available from Camping World, that provides a multistage charge, a recondition charge for depleted battery mode, and even a "supply" mode for changing out batteries and still providing power to avoid losing complicated program settings.

Onboard electrical converter/battery chargers can provide continual high-voltage levels that create battery gassing and loss of water in a flooded

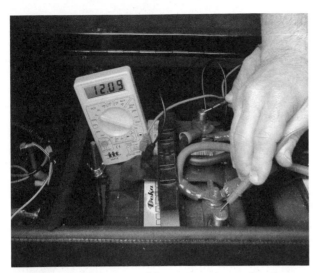

**FIGURE 10.10** Use a multimeter to determine the charge rate from a 120-volt source or 12-volt automotive engine battery.

battery, while gel-cell and AGM batteries could experience dangerous expulsion of electrolyte. Voltage should not be higher than 13.8 for long-term use with conventional open-cell batteries. It can be 14 volts with maintenance-free or sealed batteries. Newer converter/battery charger units are equipped with a voltage regulator that will tapper the charge accordingly; however it's a good idea to verify the charge with a multimeter.

## TESTING FOR CHARGING EFFECTIVENESS

An accurate multimeter will give a good indication of charging effectiveness **(Figure 10.10)**. With the engine off, the shoreline power unplugged, and generator off:

1. Set your multimeter to the 12-volt DC setting.
2. Connect the black probe to the negative post of your house battery and the red to the positive post.
3. Take the current reading of your battery.
4. Start the engine battery and wait for the battery isolator to click or open. Notice

the voltage increase. This is the charging voltage being supplied by your engine alternator. This can also be conducted on a trailer with the tow vehicle connected.

5. Shut off the engine and start the generator. Notice the reading; this is the charge being provided by the generator via the converter/charger.
6. Shut off the generator and plug the shoreline into 120-volt/30-amp service and note the reading. This is the charge voltage provided by the converter/ charger by shoreline power.

To test the effectiveness of your converter/charger turn on several lights and other 12-volt appliances and note if the charge capacity drops. This will give you an idea of what output your converter/charge has.

It is also important to note that if your batteries are fully charged at 12.6 volts and your converter/charger is providing a constant 14 to 15 volts, you may need to have your voltage regulator checked as this will "boil" the batteries and cause battery depletion.

## ACCURATE BATTERY MONITORING

There are a few essential tools that make it easier to understand, maintain, and troubleshoot bat-

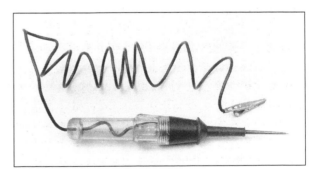

**FIGURE 10.11** A simple 12-volt test light will help when troubleshooting faulty ground.

teries and charging systems. A multimeter can perform a number of functions, including voltage measurement of both direct-current (DC) and alternating-current (AC) systems, as well as measurement of electrical resistance. It allows you to monitor the state of charge, check loads, and battery depletion. Digital multimeters are available at most hardware stores or in the electrical department of home improvement stores.

## 12-VOLT TEST LIGHT

Twelve-volt test lights have a multitude of uses, such as checking power at a 12-volt DC appliance or a light switch (**Figure 10.11**). Caution must be taken to ensure that a 12-volt DC circuit is being tested, not a 120-volt AC circuit.

**CAUTION:** Inserting the probe of a 12-volt DC test light into a 120-volt AC wall outlet can cause a dangerous electrical shock.

Most test lights consist of a plastic handle with a small bulb inside. A wire lead with an alligator clip at the end protrudes from the handle and a sharp probe is used as the tester. This is designed to pierce thru wire insulation to test for voltage in-line.

To test for power:

1. Connect the ground wire of the tester to a clean, bare metal ground such as the chassis or the negative post of the house battery.
2. Touch the probe to a 12-volt, positive terminal, usually identified by the + marking or a red 12-volt wire connected to it.
3. The bulb should light if there is sufficient voltage.
4. After testing is complete, tape any wires that may have been exposed by piercing the probe.

Although accurate voltage measurements are not possible with a test light, large differences may be detected by the relative brightness of the lighted bulb. Before using a test light for diagnosis, check it by connecting it to a known power source to ensure that the bulb is functioning properly.

## BATTERY-DEPLETION TEST

As stated earlier, most deep-cycle batteries are rated by their respective manufacturers as to how long they will sustain a specific load. It is a good idea to conduct your own battery depletion test to compare actual performance. If you find your battery will sustain considerably less load than the performance figures indicate, check for corrosion and/or inadequate charging.

1. The battery should be fully charged for an appropriate amount of time to assure full-charge status. Use a multimeter or hydrometer to confirm.
2. Turn on the interior lights until you create a 5-amp load. This can be measured with the ammeter function of your multimeter. Record the time. This is a good exercise to determine what type of load lights and other 12-volt functions of your RV draw. Record the time.
3. Monitor time and voltage until voltage drops to 10.5. Compare this to your battery rating.

## CHECKING DC VOLTAGE

To check DC voltage, follow these steps:

1. Connect the probes in the multimeter first. Set the range selector to a position that includes 12-volt DC. Usually the value here will be higher.
2. Touch the red probe to the positive side of the switch, accessory, or wire and the black probe to the negative side or ground location.
3. With the power on, read the voltage. Voltage will vary from near 0 (dead bat-

tery) to nearly 15 (output of an alternator in cold weather), depending on conditions and type of equipment used. For example, a fully charged battery that is not connected to a load will produce voltage readings of about 12.6. Appliances will not operate properly when voltage drops below 10.5. RV converters/battery chargers will produce 13.8 to 14 volts and alternator power should produce between 13.5 and 15, depending on how much current the alternator is producing and ambient temperature.

## BATTERY TESTING/INSPECTION

Batteries are housed in a closed, vented compartment and generally only inspected when all of a sudden they are dead. Proper maintenance and inspection is critical for optimum battery performance and longevity.

### INSPECTION

Examine the outside for cracks, bulges, and signs of acid that may have leaked or spilled out. Clean the terminals as this can derate the battery to a fraction of its original capacity. Disconnect the terminals and clean the post and connections even if they look clean, as corrosion can build and limit the connectivity.

Many people like to use a baking-soda-and-water solution; however, a spray-on battery-cleaning solution is easier and creates less mess. Reconnect the cables, tighten to the manufacturer's torque specification, and apply a thin coat of petroleum jelly to prevent corrosion.

### WATER LEVELS

Flooded-cell batteries will need water, but it is important to know when, what, and how much water to add. Water should not be added to a depleted

FIGURE 10.12 Distilled water can be added by an automotive fill bottle that shuts off at the desired level.

battery unless the plates are exposed; then only add enough to cover the plates. Fully charge the batteries, then add the proper amount (usually ⅛ inch below the bottom of the vent well). Only add distilled water; tap water contains a high mineral content (**Figure 10.12**). Adding too much water will cause acid overflow. Use a mirror for checking levels in a tight compartment (**Figure 10.13**).

Distilled water can be added by using an automotive reservoir tank, which features an automatic shutoff when the water reaches the desired height. If your batteries are located in a tight com-

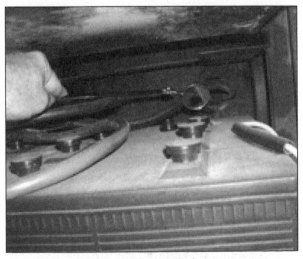

FIGURE 10.13 Checking battery fluid levels is easier with the help of an automotive mirror available at most auto-parts stores.

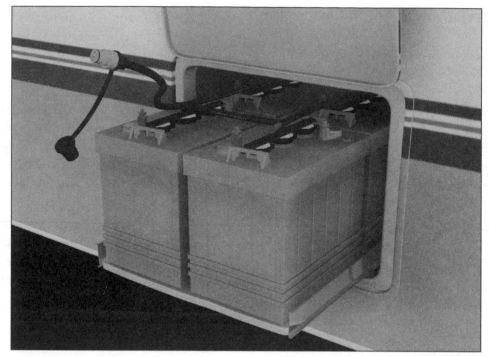

**FIGURE 10.14** Hard-to-reach batteries can be "topped off" with this easy-to-use Flow-Rite system available at Camping World.

partment that is difficult or impossible to get at, Camping World offers a handy "Flow-Rite" system, a remote battery-watering system that lets you fill all batteries to proper electrolyte levels from a single fill tube, using a simple hand pump **(Figure 10.14)**. This automatically sends water only to low cells, and an automatic shutoff at each cell prevents overfill.

drometer must be used. This test should be conducted several hours after a full charge. Some manufacturers recommend more than 12 hours, with the surface charge removed. This can be done by turning on an interior light for a few minutes. Test each cell; there should not be a difference greater than .05 between cells.

## TESTING THE BATTERY

There are three methods for testing a battery: using a hydrometer (specific gravity test), voltage measurement, and load testing **(Figure 10.15)**.

### Hydrometer

A hydrometer measures the battery's state of charge by comparing the weight of the electrolyte to the weight of water. Because temperature affects specific gravity, a temperature-correcting hy-

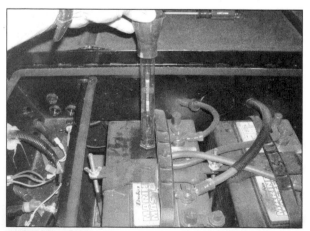

**FIGURE 10.15** Checking wet-cell specific gravity with a hydrometer.

### Open-Circuit Voltage Test

To check a battery's open-circuit voltage, follow these steps:

1. Perform this test only if the battery has not been charged within the previous twenty-four hours (so the surface charge is removed).
2. Remove the negative battery cable to make sure no load is on the battery.
3. Read the voltage with an accurate voltmeter.
4. Reconnect the battery cable.

Battery state of charge can be determined by comparing voltage to the percentage of charge listed in the open-circuit voltage chart. For example, if the voltage read at the voltmeter is 12.6 volts or higher, the battery is fully charged. A battery is completely discharged at 11.7 volts.

One of the most effective methods of testing a battery is a load test. Professional load testers are only available at service locations and some auto-parts stores. Smaller, hand-held, "coiled-" style testers will not provide an accurate reading.

## 12-VOLT TROUBLESHOOTING

The goal of any electrical diagnosis is to find the faulty component that keeps the current from flowing through the circuit as originally designed. An organized and logical approach to diagnosis is essential, which includes the proper test equipment, an owner's manual, and wiring diagrams if available.

An owner's manual? Who reads that? Every RV manufacturer designs, engineers, and builds its RV in different manner and functionality. Some utilize a residential-style three-way light switch that allows an owner to turn the light on when entering the rig and turn the same one off at a switch back by the bedroom.

Another example is multiple locations for the water-pump switch, one in the bathroom, another on the monitor panel, and a third in the service center. One loose wire will create a day's worth of "gremlin" searching.

Too often we take for granted that the appliances in our RV operate like those in our home. However, even though the thermostat looks like the one in your house, it's connected to a furnace system that is very different. Understanding how the system works, where the power is supplied from, and what can or will shut a system down is important.

As we learned in the battery-charging section, most 12-volt-powered appliances will shut down when the batteries are depleted below 10.5 volts. Not knowing this will create another long search for what is really an easy fix.

### BREAK IT DOWN

The two most common 12-volt-related failures are due to either inadequate battery voltage or an open circuit. So you need to break it down:

- Do you have adequate voltage supplied (over 10.5) to the component? Check the batteries with a multimeter.
- Is there power to the appliance?
- Does the appliance operate on another power source such as 120-volt AC?

### TESTING FOR OPEN DC GROUND TO TEST FOR AN OPEN DC- GROUND CONNECTION

Most RV manufacturers use the chassis to ground the negative/ground from the 12-volt battery. Twelve-volt lights and appliances are generally grounded to the nearest ground source, such as a steel outrigger or other steel component rather than a protected, independent wire back to the power source. In theory, the steel chassis is welded to the outriggers and perimeter steel. However, rust, fatigue, and weld cracks due to vibration can

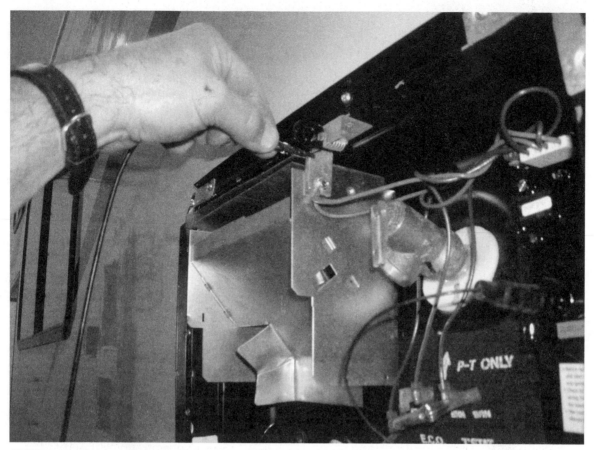

**FIGURE 10.16** A jumper wire is effective in verifying a proper ground connection.

create nightmares when it comes to grounding issues. If a light or appliance is not working, most mechanics will "hard-wire" a component, which means they run a new, dedicated ground wire to verify a good ground.

Connect a jumper wire between the component case or ground terminal and a clean, bare, metal spot on the vehicle chassis (**Figure 10.16**). If a circuit works properly with the jumper wire in place but doesn't work when the jumper wire is removed, the ground circuit has an open section that needs correction.

### Testing a Battery-Voltage-Operated Component

To take this a step further, both positive and negative dedicated wires can be used to bypass existing wire and isolate a power issue.

To test a component designed to operate on battery voltage:

1. Ground the device with a jumper as described previously and connect a fused jumper wire from the positive battery terminal to the positive terminal on the component being tested.
2. If it now works normally, remove the ground wire, and if the device stops working, repair the ground connection.
3. If the device still doesn't work, look for a break in the positive side of the circuit.
4. Due to the complexity of RV manufacturing, the short circuit may be hard or impossible to find in the myriad walls, floors, and cabinetry.
5. If you cannot find the short in a reason-

**FIGURE 10.17** To test for a parasitic drain, use a multimeter and disconnect the negative cable.

able amount of time, it would be faster and easier to run a new dedicated line by cutting off the nonworking line and splicing a new one.

## BATTERY DRAIN/PARASITIC DRAW

If your batteries are continually draining, even when you think everything is turned off, you need to conduct a battery-drain test. LP-leak detectors, radios with preset stations, and CO detectors can all draw from the battery. Some manufacturers

install a battery-disconnect switch; however, it's important to test your RV to see what may still be connected, even with this switch off.

Using a multimeter, set the meter to the 10-amp scale, make sure all 120-volt power is off, and disconnect a negative house battery cable (Figure 10.17).

This creates an open DC circuit. Touch the red probe of your multimeter to the disconnected cable and the black probe to the negative terminal on the battery. This reconnects the circuit, and your multimeter will show if there is a draw measured in amps or milliamps.

# CHAPTER ELEVEN

# AC Generators

## Choosing the Right Generator
## Generator Operation
## Breaking in a New Generator
## Exercising the Generator
## Storing the Generator
## Generator Maintenance
## Troubleshooting the Generator

**M**ost RV owners who intend to do much self-contained camping usually have either a portable or onboard AC generator designed to provide 120-volt, 60-cycle-per-second alternating power. An AC generator provides power to the distribution panel, similar to shoreline power from a campground, plus additional power on larger units for a second roof air conditioner, which we will cover later.

AC generators are sized and classified by the amount of power they are able to produce, expressed in kilowatts (thousands of watts [kW]). Those for RVs range from small 2.5kW propane-powered units to large diesel-powered units that produce up to 20kW. Determining the type and power rating of your AC generator is easy. A nameplate affixed to the side of the unit contains the following information: model and serial number, AC voltage output, phase, kilowatts (sometimes expressed as kVA, or kilovolt-ampere), ampere rating, hertz (hZ), engine-governed rpm, and type of fuel required.

## CHOOSING THE RIGHT GENERATOR

There are two types of generators that can be used for your RV power needs: portable and onboard.

### PORTABLE GENERATORS

Many smaller RVs do not have a compartment designed for an onboard generator, and the smaller power needs are generally handled by a portable generator. This generator can serve double duty as a home backup system and power an RV (**Figure 11.1**). The disadvantage of a portable or contract-grade generator is usually a louder, higher rpm engine. To soften some of this noise, RV owners with this type of unit place the genset away from the RV. However, as shown in Chapter 9, you should not use more than a 25-foot extension cord and should always make sure it's rated for the proper power.

The portable generator can be placed inside the truck bed for travel and for operation, but take care to ensure it doesn't interfere with movement of a fifth-wheeler. It can also amplify the sound through the bed, so an isolator pad may be required. Keep in mind, if you plan to take the unit out each time you set up camp, lifting a heavy generator requires two or more people.

Portable units are available in small, easy-to-carry models that will provide 900 to 1,000 watts and power items such as a computer, a television, and possibly a microwave. Consult the appliance chart, for items you will need to power (**Exhibit 11.1**); this will help you determine the size generator required. Make sure the unit is designed for continuous use and is easy to start. Some models are available with electric start and the unit should be all-states approved.

### ONBOARD MODELS

Modern technology has reduced the once bulky, noisy, and vibrating tendencies of onboard generators and provided plenty of power for total independence with all the luxuries of home (**Figure 11.2**). A variety of fuel options such as diesel, gasoline, and propane make it easy to match your generator to your specific type of RV and RV lifestyle.

Owners of gasoline-powered RVs like the convenience of utilizing the chassis-supplied fuel tank, but owner's of the larger rigs may opt for

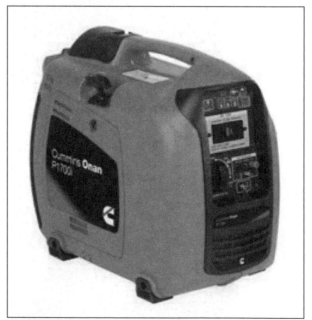

**FIGURE 11.1** A portable generator can be used for camping or for home emergencies.

**EXHIBIT 11.1** Common RV Appliances and Their Power Requirements

| Appliance | Wattage | 5 mins | 15 mins | 30 mins | 1 hour | 2 hours |
|---|---|---|---|---|---|---|
| Color TV, 13 inch | 50 | .33 | 1 | 2 | 4 | 8 |
| Color TV, 19 inch | 100 | .66 | 2 | 4 | 8 | 16 |
| Color TV, LCD, 32 inch | 125 | .75 | 2.25 | 5 | 10 | 20 |
| DVD player | 50 | .33 | 1 | 2 | 4 | 8 |
| Blender | 300 | 2 | 6 | 12 | | |
| Power drill | 500 | 3.3 | 10 | 20 | | |
| Coffee maker | 1,000 | 6.6 | 20 | 40 | 80 | 160 |
| Refrigerator, 3 cu. ft. | 150 | | | 2 | 4 | 8 |
| Refrigerator, 20 cu. ft. | 750 | | | 21 | 42 | 84 |
| Toaster | 1,000 | 6.6 | 20 | | | |
| Microwave | 1,500 | 10 | 30 | 60 | 120 | 240 |
| Air conditioner | 1,500 | 10 | 30 | 60 | 120 | 240 |
| Cell phone charger | 15 | 10 | 20 | 40 | 80 | 16 |
| Electric ceramic heater | 1,500 | 10 | 30 | 60 | 120 | 240 |
| Lamp | 100 | .66 | 2 | 4 | 8 | 16 |

**FIGURE 11.2** Typical Onboard Generator

the propane model because there is no available gasoline tank designed into the unit. Diesel-pusher RVs can utilize the chassis-supplied diesel tank and save precious propane during cold weather camping.

Once again, determining your power requirements and checking the appliance wattage chart will help in choosing the right size generator for your needs.

## GENERATOR OPERATION

An RV generator will provide power through the distribution center. In the case of a portable generator, a 120-volt AC plug is provided on the generator. The RV shoreline power must be plugged directly into the outlet; an adapter will be required for most systems over 15-amps **(Figure 11.3)**. Onboard generators are hard-wired, with an electrical receptacle located in the service compart-ment **(Figure 11.4)** or with an automatic-switch-ing system that senses AC power from the generator and switches to that mode **(Figure 11.5)**. Automatic-switching systems will often take several seconds to identify power and make the switch,

Larger onboard generators will have a second power line and fuse that supplies the rear air conditioner, allowing the use of both AC units on a 30-amp system.

Located on the generator control panel, the control switch is used to prime the fuel system (gas models), start the generator, and display a fault code. Most vehicles also have a remote-control panel located somewhere inside the RV with a second or third start switch **(Figure 11.6)**. These do not have the prime or fault-code feature. Hold the switch in the start position to start the generator, in the stop position to stop it, and the stop/prime for 2 seconds (gas models) to prime.

The status-indicator light will blink rapidly

**FIGURE 11.3** The shoreline cord must be plugged into a portable generator. A 30/15 amp adapter is required on this model.

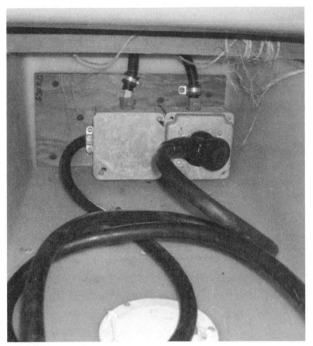

**FIGURE 11.4** The shoreline cord must be plugged into the generator receptacle in this RV.

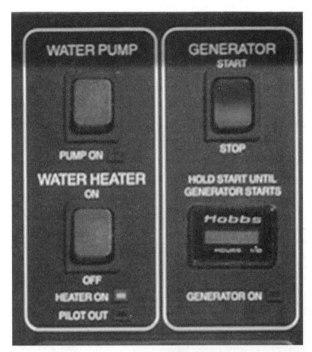

**FIGURE 11.6** A second generator stop/start switch is usually located on the dash or in the monitor panel, sometimes in both locations.

while attempting to start and turn to a solid display when running. If the generator should stop running, this will blink a fault code. These codes are listed in your owner's manual.

Line circuit breakers protect the AC power leads connected to the generator from overloads.

Before the first start of the day and after every

**FIGURE 11.5** No need to plug in the shoreline cord with an automatic-switching system.

8 hours of operation, inspect the generator for oil level, exhaust leaks, and battery condition. Make sure all carbon monoxide (CO) detectors are working, and shut off all large appliances such as the air conditioners that would put an immediate load on the generator.

Push and hold the start switch until the generator starts to run and the indicator light stays on **(Figure 11.7)**. The generator will stop cranking automatically if it does not start within 30 seconds to protect the starter solenoid, and the fault code will blink number 4. Wait 5 seconds and retry. After three attempts, consult the troubleshooting section on **page 154**.

It is recommended to let the generator warm up for 2 minutes before connecting appliances, especially in cold weather. The same goes for shutting the unit down. Disconnect appliances and let the generator run for 2 minutes to cool down before shutting it off.

Usually the generator circuit breakers will trip when an overload occurs, but the generator itself may shut down in this situation, especially

**FIGURE 11.7** Generator start switch with indicator light.

when a large motor-driven appliance is started last. Refer to the appliance rating on the data plate to obtain individual appliance loads.

Higher altitude can also decrease the generator's rated power, limiting your usage of appliances. Consult your owner's manual for "Power Versus Altitude" ratings. For example, the Onan 7kW is rated at 7,000 watts up to 3,000 feet and decreases to 6,510 watts at 5,000 feet. Therefore, it may be necessary to run fewer appliances at higher altitudes. Temperature has little effect on ratings as engines can maintain ratings up to 120°F.

If a circuit breaker on the generator has tripped, either an overload situation has occurred, or there is a short in the distribution center **(Figure 11.8)**. Disconnect or shut off all appliances possible and reset the breaker. If it continues to trip, it's time to troubleshoot or call a qualified technician. If it doesn't, reconnect the appliances individually; if the breaker trips when an appliance is connected, that appliance needs attention.

When operating a generator in adverse conditions, it's important to follow these procedures:

Cold Weather
- Verify the proper oil viscosity.
- Perform recommended spark-plug and battery maintenance.
- Check for Winter/Summer adjustment setting.
- Verify proper fuel mixture.

Hot Weather
- Make sure nothing blocks the air intake.
- Verify the proper oil viscosity.
- Perform recommended maintenance.
- Check for "Winter/Summer" adjustment setting.

## BREAKING IN A NEW GENERATOR

Most generator manufacturers have a recommended break-in procedure to ensure optimum performance and longevity. For example, Onan recommends running the generator at half the rated load for 1 hour, then three quarters the rated load for another hour. They also recommend checking the oil every 4 hours of operation for the first 20 hours total, and changing engine oil after 20 hours.

**FIGURE 11.8** A generator's onboard circuit breakers

## EXERCISING THE GENERATOR

Gasoline generators are prone to varnish buildup and must be exercised at least 1 hour per month under at least half the rated load. This helps drive out moisture and replaces stale fuel in fuel lines and carburetor and removes oxides from electrical contacts. The results are better starting, increased efficiency, and a longer-lasting generator.

## STORING THE GENERATOR

If you cannot exercise your generator and must store your RV and generator for more than 120 days, the following procedure is recommended by Onan:

1. Gasoline Models Only—Fill the fuel tank with fresh fuel and add a fuel stabilizer such as Sta-bil from Camping World, or Onan's Ona-Fresh. Without stabilizer, gasoline in a fuel system will deteriorate, causing fuel-system corrosion, gum formation, and varnish-like deposits that can lead to hard starting, rough operation, or even a no-start situation. After adding stabilizer, run the generator for 10 minutes at half load, which will fill the lines and carburetor with the stabilized fuel.
2. All Models—Change the engine oil and add a tag indicating viscosity.
3. All Models—Remove the air cleaner and restart the generator. With the engine running, spray an engine fogger such as Amsoil or Onan's OnaGard into the carburetor and stop the generator. This leaves a protective coat of oil on the internal engine parts.
4. Gasoline Models with Carburetor—Drain the carburetor-float bowl (check your owner's manual for location) into a container and properly dispose at an EPA location. This prevents deposits of gum from forming in the tiny passages as the gasoline evaporates.
5. High Pressure LP Models—Open the LP-gas oil-drain valve (check your owner's manual for location) to drain the oil-like substance evident in the clear drain line. Oil-like sludge can migrate from the LP-gas system and cause hard starting and rough operation. The oil drains out through the engine-oil drain hose. Make sure you close the valve when finished.
6. All Models—Disconnect the start battery according to the storage procedure in Chapter 10.
7. All Models—Plug the exhaust pipe to keep out dust, bugs, and rodents.
8. All Models—Shut off the supply valve if so equipped.

When returning the generator to service, check the oil viscosity for the current temperature and open all valves, unplug the exhaust pipe, and connect the battery. Run the generator for a few minutes with no load by tripping the breakers on the generator.

## GENERATOR MAINTENANCE

It is important to keep the AC generator well maintained for optimum performance. Maintenance procedures and time intervals vary from manufacturer to manufacturer. Make sure to refer to the owner's manual for your particular model and follow the recommended procedure carefully.

Inspect your generator every day; make it part of your pretrip and daily inspection schedule.

Check the engine oil and specifically look for the following:

*Exhaust*—check for exhaust leaks, bent or crimped pipe, and obstructions such as walls, trees, or objects that would block the exhaust.

*Fuel System*—check for fuel leaks on fuel lines, connection, or on the ground. Check hoses for cuts, cracks, or abrasions, and have them replaced if suspect.

*Battery Connections*—check the start batteries (usually the house batteries) for proper voltage levels, corrosion, and a solid connection at the battery and the generator.

*Mechanical*—check to ensure all air intakes and outlets are clear from dust, debris, and rodents. Cooling air is drawn over the AC generator, then exits by passing over the engine. For liquid-cooled generators, check the radiator for signs of debris buildup that can lead to overheating.

*Liquid-Cooled Models*—liquid-cooled models have a few more maintenance requirements since the water pump and cooling fan are driven by a fan belt. This should be inspected at regular intervals, looking for signs of cracking, tension, abnormal wear on one side or another, fraying, and age. Check your generator owner's manual for the life cycle of belts as most manufacturers recommend replacement every three to four years regardless of hours of operation. Engine coolant should be checked by a qualified technician to ensure it provides enough freezing/boiling protection.

## CRANKCASE-OIL LEVELS

When checking the oil level, make sure you follow the AC-generator manufacturer's recommendations **(Figure 11.9)**. Onan requires the cap to be securely seated before reading the dipstick. Older-model Kohler generators require the cap to be resting on the oil-shaft collar. It is important to consult the owner's manual for your specific generator's visual recommendations as well as correct viscosity and API- (American Petroleum Institute) rated oil if additional oil is required.

## CHANGING OIL

Most manufacturers recommend that oil changes should be performed every 100 hours (except for

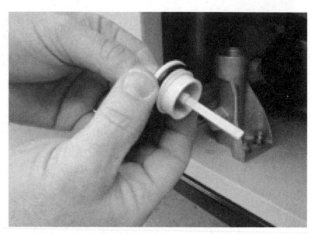

**FIGURE 11.9** Check oil levels periodically.

break-in at 20 hours) or once every 12 months. Drain the oil while the engine is warm, after running the generator at one-half load for 30 minutes. Check your owner's manual for the specific location of the drain plug/valve and oil filter. Some models may require removal of protective shields or plates.

1.  Stop the AC generator (caution must be taken as exhaust pipe and oil may be hot).
2.  Remove the oil-filler cap and open the drain plug. Drain oil completely and dispose of properly.
3.  Remove the oil filter.
4.  Clean the filter base on the engine.
5.  Apply a film of oil to the new filter gasket.
6.  Screw the new filter to the base until the gasket contacts, then tighten an additional half-turn.
7.  Replace drain plug or close valve.
8.  Refill the crankcase to the proper level with the recommended grade and weight of oil.
9.  Start the engine and run for a few minutes, checking for leaks at the filter base and drain plug or valve.
10.  Recheck the oil level and record the hour-meter time of oil change for maintenance records.

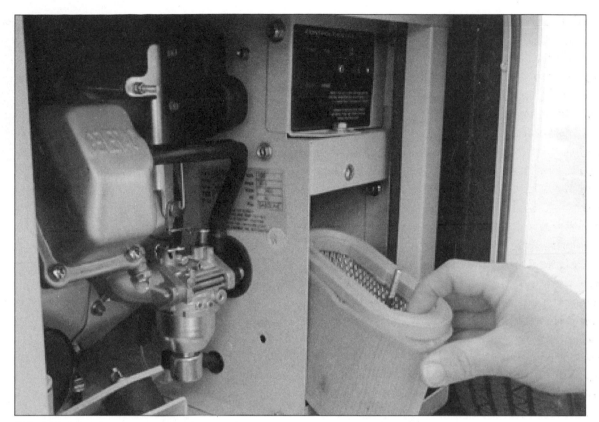

**FIGURE 11.10** Clean or replace the air filter after approximately 50 hours of service.

## AIR CLEANER

Most AC generators utilize a pleated or foam air-cleaner element that requires service approximately every 50 hours; some dusty conditions may require sooner intervals **(Figure 11.10)**. Check your owner's manual for specific details on maintenance intervals, location, and filter specifics. Most filters can be cleaned after the first 50 hours by lightly tapping against a flat surface to dislodge any loose dirt and dust. It is not recommended to use an air hose because the pressure may damage the air filter. Remove the filter, clean the sealing surface of the housing, and replace with a clean or new gasket.

## SPARK PLUGS

Spark plugs should be visually checked once each year for signs of deposits, cracked insulator, or burning **(Figure 11.11)**. Check your maintenance schedule for recommended replacement, Onan recommends every 450 hours. However, spark plugs that show heavy, black-colored deposits could indicate excessive oil consumption or a rich fuel mixture. Always check the gap because recommendations vary between generators, and spark plugs are factory set for generic usage. When replacing, always tighten by hand first to reduce stripping the threads. Then torque to the manufacturer's recommendation (usually 10 pound-feet).

### Spark-Plug Arrestor

Most generators have a spark-plug arrestor that requires a cleaning procedure at approximately 100 hours. Check your owner's manual for location and procedure. Find a level surface away from grass or material that can be ignited by sparks, such as a concrete or blacktop parking lot. Remove the screw(s) from the muffler end of the

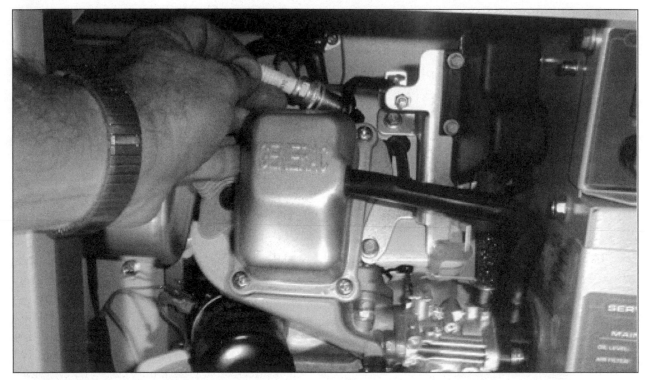

**FIGURE 11.11** Check your spark plug every year for signs of deposits, cracked insulator, or burning.

generator; you may need to add a swivel end or extension for hard-to-reach locations. Start the generator and apply a load, letting it run for about 5 minutes to remove the soot. Some manufacturers recommend using a wire brush instead of running the generator. Refer to your model's recommendations. Shut off the generator and let it cool down. Then replace the screw.

## TROUBLESHOOTING THE GENERATOR

When troubleshooting an AC generator, start by looking for the obvious. If the generator will not start, the basics of troubleshooting an engine malfunction are fuel and spark. First, do you have enough fuel?

Most gasoline and diesel onboard models are "plumbed" into the main fuel tank up at approximately one-quarter of the fuel level. This will vary between manufacturers and even models. Make sure you have adequate fuel and it is being de-livered to the unit, since a plugged fuel filter will impede the delivery of fuel.

- If the engine will not crank, check for low batteries, a blown fuse, or a faulty switch. If it will not crank using the remote switch, try another switch, preferably the one located on the generator.
- If the engine cranks but will not start and you have verified a fuel source, check for a plugged air filter, loose or fouled spark plug, or altitude/temperature adjustment. For other repairs, consult the owner's manual for specific code references.
- If the generator runs, but there is no power to the unit, check the onboard circuit breakers, verify the power cord is plugged into the generator outlet, or the automatic-switching system is operable, and check the circuit breaker at the distribution center. For further diagnostic information, consult the owner's manual.

## PORTABLE GENERATOR
## MAINTENANCE AND TROUBLESHOOTING

Owner maintenance and service of these small, portable generators are usually limited to oil changes, spark-plug replacement, and air-filter cleaning or replacement. Check the oil before each use and every 8 hours if used continually. Check the manufacturer's recommended procedure because some models require the dipstick to be threaded to contact and removed for proper readings, while others require the dipstick be inserted but not threaded.

Changing oil often requires removal of an engine cover, oil-filler cap, and drain valve. Make sure the engine switch and any vent lever are in the off position, and tip the generator to assure all oil is drained. Refill to the recommended level with the appropriate weight and grade oil for the temperature.

Air-cleaner and spark-plug replacement is very straightforward. Consult your owner's manual for location and specific recommendations for cleaning or replacement. Some air filters can be cleaned by using a detergent soap-and-water solution. Let it dry, then soak the filter in clean engine oil and squeeze out the excess oil. It is important to verify the cleaning/replacement procedure for your specific manufacturer and model.

If the generator is to be stored for less than 30 days, the fuel tank should be filled with fresh gasoline and fuel stabilizer added. For storage periods beyond 30 days, the fuel should be drained from the fuel system, including the engine. Use a hand siphon to remove the fuel from the tank. Most generators have a fuel-drain tube or valve to help remove the fuel in the lines. Remove the spark-plug cable, open the drain valve, and remove all fuel available. Turn the engine switch to the off position and pull the starter rope or crank the engine three to four times to empty the fuel pump. Replace the spark-plug cable and close any engine compartments.

# CHAPTER TWELVE

# Propane Use and Safety

## Propane—The Fuel
## How the Propane System Works
## Propane-Storage Containers
## Properly Filling Containers
## The Overfilling-Protection Device (OPD)
## Testing and Inspecting Propane Systems
## Traveling with Propane

According to the National Propane Gas Association (NPGA), propane supplies 3 to 4 percent of our total energy needs with nearly 11 billion gallons consumed annually by more than 50 million Americans. Propane is used every day, not only in RVs and homes, but also on the farm and even in automobiles. This cost-effective energy source has been used in RVs for decades for cooking, heating, and refrigeration. Propane is produced from both natural gas and crude oil refining. It is nontoxic, colorless, and virtually odorless, so a strong identifying odor is added for leak detection.

Of course, propane can be dangerous if handled carelessly or used improperly—very dangerous; so can gasoline. Therefore, safety begins with education about handling, use, and maintenance of your propane system.

## PROPANE—THE FUEL

Liquefied petroleum gas (LP gas) consists of a number of hydrocarbon gases that will turn to liquid under pressure. The gas used in RVs is called *commercial propane*. It consists of 95 percent propane and/or propylene and 5 percent other gases, mainly of the butane family. All of these gases are petroleum products separated out of the natural gas—or crude-oil streams. Butane is another form of liquefied petroleum but not normally used in RVs as it has no vapor pressure below 31°F. Propane is usable down to a temperature of −44°F, which makes it more usable in the climates of North America.

Make sure you are familiar with the distinctive added odor (it smells similar to rotten eggs) and be aware that smells can be deceiving. Your local propane retailer should have a scratch-and-sniff brochure provided by the National Propane Gas Association (NPGA) for you and those traveling with you to become familiar with the smell **(Figure 12.1)**. All RVs should have an LP-leak detector installed to detect a propane leak because your sense of smell could be diminished.

Since propane boils at −50°F, the liquid absorbs heat when the pressure is released. You have seen the stream of liquid at your fill valve when the tank is being filled. It looks like steam but instead of being hot, it is very cold. Remember, it's flammable, it's under pressure, and it can freeze your skin.

### EXPANDING LIQUID = GAS

Liquid propane expands 270 times to form the gas. One gallon of liquid propane makes 36.6 cubic feet

**FIGURE 12.1** Propane has a distinctive odor to it; and should only be filled by a certified technician.

of gas with 2,500 Btus. Natural gas has 1,000 Btus per cubic foot, so propane has twice that. Propane will produce approximately 91,500 Btus of energy for each gallon burned. Even a small 20-pound cylinder (BBQ-grill size), properly filled to 80 percent, offers approximately 430,000 Btus of heat. This is enough to operate a 25,000 Btu/hour furnace continuously for more than 17 hours.

Liquid propane weighs 4.24 pounds per gallon, about half the weight of water. Propane liquid expands dramatically when it warms, growing 1.5 times bigger for each 10°F it is warmed. This is why we only fill propane cylinders and tanks 80 percent full, which is regulated by the overfilling protection device (OPD) valve.

## HOW THE PROPANE SYSTEM WORKS

Most RV propane systems operate in a similar manner, starting with either one or two cylinders used on trailers with a two-stage automatic changeover regulator and the horizontally posi-

FIGURE 12.2 Travel trailers typically use a two-cylinder LP-gas system with a two-stage automatic-changeover regulator. Motorhomes use an ASME tank and a two-stage regulator.

- Extinguish any open flames, pilot lights, and all smoking materials.
- Shut off the gas supply at the tank/cylinder valve(s) or gas-supply connection.
- Open doors and other ventilating openings.
- Leave the area until the odor clears.
- Have the gas system checked for leaks.

## PROPANE-STORAGE CONTAINERS

As mentioned earlier, there are two types of containers used to store LP gas in RVs: Department of Transportation (DOT) cylinders used on travel trailers and fifth-wheels, and the ASME tanks used on motorhomes, which are usually permanently mounted. ASME tanks are usually horizontally mounted and have a separate port for filling, and may have vapor and/or liquid service ports.

All propane containers are protected by pressure-relief valves. These valves protect the container in a fire environment or in the case of an overfill. Propane containers are intended to be free of air. New containers should either be purged with propane vapor or evacuated with a vacuum compressor before filling for the first time. This procedure should be done by a trained technician.

tioned ASME tank in motorhomes with a two-stage regulator **(Figure 12.2)**. The regulators are used to reduce the high tank pressure to an approximate pressure of 11 inches of water column for use at the appliances. The fuel is then supplied to individual appliances through industry-approved lines, such as black-steel piping, copper, and steel-braided lines.

The one characteristic everyone seems to know about propane is that it's heavier than air—about 1.5 times as heavy, while natural gas is about half as heavy as air.

Because of this, LP-leak detectors are commonly located close to the floor, but keep in mind that due to constantly moving air currents, fumes can collect almost anywhere. Therefore, regardless of where you might smell the odor of propane, take precautions:

Don't turn on any light switches, don't light a match, don't provide any source of ignition—high or low—when you detect or suspect any leaking gas.

The National Fire Protection Association (NFPA) states that if you have a leak you should:

### DOT CYLINDERS

Department of Transportation (DOT) designed cylinders are used typically for travel trailers, fifth-wheel trailers, pickup campers, tent trailers, and even barbecue grills **(Figure 12.3)**. DOT cylinders come in a variety sizes, with the most common for RVs in 20-, 30-, and 40-pound capacities. DOT cylinders for RV use are vapor service only. These cylinders come in horizontal and vertical configurations and are typically secured to the A-frame on the tongue of a trailer, or in a separate vented compartment secure from the inside in larger trailers and fifth-wheels.

**FIGURE 12.3** A DOT Cylinder Used on a Travel Trailer

DOT cylinders can usually be removed for filling rather than taking the RV to the filling location. Propane container capacity may be designated in pounds or gallons since it is stored as a liquid. A 20-pound tank will hold 4.8 gallons at 80 percent capacity, a 30-pound tank = 7.2 gallons, and a 40-pound tank = 9.2. This is important to remember when filling, as some locations charge by the gallon, others by weighing the cylinder before and after and charging by weight.

It is important to periodically inspect your DOT cylinder for rust, gouges, scraps, or dents, especially underneath where condensation collects and is out of sight. DOT code requires visually checking each tank for defects and leaking before filling. Furthermore, filling personnel are not allowed to fill a DOT cylinder that has a crack or leak, a bulge, a defective valve, or shows sign of physical abuse. These cylinders must also be recertified after twelve years from the date of manufacture. Tanks can either be rejected, which means they can be repaired and recertified by an authorized technician, or condemned, which means they must be scrapped. The process of repairing and requalifying usually is more expensive than just buying a new cylinder. They should always be transported in their respective positions for filling and secured to the bed of a pickup.

The racks that hold cylinders on a trailer A-frame are designed to hold eight times the filled containers' weight. (Old racks were designed for four times filled weight). Make sure your hold-down bars are properly positioned and the wing nut is securely tightened before travel. Make this part of your pretrip inspection list.

Mount your cylinders with the openings of the relief valves pointing away from the trailer. The guard opening will be toward the trailer, allowing better protection for the valve from flying debris; the regulator will also be better protected between the cylinders and the trailer wall. A fairly common service-valve complaint is a leak around the valve stem. When the O-ring seal becomes cold, dirty, old, or worn, it may leak at the stem threads. Fortunately this leak can be controlled by opening or closing the valve all the way. Gently backseat the valve stem when opening to prevent stem leakage; you can then operate safely until proper repair or replacement can be made. Sometimes opening and closing the valve a few times will remove dirt from the internal O-ring. The service valve should close off gas flow when hand tight; avoid the use of tools. If tools are required, the valve should be replaced.

**DOT Valve and Connector**

Historically a left-hand-threaded, bullet-nosed, brass Prest-O-Lite (POL) connector was used on cylinders until 1998 when the hand-tightening, Type 1 ACME, or quick-closing coupling (QCC) became mandatory **(Figure 12.4)**. The early versions features a thermally sensitive bushing that would melt in extreme temperatures, pushing the connection away from the valve and the spring-loaded positive-seal module, which shuts

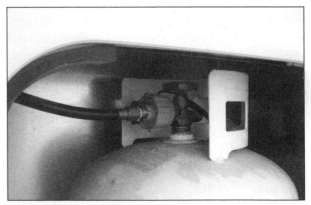

**FIGURE 12.4** Type 1 ACME or Quick Closing Coupling (QCC)

off the flow of LP gas. This valve is identified by a black bushing found between the hose and the nut. Current models are green in color and feature an internal thermal sensor without the visible bushing; this feature also prevents LP flow if the connector is not properly seated to the valve.

Engineered inside this connector is a spring-loaded excess-flow valve designed to restrict LP-gas flow in the case of a damaged line or leak. A small ball bearing in the assembly is pushed forward and seats against a housing that restricts the flow of LP gas. This has been a source of confusion for owners as they open a newly filled tank and the initial pressure pushes the ball forward. By design, this does not totally shut off the gas but rather allows a small amount of gas to go into the propane system and create back pressure that equalizes the pressure and pushes the ball off the seat. This usually happens within 5 to 10 seconds without the owner realizing what is happening.

However, if an appliance is inadvertently turned on, such as the stove, outside grill, or even a pilot light, the flow cannot create the back pressure since the flow goes out the open pilot. In some cases, the stove will light and operate until another appliance fires up, such as the furnace, refrigerator, or water heater, and everything starts to starve out because the back pressure has not equalized the system. In other situations, nothing will light because the flow is too restricted.

To fix the situation, turn off all the appliances and pilot lights and wait 5 to 10 minutes. If there is a crack or slight leak in the system, it will not equalize the pressure and must be repaired. This situation occurs more often when owners open the valves and try to use an exterior grill located very close to the cylinders. It can also take longer for a system that has two cylinders located on opposite sides of the RV. Opening the LP valve very slowly will reduce the chance of this occurring as well.

### Automatic-Switchover Regulator

An automatic-switchover regulator is used on a two-cylinder system in trailers connected by high-pressure lines called *pigtails* (**Figure 12.5**). With both valves turned on, the regulator will use the cylinder indicated as the service cylinder by the arrow or marker. As long as there is fuel in the service cylinder, the full–empty indicator on top of the regulator will show white (some show green). When the service cylinder goes empty, the indicator will turn red, and the regulator will change the fuel supply to the reserve cylinder without interruption.

When you observe the red indicator, you may close the service-cylinder valve. Rotate the selector knob so the arrow/marker points to the reserve cylinder. This transforms the reserve cylinder to the service cylinder and is important before disconnecting the empty tank to prevent gas from leaking out the disconnected pigtail. You can now fill the empty cylinder without interruption of service, and reconnect, open the valve, test the connection, and have a full tank in reserve again.

You can also use this feature as a leak-detection device by following this procedure:

1. Shut off both cylinder valves.
2. Make sure all burners and pilots are off.
3. Momentarily turn on the in-use cylinder valve as indicated by the regulator selector. The red indicator should switch to green.
4. Have an assistant turn on a stove burner until the red indicator starts to appear in the sight glass.
5. Observe the full–empty indicator for 3 minutes. If the red/green position does not change, the system is free of leaks.

### ASME (MOTORHOME) TANKS

ASME tanks are permanently mounted and feature a fill valve with an 80 percent stop-fill valve, bleeder valve, service valve, POL connection with excess-flow valve, relief valve, and a visible sight gauge (**Figure 12.6**).

**FIGURE 12.5** Two-Stage Automatic Changeover Regulator Used on Travel Trailers.

### Fill Valve

Since 1983, ASME tanks have been required to include the 10 percent stop-fill valve, which limits filling.

### Bleeder Valve

Officially called the *fixed liquid level gauge*, the bleeder valve is a screw valve that is opened while filling to not only bleed air out but also to exhaust propane when overfilling occurs. A steady white mist indicates propane level is above 80 percent.

### POL Connection

ASME tanks still use the Prest-O-Lite or POL-type connection to the service valve rather than the hand-tightened ACME style used on cylinders, because the ASME tanks are filled from the separate fill valve and are not removed for filling **(Figure 12.7)**. Inside the POL valve is the excess-flow device, which is spring loaded, and a check valve and retainer to reduce the flow of gas in the event of a leak.

### Service Valve

This is the on/off valve that provides vapor withdrawal for use inside the RV.

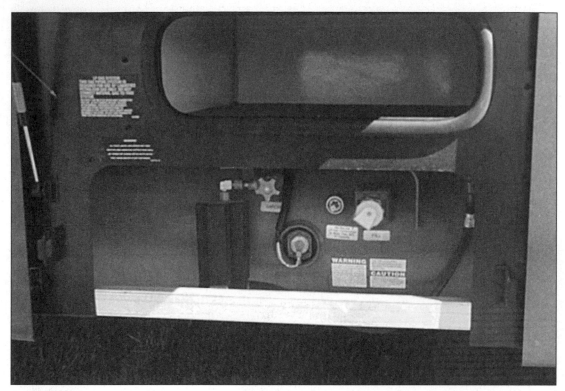

**FIGURE 12.6** ASME tank used on motorhomes.

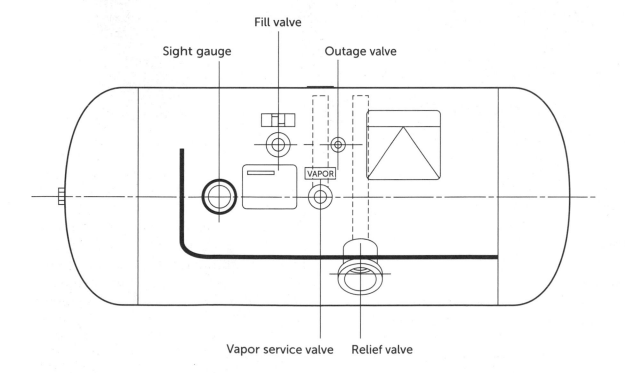

**FIGURE 12.7** Fill valve, bleeder valve, POL connection and relief valve locations as shown in this diagram..

### Relief Valve

Usually located underneath the tank, the relief valve will discharge propane if the pressure in the container is too high. The relief valve on a DOT cylinder is set at 375 psi, while AMSE tanks are set at 312 psi. Discharge can occur from expansion during increased temperature as discussed earlier. If propane is discharging, take evacuation measures as noted.

### Visual Sight Gauge

This gauge is designed as a quick reference for fuel levels during operation only and should not be used for filling purposes. The fixed liquid-level gauge or bleeder valve is a screw-type valve that also ensures proper filling by purging air and vapors. The excessive-flow valve is located in the POL fitting and operates similar to the DOT excess cylinder version. The AMSE tanks do not require the twelve-year requalification; however, it is a good idea to annually inspect your tank. Look for rust and leaks, check the mounting brackets and bolts, and look for stress cracks.

## PRESSURE REGULATORS

On both the DOT cylinder and ASME tank, the pressure regulator controls or reduces the internal tank pressure to the correct vapor pressure supplied to the appliances. It is a very critical component in the LP-system as tank pressure fluctuates. However, the regulator must maintain a constant pressure of 11 inches water-column (WC) or about $\frac{1}{3}$ of a pound. A manometer is used to measure the amount of pressure in the system, to check for leaks, and for setting the regulator flow pressure. This should only be performed by a trained technician.

Early regulators experienced difficulty maintaining a constant outlet pressure in cold weather with low inlet pressures. In 1977 the design code was changed to require the use of two-stage regulators. These are really two regulators in one; the first stage reduces the varying tank pressures to about 10–15 pounds, and the second stage reduces pressure to the desired 11 inches WC pressure. The first stage can take the form of an automatic cylinder changeover device on trailers or a rectangular section attached to the second stage on units that don't have automatic changers.

Pressure-regulator life is generally not more than fifteen years due to intermittent use, exposure to road spray (salt), and contaminants that come loose from the vibration and shaking. Regulator failure may not only cause inconvenience but is dangerous. Don't wait until you have trouble. Each time you turn on the container, open it slowly since quick openings cause excess pressure and may cause regulator-diaphragm leaks.

Regulator vents must point downward within 45 degrees of vertical to drain any moisture from the diaphragm. The drip-lip design on the vent prevents ice from forming over the vent screen. You must select the correct design for your application. A motorhome regulator will have vents on the side, and an automatic regulator will have a vent on the bottom, next to the gas outlet. Water from wheel spray can otherwise collect in the diaphragm area, causing rust on the metal parts and rotting the diaphragm rubber, thus reducing useful life.

Regulators that are not enclosed in compartments, such as the cylinders located on the tongue, are required to have covers. It is important to inspect these covers for cracked or broken pieces and always to ensure the cover is in place. Regulator manufacturers do not make any replacement parts and specifically advise against attempting any repairs. If you have reason to suspect your regulator is faulty, have it inspected or replaced by a qualified service technician.

Another problem can occur when water contaminates the propane and causes the regulator to freeze from the inside. When this happens, the flow of propane will be restricted or stop. A test for a frozen regulator is to apply heat to the regulator using a hot-water bottle or other method of indirect heat. Once the regulator is warmed above freezing, the ice will melt and the gas flow will be restored. If you do have this condition, take it to a qualified technician who can inject the appropriate amount of anhydrous methyl alcohol into your propane system.

## PROPERLY FILLING CONTAINERS

NFPA, Code 58, requires that dispenser operators must have documented training to fill any container. Even so, some propane-dispenser operators have made mistakes by filling containers beyond the 80 percent level. It is your job to observe and make sure the procedure is done properly. The activation of the relief valve signifies a potentially serious problem.

The trained filler will first inspect your container for damage, excessive rust or pitting, absence of brackets and covers, the manufacture date or recertification stamp, and OPD valve. Following the visual inspection, the filler will look for the water capacity (WC) and the tare weight (TW). The water capacity is how much water the container will hold in pounds, which is stamped as WC and followed by the capacity, such as 47.6, meaning the container can hold 47.6 pounds of water. The tare weight is indicated by a stamped TW and indicates the weight of an empty cylinder used for removable trailer containers **(Figure 12.8)**. These numbers provide proper filling-capacity information, and a filling chart will convert water capacity to pounds of propane at 1 pound propane to 2.39 pounds of water. The scale can then be adjusted to the tare weight and the supply line connected. Next, the bleeder valve will be opened and begin pumping. Pumping must be stopped when the bleeder valve starts to spew liquid, the scale indicates legal capacity, or the OPD valve shuts off the flow.

**CAUTION:** Don't allow overfilling of any of your tanks or cylinders! This is the most common

**FIGURE 12.8** The Water Capacity (WC) and Tare Weight (TW) are stamped on the container.

cause of accidents. Due to the previously discussed natural expansion of the fuel in response to temperature changes, the relief valve of an overfilled cylinder or tank that is subjected to a large temperature change may open and release a potentially large amount of gas.

For example, a container being filled in the early morning will have low temperatures, sometimes even below freezing. The next day, the RVer may travel several hundred miles and the daytime temperature could reach upward of 90°F. If little or no propane is used, the volume of fuel in the overfilled container will increase ten to twelve times, forcing the relief valve to open and release gas. When that happens, all that is needed to start a fire is a small spark or flame such as pilot lights or appliance spark igniters.

Do not rely on the gauge (if applicable): this is only for a quick reference for owners. Even a slight change in temperature can make a gauge change as much as 10 percent from a cool night to a warm day. Use the gauge only to check when you are running low and need to refill. Only three methods are used to determine when a container is full: when white liquid appears at the outage (20 percent) valve, when the OPD valve automatically shuts off the gas flow, or when the filling station is equipped with an accurate scale to weigh a cylinder. When the appearance of white liquid at an outage valve indicates a full tank, the filling service should be shut off immediately. Any delay will require that the excess fuel be bled off.

## THE OVERFILLING-PROTECTION DEVICE (OPD)

Since propane dramatically expands when it gets warm, containers are limited to 80 percent fill capacity, leaving room for vapor outage. American Society of Mechanical Engineering (ASME) tanks have been equipped with 80 percent stop-fill valves since 1983, and, starting in October 1998, new propane cylinders are required to have an OPD **(Figure 12.9)**. It is now illegal for any propane retailer to fill a container that does not have an OPD according to the National Fire Protection Association. These older containers can be retrofitted, but it's usually more expensive than purchasing a new cylinder. The new OPD valves are identifiable by the triangle-styled handle. A float gauge connected to the valve raises during filling and when it hits the pre-engineered 80 percent level, closes a valve, thus preventing overfilling the container.

## TESTING AND INSPECTING PROPANE SYSTEMS

There are several testing and inspection procedures that are necessary for both safe and efficient operation of propane systems.

### CHECKING FOR LEAKS

As stated earlier, it is important to become familiar with the distinct smell that has been added to propane and to take precautions if you detect a leak. You can check connections at valves, containers, and appliances by using a small amount of dish-

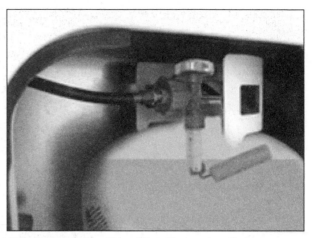

**FIGURE 12.9** The Overfilling Protection Device (OPD) limits capacity to 80%.

water detergent mixed with water and soaking the connection area with a spray or by using a sponge **(Figure 12.10)**. Several companies offer an actual propane-leak detection kit that comes with an applicator. The soapy mixture will bubble if there is a leak in a connection. Leaks at the diaphragm seal or vents indicate the regulator should be replaced.

If you find a leak using the soapy-water method, turn off the LP line immediately. Most appliances have an in-line shutoff valve close to the appliance that can disconnect the flow of LP to that specific appliance. This would allow you to use other appliances until you can get the faulty appliance serviced.

### TESTING WITH A MANOMETER

Regulators should be checked with an instrument called a *manometer*, which measures gas pressure in inches of water column. The pressure output should be 10.5 to 11.5 inches of water column (WC) pressure when about half your appliances are operating (measured by Btu rating). Simply put, this means enough pressure to raise an actual column of water 10.5 to 11.5 inches on the device. When everything is off, the "lock-up" pressure can be measured. This must not exceed 14 inches WC or one-half pound. Another type of manometer is the dial

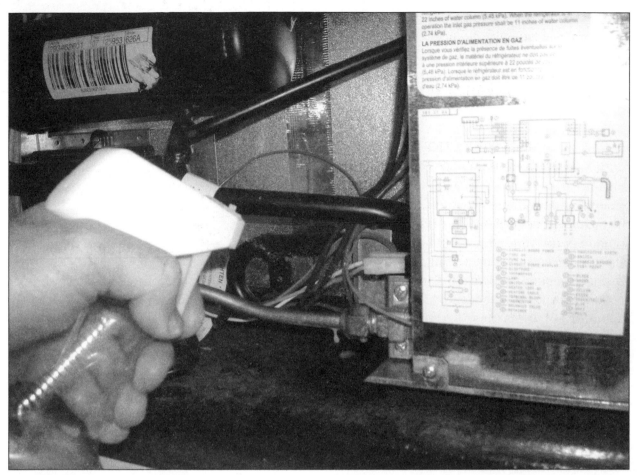

**FIGURE 12.10** A simple test for leaks can be performed with a soapy mixture.

gauge with rubber tubing or in-line model that will directly show the WC pressure.

A manometer leak test is required when a gas line is temporarily disconnected; be sure this test is performed by a qualified technician.

A manometer must also be used to correctly set the pressure regulator because very slight changes will not be visible in an appliance flame. Once again, these tests and adjustments should only be done by a qualified technician or damage could occur to appliances.

Low operating pressure can be the result of improperly sized, damaged, or crimped pipelines. Check them if the operating pressure drops when you turn on more equipment.

Liquid propane being fed to the regulator may create interruption of flow. Liquid can enter the regulator if the tank or cylinder is used in an im-

proper position. Horizontal DOT cylinders are constructed with internal tubes so they can be used either vertically or horizontally. However, when used horizontally, they must be used in a specific, well-identified position (stickers state which position of the cylinder is "up"). Liquid propane reaching the regulator may indicate overfill. Check the liquid by using the outage valve, and bleed if necessary.

Small amounts of liquid can splash into the drop tube, the tube within the container that goes up into the vapor space of ASME tanks or horizontal cylinders.

This normally does not affect a two-stage regulator but can cause a possible gas interruption if you use an old-style single-stage regulator. Vibrations can cause a drop tube to crack or even break off. If this condition is suspected, have your tank checked by a qualified technician. Continuing regulator problems would indicate that this is a possibility. Your regulator may also show frost or feel cold even when the air temperature is above 40°F.

## CHECKING GAS QUANTITY

A test to determine the quantity of gas in a DOT container requires a scale. Merely weigh the cylinder and subtract the tare weight as stamped on the guard. For example, if your cylinder weighs 32 pounds and your tare weight is 18; you have 14 pounds of propane, or 3.33 gallons. (Propane weighs 4.2 pounds per gallon).

Moisture on your cylinder or tank may be visible on cool but not freezing mornings, after overnight use of your furnace. The visible demarcation line between the moisture and the dry upper surface of the container will indicate the liquid level. A frost line may be visible in cold weather.

In warm weather, you can pour a glass of water over your container after use and there will usually be a visible area of difference in the way the water shows bubbles, indicating the liquid level.

## TRAVELING WITH PROPANE

Traveling with propane has been a very hot topic over the years, and you will find proponents on both sides of the safety debate. Recent forum threads have gone on for several pages with owners arguing, debating, and discussing the issue. Just because you've been driving for several years without a problem, doesn't mean it's safe.

Propane lines inside an RV are generally ⅜-inch copper and often run along the inside of the exterior wall, especially to the refrigerator and range top. These lines can break or leak if an accident occurs or even from vibration and fatigue. If the service valve is open at the container, propane can leak into the RV without warning. Therefore, it is a good idea to have the service valve shut off while driving.

Here is where the debate begins. RV refrigerators operate on 120-volt AC power or propane, although a few older models and smaller ones operate on 12-volt DC power. While driving, the refrigerator would need to be operated in the LP mode for cooling since there would be no 120-volt AC power available.

Both Norcold and Dometic models manufactured after 1995 are designed to keep internal temperatures at or less than 40°F for 8 hours with the refrigerator off, and ambient interior RV temperatures under 100°F. Recently we tested a Norcold two-door refrigerator bringing the unit down to 34°F and turning it off. Each hour we recorded the temperature with a temperature probe and after six hours it maintained 40°F while ambient temperature inside the coach was 85°F.

# CHAPTER THIRTEEN

# Boondocking

**Boosting Battery Power**
**Calculating Correct Battery Capacity**
**Catalytic Heaters**
**AC Generator and Converters**
**Inverters**
**Let the Sun Shine—Solar Power**
**Wind Energy**
**Water, Water, Not Everywhere—Stretching Your Water**
**Oh, the Places You'll Go!**

**W**hether your idea of boondocking or dry camping is exploring the backroads of the foothills or simply spending the night in a superstore parking lot, life without hookups takes some preparation. Some RVers' idea of roughing it is only having 30-amp service while others take the adventure of traveling self-contained to the limit.

**FIGURE 13.1.** Boondocking off the beaten path can be a rewarding and challenging RV experience.

All the luxuries of home, cooling, heating, entertainment, and modern plumbing can all be used comfortably in every climate. The RV lifestyle offers independence, the ability to go where you want, when you want, and stay as long as you want (Figure 13.1). And although campground hookups are convenient, today's RV is designed to be fully self-contained, maybe with some limitations. However, understanding your power needs, how to get the optimum use of 12-volt DC systems, and knowing how to stretch your LP-gas, water, and holding-tank capacity will make your boondocking more enjoyable.

## BOOSTING BATTERY POWER

As we discussed in Chapter 10, the first step in boosting your battery performance is proper main-tenance, storage, and charging **(Exhibit 13.1)**. Most RV batteries are plagued by sulfation almost from the start; therefore, they are not working to their true potential. Outside of using a 120-volt generator, the 12-volt DC batteries of your RV are the lifeblood of dry camping since they provide power for the water heater, interior lights, ignition modules for LP-gas appliances, and water pump **(Figure 13.2)**. What's more, they also can provide 120-volt power through an inverter. Refer to Chapter 10, "The 12-Volt Direct-Current (DC) System," for specific information on providing optimum battery performance.

Most RV manufacturers provide a mid-level house battery as a standard feature. One group 24 deep-cycle battery has an 85-amp-hour rating, which means 1 amp for 1 hour or 10 amps for 1/10 of an hour. This may be sufficient in smaller RVs that don't have a large number of appliances or for someone who is mostly plugged into a

**EXHIBIT 13.1** Common RV Appliances and Their Power Requirements in a 24-Hour Period

| Appliance | Amps | Running Time | Amp-hours |
|-----------|------|--------------|-----------|
| Lights | 4.5 | 4.0 | 18.0 |
| Television | 4.0 | 3.0 | 9.0 |
| Water Pump | 5.0 | 0.2 | 1.5 |
| Furnace | 7.0 | 4.0 | 28.0 |
| | | Total: | 56.5 |

campground source. However, the smaller battery will probably not be sufficient for extended dry-camping trips.

The common question is, "How long will my batteries last?" This is difficult to answer because variables include the size of battery, type of battery, state of charge, battery condition, amp draw, and even temperature. However, looking at the amp draw of the appliances being used and subtracting 20 percent for these variables can give a good rough idea of the amount of time you can expect before your batteries drop below 10.5 volts.

Running a furnace, water heater, and interior lights may only last overnight in some applications.

A group 27 battery generally provides only 105 amp-hours; therefore, to boost battery capacity, rather than upgrading from a group 24, it would make sense to just add a second battery if space would allow.

## CALCULATING CORRRECT BATTERY CAPACITY

Factor in the refrigerator, water heater, coffeemaker, and possibly charging a cell phone, and you can see the group 24 battery doesn't go very far when we subtract the 20 percent ($85 - 17 = 68$ amp-hours). When adding a second battery, it's wise to use the same make, model, and age because a weaker battery will rapidly discharge the stronger one. Also, check the compartment where you are planning to install the battery to ensure it can handle the extra weight and is vented properly. Use the appropriate gauge wire to connect 12-volt batteries parallel and if installing additional 6-volt batteries, two are required wired in series. See **Exhibit 13.2**.

**FIGURE 13.2** Proper battery maintenance can prolong your dry-camping capabilities.

---

**EXHIBIT 13.2** Boondocking Tips to Extend Your Battery Life

- Charge portable items such as cell phones, laptops, and other personal devices while driving, using the engine-charging system.
- Unplug appliances when they are not in use. Several appliances draw a small amount of power even when they are off.
- Convert fluorescent bulbs to LED bulbs; they use a fraction of the power.
- Turn off lights when not needed and use rechargeable lamps whenever possible.
- Use a catalytic heater.
- Add a solar- or wind-generator system.
- Use a "French press" coffeemaker. Heat water on the stove; pour over coffee grounds in the vessel and depress the plunger (press). Conventional coffeemakers require 120-volt power, which means an inverter and battery depletion.

---

## CATALYTIC HEATERS

The onboard RV furnace, particularly the fan motor, is a power guzzler. Propane-fueled catalytic heaters produce no flame and require no electrical power, resulting in energy-saving heat for your boondocking needs. Available at camping-supply stores such as Camping World, the Olympian Wave Catalytic Safety Heater can be temporarily placed inside the RV or permanently mounted under a dinette or other secure location

FIGURE 13.3 The Olympian catalytic heater is available at Camping World and other camping-supply stores.

(**Figure 13.3**). These heaters are noiseless and draw no DC amps with a self-generating piezo starter.

**NOTE:** A by-product of catalytic-heater operation is a small amount of water vapor that can form as condensation on plastic and metal. Some RV manufacturers recommend venting the RV, but a quick check of enclosed areas such as overhead cabinets or wardrobes periodically will indicate if you need to vent or not.

## AC GENERATORS AND CONVERTERS

If you plan to get away from it all, it's wise to outfit your RV with either a portable or onboard generator to run roof air conditioners or a microwave oven. Even if you plan to really rough it without these modern conveniences of home, a generator is a good backup for battery charging. A portable generator does not have battery-charging capabilities but rather 120-volt output; therefore, a stand-alone battery charger would be needed. Onboard generators are wired through the power-distribution center and the converter typically provides some battery-charging capabilities.

As discussed in Chapter 9, "The 120-Volt Alternating Current System," dual-output converters are commonly used due to the inexpensive price. They have two output circuits, one for operating the RV appliances and one to charge the batteries. With this type of converter, battery charging is usually not very effective, as the amount of power required by the appliances is subtracted from the output available for battery charging. Running the generator may provide little or no charging ability.

A single-output converter is more efficient but usually more expensive. The battery is always online, and the voltage is filtered so that ripples and surges are minimal.

How do you know what converter your RV, or the unit you may be looking to purchase, has? Today's unit are equipped with single-output, electronic converters after dual-output converters were discontinued in the late 1990s. The best way to check older units is to look at the owner's manual for information on charging profiles. If it's a dual-output converter, rating will be listed for the separate output circuits. Another source is to check the data plate mounted directly on the converter, although this could be difficult if the con-

verter is mounted inside cabinetry.

Battery manufacturers recommend not depleting batteries much below 12.0 volts or you risk damage to the batteries. For rapid recharging in no-hookup situations, a converter with at least 20 amps of battery-charging capability is needed for a single group 27 battery, or 30 amps for two such batteries. One of the more sophisticated multistage converters, sold in RV supply stores, is recommended.

## INVERTERS

For maximum convenience and minimum AC-generator usage (noise), many RV owners install inverters that change 12-volt DC to 120-volt AC power, the opposite of the converter/charger. Inverter output ranges from 300 watts for small units that power a TV and DVD player **(Figure 13.4)**, up to 3,000 watts (2,500-watt continuous-load rated) for most appliances. Depending on the number of appliances and the amount of run time, in-

**FIGURE 13.4** A smaller 300-watt inverter will power the TV and DVD player.

**FIGURE 13.5** Roof-mounted solar panels provide additional battery-charging capabilities.

verters pull a great amount of energy from a battery. More information about inverters is provided in Chapter 9, "The 120-Volt Alternating Current System."

## LET THE SUN SHINE— SOLAR POWER

Solar power is the production of electricity by sunlight using solar panels composed of photovoltaic cells. These cells create electricity when exposed to light from the sun with no moving parts and zero emissions. As the intensity of the light increases, more current is generated.

Solar power has become popular with boondockers as the price has become more affordable and the technology more user friendly. Several

manufacturers of solar panels offer a variety of panels that range in output from a trickle of power to amounts that are limited only by the number of solar panels that will fit on the roof of an RV **(Figure 13.5)**.

Smaller panels, like the Sunforce® ⅛-watt solar panel, mount on the windshield, plug directly into a 12-volt outlet, and can provide .125 amps per hour for a convenient maintenance charge.

Larger panels such as the Sunforce 246-watt model require a controller to prevent battery overcharging. Along with the wattage, both the size and the weight are things you'll need to consider when planning your solar-power system.

The first step is to calculate how much 12-volt DC electricity you need to use in the average day and determine the number of amp-hours needed in the battery bank. If you plan to operate any 120-volt AC equipment from an inverter, factor this in as well.

To figure usage, multiply the consumption rate of the individual appliance by the length of time it will most likely be operated to arrive at the total ampere-hours used in a day. As daily needs change, usage will vary; therefore, it is difficult to be precise in your calculations. However, assuming you follow the conservative practice of discharging the batteries to around 25 percent of capacity, multiply the total daily ampere-hour usage by four. The resulting figure will be close to the minimum amount of ampere-hours you'll need.

Using this formula, a daily usage of 30.5 ampere-hours (Ahs) would require a battery or battery bank with at least a capacity of 100 ampere-hours, such as one group 27 battery (105 amp-hours), two group 24 batteries (80 x 2 = 160 amp-hours), or two 6-volt batteries (225 amp-hours), which is more than you would need in this example, but you must use two 6-volt batteries wired in series for 12-volt output.

Once the battery capacity is figured, you can determine how many panels you'll require to achieve the minimum charge. A good way to figure this is to allow 1 watt of solar power for every 2 ampere-hours of battery capacity. For example, pair a 50-watt panel with a 100-Ah battery. To provide extra charging capability in cloudy weather, some RVers use a formula of 2 watts of solar power for 1 Ah of battery capacity.

Even if your usage is low, you may want more than the minimum system for faster charging and for more efficient operation in low light levels. Keep in mind that you may only get an average of 6 hours or less of direct sunlight per day. Also, you can add more panels later if space allows because all solar panels are wired in parallel.

As a general rule of thumb, the conservative RVer's power consumption might only total 20 ampere-hours per day, while the owner of a large motorhome equipped with all the comforts of home and using an inverter might need 60 to 70 ampere-hours per day. Some people want to live in their RV exactly like they live in their home.

Mount the panel(s) on the roof, as near the refrigerator vent as practical, to minimize the length of wire needed to reach the charge controller installed inside the coach. For the amount of current involved, 12-gauge wire is specified; however many technicians prefer larger wire to hold voltage drop to a minimum.

**NOTE:** Whenever panels are exposed to sunlight they produce electricity, so, to be safe, cover the panels with a blanket or large piece of cardboard before working with them. Follow the instructions provided by the solar-panel manufacturer and always caulk any screws put into the roof before inserting and on top of the head when secured. Use a caulk that is compatible with the type of roof material on your RV.

A controller is needed to regulate voltage and prevent overcharging the batteries. It also prevents reverse flow. This occurs at night, when no light is falling on the panels and no voltage is being produced. The voltage of the battery causes current to flow back into the panels, which causes a slight battery discharge.

Solar panels require very little maintenance other than keeping them clean. When the panel becomes dirty, simply wipe it off with a sponge

**FIGURE 13.6** Wind turbines (generators) are becoming a popular item for free battery charging.

or a soft cloth and water, or use window cleaner and paper towels. Take care that nothing falls or is dropped on the surface of the panel that will break the glass. The glass is sturdy, so the occasional acorn or other small debris is unlikely to cause any damage.

Try to pick a camping place where the panel(s) will be in the sun all day. Pay attention to trees, buildings, or other structures that may block the sun during certain hours. You may wish to tilt the panel toward the sun for more efficiency by purchasing legs that attach to the side.

## WIND ENERGY

Wind turbines or wind generators are becoming more popular as a source of 12-volt power from the wind (**Figure 13.6**). Sunforce offers a 400-watt wind generator that is constructed from lightweight, weatherproof aluminum and can be roof mounted with a swivel base or manually connected to a telescoping pole. A fully integrated regulator shuts down when the battery(s) are fully charged and provides a maximum output of 400 watts or 27 amps.

## WATER, WATER, NOT EVERYWHERE— STRETCHING YOUR WATER

If battery power is the lifeblood of boondocking, then an available water supply must be the backbone. Water is an essential ingredient, not only for comfort such as personal hygiene, but as an important part of proper nutrition.

Of course, the more water you carry with you, the less you have to worry about running out. However, this creates other consequences such as additional weight (8.3 pounds/gallon), ballast as we drive down the road, and tank capacity. How much water is enough? That's a question that must be answered individually because we all have different comfort levels when it comes to water usage.

As you spend more time dry camping, you will start to find ways to conserve water such as:

- Taking shorter showers, turning off the water flow when soaping up, and even going to military-style showers
- While waiting for the water to get hot during showers or when doing dishes, capturing the cold water for use later
- Bringing along additional fresh water in containers
- Capturing rain water and using it for flushing the toilet

Water tanks come in every size and shape imaginable. Many RVs have water tanks of marginal size, and some of these tanks do not fill the compartments in which they are housed. In such cases it's wise to install the largest water tank that will fit in the compartment. Replacement tanks can be purchased from RV supply stores. Once again, check your weight ratings if adding capacity.

Generally it's better to travel with a small amount of water until you get close to your final destination rather than carrying 800-plus pounds of water weight across the country. Also, filling a water tank located in a dinette for example, will put additional weight on one side of the unit, affecting handling and tire wear. Portable tanks are available for both fresh water and waste water.

## OH, THE PLACES YOU'LL GO!

The list of places you can go to get off the beaten path is endless.

Several public campgrounds, beaches, and open areas are administered by federal agencies, such as state and national park services. (Personally, I like the beaches of Padre Island managed through the Bureau of Land Management [BLM]). Various entry points allow you to pay a minimal fee and drive down on the beach.)

If you are sixty-two years of age or older, purchasing a lifetime "America the Beautiful—National Parks and Federal Recreational Lands Pass—Senior Pass" provides a 50 percent discount on camping fees.

## US DEPARTMENT OF INTERIOR— BUREAU OF LAND MANAGEMENT (BLM)

The Bureau of Land Management Division of Recreation and Visitor Services (BLM Recreation), www.blm.gov, is the national office in Washington, D.C., that oversees recreation and visitor services on BLM-managed lands. This department assists state BLM divisions with over 256 million acres of public land where people can enjoy countless types of outdoor adventure—participating in activities as widely varied as camping, hunting, fishing, hiking, horseback riding, boating, whitewater rafting, hang gliding, off-highway vehicle driving, mountain biking, birding and wildlife viewing, photography, climbing, all types of winter sports, and visiting natural and cultural heritage sites.

**FIGURE 13.7** Some superstores offer free overnight camping, but always check for local ordinance restrictions.

### INTERNET SITES

Several popular RV forums provide information on a variety of topics, including one dedicated to the art and joy of boondocking. Fellow RVers list boondocking sites all over the country, provide tips, and share their experience. Here are a few that were listed at the time of this printing:

- www.rv.net (Click on the RV Forum tab and scroll down to Locations for discussion threads on national parks and specifically one on public lands, boondocking, and dry camping.)
- www.goodsamclub.com (Click on Forums, enter Boondocking in the search)
- www.rvnetwork.com (Escapees Club forum)

### SUPERSTORE PARKING LOTS

Many superstore chains have opened their arms and parking lots to RV owners for overnight camping. They realize that RVers will more than likely need supplies, and by offering free camping in oversized lots, they have a "captured" market. Although this is a generally accepted practice, some locations may have a city ordinance prohibiting overnight camping. It is wise to consult the store manager for permission in your area **(Figure 13.7)**.

### FRATERNAL ORGANIZATIONS

If you are a member of a fraternal organization such as Elks, Moose, Eastern Star, or Masonic Temple, check with the organization in the area you intend to travel as several offer free overnight parking/camping. Most of these organizations look forward to meeting members from other parts of the country.

# CHAPTER FOURTEEN

# General Maintenance

### Engine Maintenance
### Roof Care
### Air Conditioners
### Sidewall/Decal Maintenance
### Sealants
### Interior Care

An RV is made up of an array of many materials: fiberglass, steel, aluminum, wood, rubber, plastic, literally thousands of parts and materials that are subjected to the most extreme environments. They are run 70 miles an hour down some of the bumpiest and dirty roads on the face of the earth. Sometimes they sit unused for months on end in subzero weather. After letting them "cook" in sauna-like temperatures for days, then RVers fire up the air conditioner and expect to live comfortably like we do in our home. And the RV takes it—for the most part.

With such an array of materials and conditions, specific maintenance is critical, not only to keep us on the road, but also to prevent moisture penetration, dry rot, and premature wear.

## ENGINE MAINTENANCE

The engine in your tow vehicle or motorhome is the single most expensive component and usually requires the most maintenance. It isn't uncommon for some engines to seemingly last forever, while others break down prematurely. Although an engine requires the most maintenance, it's relatively easy, yet arguably the most important task you can perform to prolong the life of your RV.

Engine manufacturers continually strive to design engines that provide more horsepower, torque, and longevity; however, one of the primary causes of engine wear and failure is poor maintenance. Many owners try to stretch service intervals or unintentionally prolong maintenance due to unusual usage patterns such as storage and severe use **(Figure 14.1)**

Every engine manufacturer provides a recommended maintenance schedule for changing oil/filter, transmission fluid/filter, air filters,

**Figure 14.1** The engines of tow vehicles and motorhomes are generally subject to severe service-maintenance schedules.

and other components. General Motors for example, recommends oil changes every 3,000 miles or three months for severe service, such as trailer towing or heavy loads, rather than 7,500 miles or twelve months as prescribed for normal driving. (Severe service is defined as operating in dusty areas, towing a trailer, extended idling and/or frequent low-speed operation, such as in stop-and-go traffic, operating when outside temperatures remain below freezing, and when most trips are less than four miles. It seems RVs are always in the severe service category.)

RVers tend to work rigs harder for short periods of time. In fact, the average RV owner only puts approximately 3,000 miles on a rig per year. That seems like a small amount, but the tendency is to drive rigs to a designated spot and use tow/towed vehicles for touring. Therefore it's important to review the recommended maintenance schedule and to consider the usage.

Specific motorhome engine and chassis maintenance is provided in Chapter 4, "Motorhome Chassis."

## ROOF CARE

Over the years, several different materials have been used to cover the roof of an RV. In the 1970s and 1980s it was common to see a one-piece aluminum skin that would react with the elements and create hard-to-remove black spots and streaks along the sidewall of the unit. Some manufacturers changed to a two-piece fiberglass material that created a critical maintenance point along the seam down the middle of the roof. Somewhere in the late 1980s to early 1990s, companies started using a one-piece rubber membrane that was common in the commercial roofing industry, while others started using a one-piece fiberglass material. Whatever roof material your RV has, it's important to identify the proper maintenance schedule and adhere to it.

Careful inspection and cleaning are important, not only for the longevity of the roof material, but also to reduce the potential for leaks. During a typical day, temperatures can be 20°F in the morning and climb to above 75°F in the afternoon. Sealants have a tendency to expand and contract with temperature changes, and then they're driven down the road at 60 to 75 miles per hour. Check all seams along the roof to the sidewall joint. Remove and replace any sealant that has developed air pockets or has stretched. Consult your owner's manual for the proper sealant as silicone is not always the best answer. Most manufacturers publish a sealant guide for seams, windows, and air-conditioning gaskets.

Check the seals around all vents, accessories, and aftermarket items installed on the roof such as the satellite dish, CB antennae, and others. It is also critical to check the front-roof cap-to-roof seam, which is one of the biggest culprits in a leaky roof. Another area of concern is clearance lights mounted to the front cap (**Figure 14.2**). When a lens cracks or is removed to replace a bulb, the seal is broken, and it creates a potential for water infiltration. Water coming into a clearance light can migrate inside the overhead cab, through the tubular steel or aluminum framework, and follow framework all the way to the back of the rig, and leak in the bedroom. As you can see, it's better to reduce or eliminate the leak potential in the first place.

### RUBBER MATERIAL

There are two types of rubber materials that have been used in the RV industry: Ethylene propylene diene monomer (EPDM) and thermoplastic olefin (TPO). EPDM was used from the onset of rubber-roof installations in the late 1980s until approximately 1994 when the TPO material was introduced. EPDM has a tendency to oxidate slightly, causing a white, chalky substance that can run down the side of the RV. It is has poor resistance to oil or solvent-based cleaners, so the manufacturer recommends not using citrus-based cleaners or those with petroleum solvents or harsh

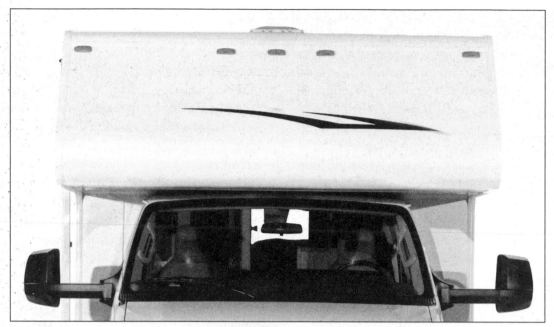

**FIGURE 14.2** Clearance lights on the front cap are common spots for moisture penetration. Check and seal the lens as well as the baseplate.

abrasives. To maintain the warranty of a EPDM and TPO roof, you are required to clean it three to four times per year with a mild household cleaner such as borax, Spic-and-Span, Murphy Oil Soap, or liquid detergent, as long as it does not contain petroleum **(Figure 14.3)**. To prevent streaking along the sidewall during cleaning, several aftermarket products are available that will not only clean the roof but also provide a treatment that will reduce chalking and streaking. Although very durable, the EPDM membrane is thin. You should always avoid low-hanging branches and be careful about dragging anything across the roof surface that could easily cut it. If necessary, rubber-roof patch kits are available from most RV-supply stores.

## ALUMINUM

As mentioned, aluminum roofs were used for several years and all that is generally needed for maintenance is to clean the material with a mild detergent soap occasionally. It's more important to check the seam, seals, and to look for scratches or dents. Older models may have an issue with electrolysis, which causes pitting in the aluminum, usually due to moisture penetration and a reaction with the aluminum.

One characteristic of an aluminum roof is black streaking caused by dirt, dust, and other materials mixing with moisture and the natural aging of the aluminum skin **(Figure 14.4)**. This creates a hard-to-remove streak on the sidewall of the unit. There are several aftermarket black-streak cleaners that make the work easier and are available at Camping World and other RV supply centers.

## FIBERGLASS

The fiberglass material used on some RVs is similar to the material used on the sidewall **(Figure 14.5)**. Most manufacturers use a matte-finish fiberglass or even a pebble-grain rather than the expensive high-gloss version commonly used on the sidewall. The fiberglass material itself requires very little maintenance other than a visual inspection of the material for any damage, blistering, or spider cracking. Spider cracks are small

**FIGURE 14.3** Rubber-roof material should be cleaned and inspected yearly.

**FIGURE 14.4** Aluminum roof material can cause hard-to-clean black streaks.

**FIGURE 14.5** Fiberglass material used on the roof is similar to the material used on most sidewalls.

web-like cracks that can occur at pressure points or a defect in the material and should be examined for potential moisture penetration. They can be sealed or repaired with a fiberglass-repair kit.

Ultraviolet (UV) rays can cause fading or oxidation, and older units are affected more severely because little UV protection was incorporated into the outer layer of the material. Fading or oxidation does not affect structural integrity, it just doesn't look good. On the top of an RV, most owners think, "out of sight, out of mind."

## ETERNABOND

One last comment on roof maintenance and repair: Not all products will stick to every type of roof material, so it's important to use the proper sealants, gaskets, and repair materials on your roof. Many seasoned RV veterans recommend Eternabond (www.eternabond.com), which is effective on almost all materials and is easy to apply.

## AIR CONDITIONERS

Another area of concern on the roof is the air conditioner, which is sealed to the roof using a sponge-rubber gasket (**Figure 14.6**). Over time, this gasket will compress and allow moisture to penetrate. All RV air-conditioning manufacturers recommend checking the tightness or torque setting of the inside fasteners.

First, visually inspect the gasket to ensure there is still at least ½ inch of gasket material between the air-conditioner unit and the roof material. Then remove the interior shroud and check the bolts for tightness. Do not overtighten; there must be a gap to allow condensation to drain from the bottom of the unit. Also, do not apply sealant around the perimeter in an attempt to seal an air-conditioner leak. This will trap moisture in the drain pan.

If you are experiencing a leak around the air-conditioning unit, check the following:

- *Is it leaking during operation due to condensation not draining?* Check the drain hole and a possible cracked drain pan.
- *Is it leaking during rain?* This would indicate a loose or defective gasket.
- *Does water pool around the unit?* Most roofs are crowned to provide water runoff; however, if water is pooling around the air conditioner or other parts of your roof, you may have roof deteriora-

**Figure 14.6** Check the sponge-rubber gasket of the air conditioner periodically to prevent moisture penetration.

tion and sagging, which traps both rain and condensation around the unit. Run a straight edge or a taut string line from one side of the RV to the other and look for sagging. If present, the air-conditioning unit and roof need to be raised. This can sometimes be done by removing the air-conditioning unit and placing shims between the roof material and roof frame. However, it generally requires more extensive repairs such as an additional arched frame rail inside the RV.

## SIDEWALL/DECAL MAINTENANCE

As with roof materials, sidewalls have evolved from aluminum skin to fiberglass over the years with a variety of styles and applications. Some manufacturers still use an aluminum exterior skin, although most have gone to a one-piece fiberglass material. Older models with an aluminum outer skin were prone to electrolysis or pitting due to the aluminum skin connected to the steel sidewall frame, or, more often, moisture penetrating the sidewall from the roof and causing a reaction. Little can be done to combat this other than eliminating the source of moisture penetration and some cosmetic surgery, such as a paint cover-up.

### ALUMINUM

Aluminum RV exterior skin will be either raw metal or painted. Care of the two surfaces is different in some respects. Harsh abrasives should not be used when cleaning unpainted aluminum because fine scratches can mar the raw metal surface. However, a painted aluminum surface can be treated just as a painted steel surface because it is the paint that is being treated and not the aluminum.

To care for and restore the luster of an unpainted aluminum surface, begin by washing thoroughly with a warm solution of automotive-wash product. Do not use strong detergents, solvents, or abrasive cleaners. Wash during the cool of the day, in the shade or on an overcast day. Never wash the aluminum skin in direct sunlight.

Begin with the roof, and wash one section at a time, rinsing to prevent the cleaning solution from drying on the surface. Dry with a chamois or soft, clean towel to prevent water spots. Road tar, bugs, and sap should be cleaned off as soon as possible, before they can harden in place. Use kerosene, turpentine, or naphtha with a soft cloth, taking care not to scratch the surface. Rinse thoroughly with clear water. Wax the affected area.

The painted aluminum skin should be waxed every three to six months or more often if necessary, as determined by exposure to the elements.

A painted aluminum skin should be washed and cleaned of road tar, sap, and bugs, using the same methods as the unpainted surface. When necessary, oxidized paint can be treated by using a polish combination, cleaner-wax, or in extreme cases a polishing compound. A good grade of automotive wax should be applied every three to six months.

Unpainted aluminum exterior siding, used on certain RVs (Airstream, for example), is treated with a protective coating. You should not wax this surface. With the passage of time, the protective coating may discolor, fade, or strip away in blotches. Before a new coating can be applied, the old material must be etched off; this requires a special chemical and a safe environment and should be left to a professional.

Aluminum skin that has been damaged cannot be repaired and must be replaced. Emergency repairs can be made to avoid moisture penetration; however, this is a temporary fix and needs to be addressed as soon as possible.

### FIBERGLASS

Fiberglass material used on the sidewall requires little maintenance, although it can be affected by UV degradation that causes fading. It is important to understand the components used in making the fiberglass panels, which consist of a fiberglass-reinforced plastic (frp) base that is usually tinted white or beige, and a clear outer resin called *gel-coat*. In recent years, fiberglass manufacturers have engineered an advanced resin system that provides added performance and durability in all types of weathering conditions.

Some sidewall fiberglass panels are painted, which requires the same maintenance as the painted aluminum or the surface of your car.

## WAXING AND DECALS

Although fiberglass manufacturers do recommend waxing the surface in their care and maintenance guides, it is critical to NOT wax over vinyl decals **(Figure 14.7)**. Sharpline Converting, Inc., a leader in RV graphics and decals, states that today's decals are designed with an ultraviolet-resistant coating, and waxing prevents the natural breathing and will enhance cracking, peeling, and fading.

With today's technology, waxing does very little for the longevity of fiberglass other than provide a protective coating for surface scratching and a shine.

Some owners wax the front fascia, making it easier to remove pesky bugs. Several aftermarket products are available that will help enhance the shine and add UV protection, such as Protect All's Fiberglass Oxidation Remover & Color Restorer, or 303 Protectant, both available at Camping World **(Figure 14.8)**.

**Figure 14.7** Most decal manufacturers discourage waxing over the decals.

## SCRATCHES AND MINOR IMPERFECTIONS

To fix those annoying little scratches, dings, and scrapes, you need to identify the severity of the problem and the material your sidewall is made of. Bare aluminum can be cleaned and polished, but it cannot be fixed with a simple topical repair. Large scratches, gouges, and punctures in fiberglass can be fixed with a repair kit or by taking it to a body shop. For minor scratches, there are several compounds that can be used with a little elbow grease to restore that showroom finish.

Always begin by washing the surface with a mild detergent or RV washing solution. Keep in mind that hard water with high mineral content will leave a residue and hard-water stains. Use soft water if possible or add a conditioner such as Meguiar's Hard Water Spot Remover. Some scratches and stains can be removed with a little more effort during the wash. After drying the unit, if the scratch is still evident, use a light swirl remover or light polish and a clean rag. For heavy scratches, rubbing compound and an electric buffing wheel may be used. Rubbing compounds should always be used conservatively because they can remove paint, gel-coat, and make the scratch even worse. Do not use rubbing compound and a buffing wheel on vinyl graphics. After buffing, use a quality swirl remover to finish the area and remove any small scratches or swirls left. Once it dries, buff off the area with a clean, soft cloth.

## SEALANTS

Moisture penetration is the leading cause of delamination and deterioration of the roof, walls, and floor of an RV. Earlier we covered what to look for on the roof of your RV. Now let's take a look at the sidewall and storage compartments.

The windows in your RV are set or installed into a cutout of the sidewall material and sealed with either butyl tape, tacky tape, silicone, or a combination of materials **(Figure 14.9)**. Just like the windows in your home, silicone can crack, shrink, or separate and needs to be checked regularly. Windows can also settle, leaving a potential for moisture penetration at the top cap. It is important to check the sealant around your windows periodically for these conditions and to make sure the weep holes on the bottom frame are open to allow moisture to drain from the frame.

Windows are installed using a clamping method: the outside frame is set, and an inside ring is attached, drawing the two pieces together tightly

**FIGURE 14.8** Protect All Inc. offers cleaning and protection solutions available at Camping World or online at: www.protectall.com.

**FIGURE 14.9** Silicone is not always the best sealant. Check the manufacturer's recommended sealant for the specific location, such as butyl tape around the windows.

in the opening. If the window is loose or the side-wall material compresses slightly, it will not seal well and will leak.

Check the screws on the inside frame to ensure they are snug but not too tight.

Check all cutouts and opening in the side-wall, such as a refrigerator vent, furnace exhaust, and especially the sidewall-to-floor joint. This seam, running the entire length of the lower section of the sidewall, is fastened with screws and covered with a molding. Make sure the molding is in place and the sealant is in good condition. Most manufacturers run a bead of silicone along the top of the molding.

With road vibration and temperature changes, this joint moves and flexes considerably and requires frequent inspection.

Some awnings are made of fabric material that is resistant to rot and mildew, while others need special care to prevent this type of damage. Rot and mildew result from moisture being trapped in the fabric. All awnings should be allowed to dry before they are rolled up. If this cannot be done, unfurl the awnings as soon as possible, clean the material off, and let them dry before storing again.

Several conditions can damage and deteriorate awning material. Air pollution, dirt and dust, debris from trees, and salt spray can all stain or damage the material. It is important to keep the material clean and to check for leaks such as tears or pinholes, which can be repaired with a vinyl liquid patch (VLP).

## INTERIOR CARE

The inside of your RV is outfitted with similar materials and components as your home, such as carpet, fabric, countertops, and wood cabinetry and furnishings. Soil and stains are the worst enemies of any RV interior, so routine cleaning is the most effective method to prevent damage and premature wear and tear.

## CARPET

Sand, dirt, and other debris tracked inside your RV will work into the pile and literally cut the fibers of your carpet, making it show wear faster. Periodic vacuuming helps reduce this effect, and easy-to-install central vacuum units make it an easy chore. There are also several 12-volt portable units available that are inexpensive and store well in an RV.

If you travel with pets, oil from their skin, especially dogs, will saturate carpet fibers and collect dirt and dust, which will matte the carpet down and cannot be restored. Several aftermarket treatments are available that coat individual carpet fibers to prevent this effect.

Most seasoned RVers never see their carpet due to the throw rugs and runners used throughout the RV. Some areas may require a runner or replacement with a material that can withstand the heavy traffic, such as the entrance door, bathroom, or kitchen. Carpet can be replaced with several new products, such as linoleum squares, Nafco synthetic tile, or even a host of synthetic wood-flooring products that are easy to install and can withstand harsh traffic.

When cleaning stains on carpet, it is important to verify what type of carpet fiber you have **(Figure 14.10)**. Nylon carpets will not accept harsh

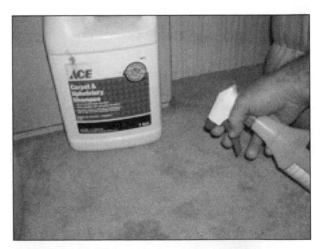

**FIGURE 14.10** When treating stains, check the type of carpet and test for color fastness.

chemicals, while Olefin carpet can be cleaned with bleach and water. You will want to test an area that is out of sight, such as underneath cabinetry, bed pedestals, or the sofa, for color fastness with different cleaners. The main rule of thumb is to act quickly, and don't let the stain dry if possible.

Carry a bottle of carpet cleaner with you, and, once you've tested it on your carpet, use it right away to clean up a spill or stain. Another product that works well is Windex®. This all-purpose cleaner is great on a majority of stains for carpets and fabrics. Always test it on your carpets, especially light-colored versions because the blue dye may create a stain.

It is best to treat a spot and work from the outside edge toward the middle. Best results are achieved by blotting or patting the spot rather than rubbing or scrubbing. Use an absorbant cloth or paper towels and lightly step on the stain after treatment.

Not all stains can be treated with the same cleaner. Check the stain- removal guide available in the appendix.

### WALLS AND CEILINGS

Dust, fingerprints, and grease from cooking can coat wall paneling and ceiling material. Routine cleaning of these surfaces with a soft cloth and mild detergent or Windex will help prevent buildup. Wall paneling is generally plywood sheeting covered with a vinyl paper, which can be cleaned easily. Wood surfaces should be cleaned with a wood cleaner such as Murphy Oil Soap or other similar product.

Ceiling fabric is usually vinyl paper, padded vinyl, or closed-cell fabric. For fabric ceilings, consult your owner's manual for cleaning instructions. Some recommend a light detergent solution while others require a bleach solution. Other campground favorites are Oxyclean and portable steam cleaners. Always test first!

**FIGURE 14.11** Solid-surface material can be buffed using a Scotch-Brite pad.

### SOLID-SURFACE COUNTER MATERIAL

Many manufacturers are using solid-surface material for the kitchen countertop, backsplash, and even in the bathroom and bedroom. Solid-surface material is available in matte and gloss finishes, and both will scratch over time.

Manufacturers recommend the following cleaning and maintenance procedures:

- For stubborn stains on a matte finish, use an abrasive cleaner and a green Scotch-Brite pad (**Figure 14.11**).
- On a glossy finish, use Soft Scrub or diluted bleach and a white Scotch-Brite pad or sponge.
- To disinfect, use a bleach solution of 1 part water/1 part bleach.
- To remove cuts and scratches on a matte finish, sand with 180-or 220-grit fine sandpaper until the cut is gone. Then restore the finish with an abrasive cleaner and a green Scotch-Brite pad. For a glossy surface, sand with 400-grit sandpaper and finish with a nonabrasive cleanser and a white Scotch-Brite pad.
- For high-gloss finish, you will need to follow the 400-grit sanding with a 600-grit

**FIGURE 14.12** A quality furniture polish or solid surface cleaner can provide a high gloss finish.

sandpaper and buff with a white polishing compound and a low-speed (1,500–2.000 rpm) polisher. Then finish with a countertop wax.

- A gloss finish can be added to a matte surface by using a high-grade furniture polish or countertop wax **(Figure 14.12)**.
- Stainless steel sinks can be cleaned and shined by using vinegar to cut lime deposits and water spots. Rubbing alcohol or baking soda can be used for stubborn stains and rinsed with hot water or a mild detergent. Do not use abrasive cleaners or pads because they will leave scratches on the surface.
- Fiberglass sinks, tubs, and showers need special care as they seldom have a thick gel-coat finish like the sidewallmaterial. Scratches, stains, and even cracks can occur and can be removed or repaired. Fiberglass-repair kits are available at most RV supply stores; however, it is often difficult to match the original color. Use only nonabrasive cleaners that are fiberglass-safe and apply a coat of fiberglass wax or protectant. This will help reduce water deposits, discoloration, and stains. Do not wax or apply protectant to the floor of the shower. This will become slippery.
- Windows can be cleaned with a cleaner such as Windex or a good homemade solution of ⅔ cup ammonia, ¾ cup vinegar, and 1 gallon of water. This is an all-purpose cleaner. It contains no dye or coloration. Always test on any surface prior to cleaning. Avoid using abrasive pads or cleaners, especially on tinted windows where a light film could be scratched.

# CHAPTER FIFTEEN

# Driving an RV—
# Different, Not Difficult

## Getting to Know Your RV
## Mirror Adjustment
## Vehicle Size and Handling Characteristics
## Mountain Driving
## Driving Basics

**D**riving or towing a recreational vehicle is not difficult; it's just different than any type of driving you may have experienced before and requires new skills. Most of us feel we can jump behind the wheel of any vehicle and drive it, which is probably true. Anyone can drive; however, there is a big difference between driving and driving without hitting something.

My first experience with RV driving was pulling a trailer at the age of fourteen on I-80 with a learner's permit on a family vacation to the East Coast. The tow vehicle was a new '74 baby-blue Ford LTD 2 and the RV was a 20-foot travel trailer. Since there was no traffic, my dad let me drive on the open road just outside of the Iowa border into Illinois, and it was actually easier than pulling a manure spreader with a John Deere 4020.

Suddenly we were in downtown Chicago during rush hour, and there was no place to pull over and change drivers. My dad may argue this, but I think I might have been the best qualified driver in that situation. It was probably the most traumatic experience of my life to that point (there were many more after); however, it was one of those life lessons that I will never forget—awareness and preparation!

## GETTING TO KNOW YOUR RV

For the first-time RVer or one buying a new unit, it's important to become familiar with all the operations of the new rig before a driving emergency presents itself. Knowing where the windshield-wiper switch is located, how to turn down the radio, or how tall your unit really is can be the difference between an enjoyable RV experience and getting to know your roadside assistance company.

### DIMENSIONS

The width and height of your RV listed in the brochure or even on the price sheet may only be an estimate, not the actual dimension. Plus, it does not take into account aftermarket items added by a dealer or yourself, such as vent covers or a satellite dish.

*Height*—Check the measurement at the highest point, such as air conditioner, ladder, or satellite dish. Over 25 percent of RV insurance claims are due to overhead obstruction damage (**Figure 15.1**).

*Width*—Measure to the outermost points, such as assist handles, awnings, or mirrors.

*Length*—Measure from the front of the vehicle to the end of the towed vehicle. Often a manufacturer's 34-foot model is really longer after bumpers and tow hitches are factored in.

*Weight*—Total weight of all vehicles, including passengers and "stuff." Please refer to Chapter 2, "Understanding Weight Ratings."

Write these measurements down and have them visible on the dash for a quick reference (**Figure 15.2**).

## GETTING THE RIGHT FIT WITH YOUR VEHICLE

Make sure you and your vehicle fit well together and that you have a clear line of sight to the side mirrors without obstruction from the front pillar or window frames.

There should be at least 10 inches of room between your chest and the steering wheel, and your hands placed at 9 o'clock and 3 o'clock. This is a departure from what we learned early in life; however, this position is better for quick-turning reaction time, and it keeps the hands/arms clear in the unlikely event of an airbag deployment.

If the steering wheel blocks your speedometer or warning lights, try adjusting the tilt (telescope if applicable) or moving the seat forward, back, up, or down. In some cases it may be impossible to see all gauges; therefore, adjust for optimum viewing and determine the critical gauges, such as the speedometer, engine oil, air pressure if air assisted, and engine temperature.

Items like seat belts and head restraints should be adjusted to your specific height and driving position. Most seat belts are adjustable by either sliding the D-ring at the pillar, or by using the plastic "fingers" to position the belt across the chest. Adjust the head restraint to the proper position with the center of the head restraint at ear level on the back of your head.

**FIGURE 15.1** Know the actual height of your rig; don't guess!

Also, check your visors before you take to the road. With today's bus-style RVs, there is a tremendous amount of windshield to shade. Make sure your sun visor is adequate for your application. You may wish to purchase an aftermarket shade to assist during high-glare driving situations. Also, make sure the visor can be adjusted as your direction of travel changes.

## MIRROR ADJUSTMENT

Mirrors play an important role in driving an RV because there are more blind spots to deal with than in ordinary vehicles (**Figure 15.3**). In our cars and trucks we have windows all around the vehicle with a few frames limiting vision. In an RV we seldom have a back window or one that allows us to see directly behind us. We also have limited or no side vision past the driver and passenger windows.

Mirrors generally come with a flat upper section that shows a true reflection and a convex mirror that provides a wider angle that is more distorted. The flat upper mirror should be adjusted so that the RV can be seen in the first 1 inch of the mirror. Never adjust a motorized mirror by pushing on the glass itself; you could damage the motor. Either use the power buttons or adjust the entire mirror head. Now adjust the mirror vertically to

| My RV Dimensions Are: | | |
|---|---|---|
| | **English** | **Metric** |
| **Weight** | _____ | _____ |
| **Height** | _____ | _____ |
| **GVWR** | _____ | _____ |
| **Width** | _____ | _____ |
| **Length** | _____ | _____ |
| **W/Towed** | _____ | _____ |

**FIGURE 15.2** A sticker on the dash like this from the RV Safety & Education Foundation provides a quick reference of dimensions.

**FIGURE 15.3** Get to know what areas each mirror covers!

view the top of your RV while the bottom shows the approximate location of the back wheel. Since you cannot see the back-tire position in your side mirrors, you should place a reference mark on the side of your RV that is visible. Place a construction cone next to the tire and look in the mirror for a spot close to the cone that is visible.

Adjust your convex mirror to see 1 inch of RV on the inside and a wide-angle view of the other lane. This mirror should be adjusted down to provide a better view of passing traffic.

Even with proper adjustment, you will have blind spots, which are important to identify. Have a partner walk along the side of your unit until you can no longer see the person in either mirror. This will help when trying to pass or being passed while you are driving **(Figure 15.4)**.

## VEHICLE SIZE AND HANDLING CHARACTERISTICS

Most of us drive passenger cars or light trucks more frequently and switch to our RVs only occasionally. Thus, it's always necessary to make a mental transition and keep the size and handling characteristics of the larger rig in mind. Failing

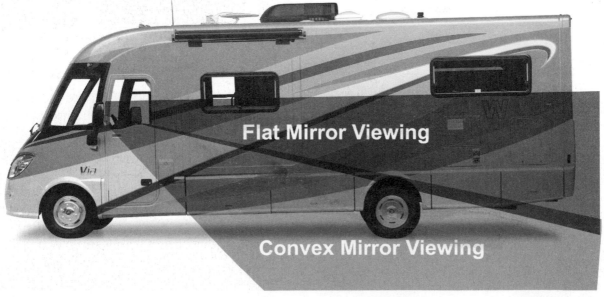

**FIGURE 15.4** Get to know what each mirror covers.

to do so may result in a tendency to make turns too tightly, run over curbs, hit stationary objects, or crowd other traffic.

## PRACTICE YOUR DRIVING

For the novice RVer, it's important to practice and understand the specific handling characteristics of the RV, such as the amount of swing in the back, cornering, and backing up. Becoming confident in your ability to make a tight turn or maneuver through construction will make it easier when a situation presents itself. Practice also helps improve your judgment in making sure you don't hit overhanging tree limbs or other obstructions.

Find a wide-open space to practice such as a church parking lot during the week or a public school or junior college parking lot during the weekend **(Figure 15.5)**. Buy a set of orange construction cones and a box of clay pigeons used for target shooting to use as road borders.

## HANDLING TURNS

A right turn is the most difficult for RVers because it is the tightest turn, and the back tires of your rig do not follow the same line as the front tires (known as off-tracking). You will need to develop a reference system depending on the turning radius of your vehicle. The typical lane of a city/residential street is 12 to 12.5 feet wide, while larger highways and interstate roads are 14 feet wide. Placing the clay discs in line, 12 to 14 feet wide, you can simulate a road and even an intersection **(Figure 15.6)**.

## HANDLING MOTORHOMES

Motorhomes will have a turning radius of 45, 50, or even 60 degrees **(Figure 15.7)**. Knowing what degree turning radius will provide the proper reference point for your rig. With a 45-degree radius, use the front bumper as the reference point; once

**FIGURE 15.5** Find an empty parking lot to practice before hitting the road—literally!

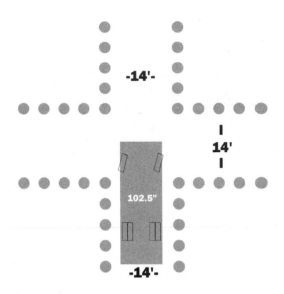

**FIGURE 15.6** Tight ride hand turns are the hardest to negotiate. Practice with clay pigeons before jumping into a critical situation.

this point passes the curb or shoulder you need to clear, start your turn. This will provide enough room for the back tires to clear any obstructions. A 50-degree turning radius will use the front wheels as the reference point; however, since you cannot see the actual wheel location on the right side of your RV, using your seat position usually works. Practice making a turn using either the bumper or front wheel as the reference point. If

a wheel comes in contact with the disc, it will break, letting you know to adjust your reference point. Being able to see your tire position will help identify if it has cleared the curb or not. Also, placing a few cones along the left side of your simulated road will help identify how far the back end swings as you turn. This information will be valuable when maneuvering around campgrounds, in parking lots, and at service stations.

Some right hand turns are impossible to "legally" negotiate, which means staying in your own lane **(Figure 15.8)**. For longer wheelbase coaches, the turn is too tight to make without either swinging wide to the left before the turn or protruding into the left lane after the turn. In either case, be prepared, look for oncoming traffic, and if you get stuck, don't panic; wait for traffic to move around you and negotiate out of the situation.

Most new motorhome drivers have a tendency to hug the shoulder or right side of the road as they feel the need to position themselves like they would in a car. Since the motorhome is much wider, this puts the passenger and the right wheel out on the shoulder. It takes some practice to

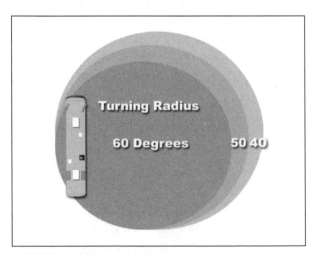

**FIGURE 15.7** Determine if your motorhome has a 40-50-or 60-degree turning radius.

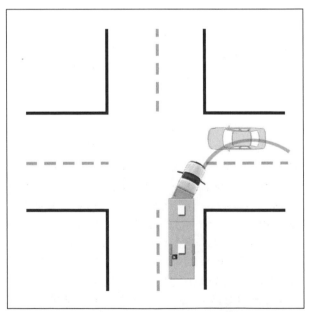

**FIGURE 15.8** Sometimes making a legal right-hand turn is impossible without using another lane.

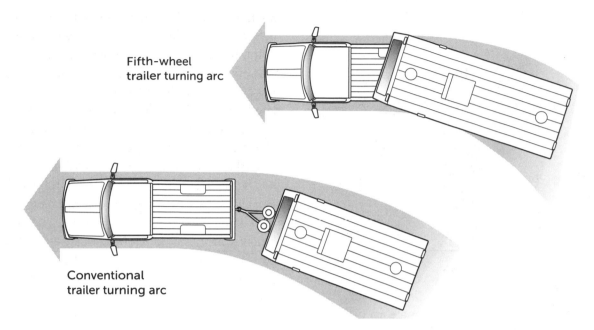

Fifth-wheel
trailer turning arc

Conventional
trailer turning arc

FIGURE 15.9 Fifth-wheel trailers track to the inside of the turn as the pivot point is over the rear axle.

get the feel for the right position and to center the RV in the lane. Use your mirrors to verify the same amount of space on each side; a rear-view monitor helps as well.

Negotiating a curve on a highway can be challenging due to the off-tracking of the rear wheels. With a little practice, you will be able to identify a reference point on the windshield or dash that can act as a guide. While turning left, keep the reference point on the edge of the road; this will help keep the back wheels on the road.

## HANDLING TOW VEHICLES AND TRAILERS

Making turns with trailers requires more practice and more visualizing because it's necessary to learn how the tow vehicle and trailer respond to steering input. Small- to medium-length travel trailers will follow closely in the tracks of the tow vehicle in turns, so the tow vehicle needn't be steered exceptionally wide in turns. A long travel trailer will track moderately on the inside of the turn, requiring more space. A fifth-wheel trailer tracks considerably farther to the inside of the

turn, so a turn that is not taken rather wide will result in the trailer's tires climbing the curb. The reason for this is that a fifth-wheel trailer's hitch point is directly above the rear axle of the tow vehicle, whereas the pivot point of a travel trailer is 4 to 5 feet behind the tow vehicle's rear bumper **(Figure 15.9)**. The tow vehicle's tail swing tends to make a travel trailer follow closely in the tow vehicle's tracks. But tow-vehicle tail swing does not steer a fifth-wheel trailer, so it tracks farther to the inside of the turn.

Tail swing is an RV handling characteristic that causes quite a number of dings and scrapes. It occurs during tight, slow-speed maneuvers when the rear of a trailer swings opposite the direction you are steering. Tail swing can be monitored in the mirrors of a motorhome, allowing you to avoid costly repairs. But with a tow vehicle and trailer, you're blind on the right side during left turns. Also, while backing to the left, you can see where you're going on that side, but you can't see the right side of the trailer. Pulling forward sharply to the left and then straightening the wheel can swing the trailer's rear to the right—into a post, tree, or other obstacle.

FIGURE 15.10 Backing a trailer takes practice and patience.

FIGURE 15.11 Place your hand at the bottom of the wheel when backing a trailer. The trailer will move in the same direction you move your hand.

The best defense is to practice and observe how the vehicle's rear changes position. With a tow vehicle and trailer, have someone else drive while you watch what happens in tight turns. Using the clay-pigeon method will help identify the specific tracking and turning characteristics of your tow vehicle and trailer( **Figure 15.10**).

## TRAILER BACKING

With conventionally hitched trailers, ease of backing increases with trailer length, which is the opposite of what most novices assume. A utility trailer is much more difficult to back; its short ball-to-axle distance causes it to react swiftly to tow-vehicle-steering input, while a longer trailer will react gradually. Fifth-wheel trailers are more difficult to back than conventional trailers, requiring more patience. Once again, use clay pigeons in a parking lot and practice backing into the spot.

Here are some general guidelines for backing a trailer:

- At the site, inspect the area for an obstruction above and to the side. Scribe a line with a stick or run a white string from the left rear tire of the trailer along the path you want the tire to follow into the final position. Backing to the left is easiest as you will be able to see this tire in your left side mirror.
- When you are ready to begin backing, place your hand at the bottom of the steering wheel. Then move it in the direction you want your trailer to go **(Figure 15.11)**. This is more effective with conventional trailers than with fifth-wheelers, which require more turning of the steering wheel.
- Isolate the left tire in the rearview mirror along intended backing path, making slow adjustments as needed. This will help eliminate what I call directional distractions, such as where tow vehicle's tailgate, bumper, and trailer's side wall are going.
- GET HELP! A set of handheld two-way radios and an assistant can help talk you through the most challenging maneuvers.
- With or without radios, make sure you are communicating properly. Develop a simplified set of hand and verbal signals that you are both comfortable with.

Scribing a line with chalk or using a stick in gravel from your back left tire along the ground to the final parking spot helps isolate the path and makes it easier for beginners.

## FIFTH-WHEEL BACKING

When you are backing a fifth-wheeler, follow these procedures:

- Watch your outside mirrors and when you see the trailer moving where you don't want it to go, turn the steering wheel in that direction. For example, while looking in the left mirror, if you see the trailer moving toward that side and you don't want it to go in that direction, turn the wheel to the left. Position someone near the rear of the trailer, in the driver's view, to watch for obstructions.
- Remember that you have no tail-swing leverage to help you steer the fifth-wheeler while backing, as one has with a ball-mounted trailer. Therefore, the tow vehicle must be at a significant angle to the trailer before any turning occurs. This does not necessarily mean that extreme winding of the steering wheel is required, but it does mean that turns must be started before you get to the slot into which you're trying to move. The trick is figuring how much earlier. Each time you pull out of a slot, observe the path the trailer wheels make, and pay particular attention to the surprisingly long way you go before the trailer is aligned straight behind the tow vehicle. That is the magical point at which you should start to turn if you were to reverse the process and back into that slot.

## MOUNTAIN DRIVING

RV drivers often overheat and damage their vehicle's braking systems by improper braking techniques such as riding the brakes or improper braking going down a mountain pass. The following information was provided by Workhorse Custom Chassis and contains recommendations outlined in the Department of Transportation (DOT) commercial driver's license manual.

In mountain driving, gravity plays a major role. On any upgrade, gravity slows you down. The steeper the grade, the longer the grade, and/or the heavier the load, the more you will have to use lower gears to climb hills or mountains. In coming down long, steep downgrades, gravity causes the speed of your vehicle to increase. You must select an appropriate safe speed, and then use a low gear and proper braking techniques **(Figure 15.12)**.

You should plan ahead and obtain information about any long, steep grades along your planned route of travel. If possible, talk to other motorhome or truck drivers who are familiar with the grades to find out what speeds are safe. You must utilize engine-braking techniques to go slowly enough so your brakes can be utilized for speed reduction without getting too hot. If the brakes become too hot, they may start to fade. This means you have to apply them harder and harder to get the same stopping power. If you continue to brake hard, the brakes can keep fading until you cannot slow down or stop at all.

## SELECT A "SAFE" SPEED

Your most important consideration is to select a speed that is not too fast for the:

- Total vehicle and cargo weight
- Length of grade
- Steepness of grade
- Road condition
- Weather

If a speed limit is posted or there is a sign indicating "Maximum Safe Speed," never exceed the speed shown.

Also, look for and heed warning signs indicating the length and steepness of the grade **(Figure 15.13)**. You must use the braking effect of the engine as the principal way of controlling your

**FIGURE 15.12** Select a proper speed in mountain driving when coming down steep grades.

speed. The braking effect of the engine is greatest when it is near the governed rpms and the transmission is in the lower gears. Save your brakes so you will be able to slow or stop as required by road and traffic conditions.

## SELECT THE RIGHT GEAR BEFORE STARTING DOWN THE GRADE

Shift the transmission to a low gear before starting down the grade. Pay close attention to the gear that is required to climb the grade prior to descent. For example, if the gear required to climb the grade is third gear, then third gear should be selected prior to the descent as a baseline to control your vehicle speed. Do not try to downshift after your speed has already built up above the safe posted speed limit. Once your speed has increased over the safe posted speed limit, you may not be able to shift into a lower gear. You may

not even be able to get back into any gear and all engine braking effect will be lost.

With motorhomes, a rule for choosing gears has been to use the same gear going down a hill that you would to climb the hill. However, newer motorhomes have low friction parts and streamlined shapes for fuel economy. They may also have more powerful engines. This means they can go up hills in higher gears and have less friction and air drag to hold them back going down hills. For this reason, drivers of newer motorhomes may have to use lower gears going down a hill than would be required to go up the hill. Usually you want the lowest gear that will keep the motorhome at or near the speed you want in negotiating the downhill. For example, if you're going down a 6 percent grade and want to go 35 miles an hour, you would start downshifting and using the brakes to get to an engine rpm that will enable you to maintain a speed at or near 35 miles per hour.

**FIGURE 15.13** Heed the steepness of the grade!

## PROPER BRAKING TECHNIQUE

Remember, the use of brakes on a long and/or steep downgrade is only a supplement to the braking effect of the engine. Once the vehicle is in the proper low gear, the following is the proper braking technique:

1. When your speed increases to or above your "safe" speed, apply the brakes aggressively enough to feel a definite slowdown.
2. When your speed has been reduced to approximately 5 mph below your safe speed, release the brakes. (This brake application should last for about 3 seconds.)
3. When your speed increases again to your safe speed, repeat steps 1 and 2.

For example, if your safe speed is 40 mph, you would not apply the brakes to any increase in speed until you reach 40 mph. Then you apply the brakes aggressively enough to gradually reduce your speed to 35 mph and then release the brakes. Repeat this as often as necessary until you have reached the end of the downgrade.

## BRAKE FADE OR FAILURE

Your brakes by design operate utilizing brake pads that rub against the brake discs to slow the vehicle during brake application. This braking function creates heat, which the brake system can dissipate during normal brake applications. However, brakes can fade or fail from excessive heat caused by improper use or dragging the brake to slow the vehicle. Every braking mechanism must do its share of the work. Brakes with excessively worn pads or rotors will not provide the same degree of braking power.

If you are not sure about the condition of your braking system, have it inspected by a qualified service center.

## BRAKE-FLUID INSPECTION AND TESTING

Most of us take our brake fluid for granted, occasionally checking it, but often never changing it. The average motorist that drives 10,000 to 15,000 miles a year uses his or her brakes an average of 75,000 times. After three years of service, the average boiling point of the brake fluid has dropped to a potentially dangerous level because of moisture contamination and may not meet minimum federal requirements for brake fluid.

Since you can't tell how badly contaminated brake fluid is by its appearance alone (unless the fluid is full of rust or is muddy), the fluid should be tested by a qualified technician. If it needs to be changed, only use the fluid type (DOT 3 or 4) recommended by your vehicle manufacturer.

Brake fluid is not a generic term and even though some economical brands may meet DOT

3 and 4 standards, they may not tolerate moisture or provide the same degree of corrosion protection. Your RV brakes are working hard for you; always use the highest quality fluid.

## ESCAPE RAMPS OR RUNAWAY-TRUCK RAMPS

Escape ramps, also known as runaway-truck ramps, have been built on many steep mountain downgrades. Escape ramps are made to stop runaway vehicles safely without injuring drivers and passengers. Escape ramps use a long bed of loose, soft material to slow a runaway vehicle, sometimes in combination with an upgrade. Know escape-ramp locations on your route. Signs show drivers where ramps are located.

## DRIVING BASICS

You may be a good driver, maybe a great driver, however, not everyone on the road is, and you can't control that. In the last forty years, traffic has increased 78 percent, while the number of highways has only increased by 2 percent. For those of us who have never had our license suspended, we have never really updated or educated ourselves regarding the changes in driving regulations and the challenges associated with driving in today's world.

There are several driving-safety classes available through insurance companies, such as the Good Sam VIP, and on-line classes, such as the American Safety Council. Some may even qualify you for insurance discounts. A few hands-on classes are also available, such as the Recreational Vehicle Safety & Education Foundation, which offers classroom education, as well as an actual driving session at the Lifestyle, Education, and Safety Conference. More information is available at www.rvsafety.com.

## SCANNING

Scanning is a way to view the total traffic scene as you drive **(Figure 15.14)**. Developing good scanning habits prevents tunnel vision that can isolate you from what is going on in the distance as well as all around your vehicle. Look at least

**FIGURE 15.14** Scanning and a safe following distance are important factors in driving awareness.

one block ahead or one-quarter mile ahead if you are in a rural setting. Glance slightly left and right to look for approaching danger, and check your side mirrors often.

## SAFE FOLLOWING DISTANCE

When we were younger, we learned that the safe following distance was one car length for every 10 miles per hour. As we stated earlier, things have changed. According to the National Safety Council, we need at least a three-second distance in normal driving conditions.

Here is how you can determine your following distance. When the car ahead of you passes a fixed object like a sign or marking, begin counting "1,001, 1,002, 1,003." If your vehicle passes the same fixed point as you hit 1,003, you have a safe following distance. Now that is in a normal driving situation.

If it's raining, add another section. If it's snowing, add two more, or turn your map around; you've gone in the wrong direction!

Now you might be saying to yourself, "If I leave a three-second gap, someone will come ahead of me and pull into it!" That is a challenge we all face. Remain calm, reduce your speed, and develop a three-second distance. Remember, you should not be in a hurry to get somewhere; after all, it is called *a recreation vehicle*.

## SKIDS

If a breaking-loose situation or skid occurs, staying calm and being prepared are important **(Figure 15.15)**. Know what caused the skid and what you need to do to regain control without drastic inputs. Let off the accelerator, grasp the steering wheel firmly, and steer in the direction of the skid or turn the wheel in the direction the back end is going. Braking hard increases the dynamics of the skid.

## INTERSECTIONS

Intersections are busy places with many hazards. For drivers seventy-five years and older, at least 40 percent of fatal crashes occur in an intersection and that increases with age. One misconception regarding intersections is that someone has the right of way. Traffic regulations state only who must YIELD the right of way.

Utilize delayed acceleration at intersections. Look left, then right, then straight ahead, and scan left again. This two-second delay may save your life if someone tries to squeeze through the yellow light. Never enter an intersection that you cannot exit. You could get stuck in the intersection and cross traffic may be "timing" the light. Never turn your wheel before actually making the turn. A rear-end crash will push you into oncoming traffic.

## SHARE THE ROAD

The Federal Motor Carrier Safety Administration, in partnership with the trucking industry and highway safety organizations, is working to make our roads safer for everyone. The "Share the Road Safely" campaign is sponsored by the Federal Highway Administration and its goal is to reduce truck-related fatalities by 50 percent by the year 2011.

Your commitment as an RV owner/driver to share the road safely will help achieve this objective.

Large trucks do not operate as cars do. Because they are large, accelerating, slowing down, and stopping take more time and much more space than for any other vehicle on the road. Average truck weight loaded—80,000 pounds.

Stopping distance at 55 miles per hour: The length of a football field (300 yards/900 feet) **Figure 15.16)**.

Anticipate the flow of traffic before pulling in front of trucks. More than 60 percent of fatal truck crashes involve impacts with the front of the truck. Trucks are not equipped with the same

**BRAKING SLIDE (WITHOUT ABS)**

**REAR END BREAK LOOSE**

**TAKE YOUR FOOT OFF THE BRAKE**

**APPLY BRAKES WITHOUT LOCKING WHEELS**

**APPLY THE TRAILER BRAKES**

**POWER SLIDE**

**MOMENTUM SLIDE**

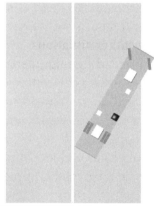

**DON'T BRAKE, SIMPLY REMOVE YOUR FOOT FROM THE ACCELERATOR**

**DON'T BRAKE, SLOW DOWN AND GET THE WHEELS TO GO IN THE DIRECTION THEY ARE POINTED**

**FIGURE 15.15** Rear End Break Loose

type of energy-absorbing bumpers as cars. When a car is hit from behind by a truck, the results are too often deadly.

Large trucks are as wide as your lane of travel. Driving too close behind one prevents you from reacting to changing traffic conditions. If you are too close to the rear of a truck and there is a slow-down on the highway, debris on the road, or an accident, you won't notice it until it is a braking emergency.

## DRIVING AND AGING

Depth perception and peripheral vision decrease as we age, making distances and speeds of vehicles more difficult to judge, and objects coming from the sides of our field of vision may surprise us. Have your eyes checked regularly and identify areas that need addressing, possibly reducing night driving, and use caution in rain, fog, or and other bad-weather situations.

Our sense of hearing helps alert us to situations in and around our vehicle that may require us to respond, such as honking horns, engine sounds, and emergency vehicles. As we age, our hearing may gradually become diminished and we may miss cues that we used to routinely hear. Have your hearing checked regularly and avoid loud sounds, music, or conversation levels that can distract you.

Reaction time involves seeing and/or hearing something in our environment, our minds deciding what to do, and our brains telling our bodies to take action. Studies indicate that as we age, reaction time typically takes longer, about $3/10$ of a second. This doesn't sound like much, but it can mean the difference between having and avoiding an accident. Check your mirrors every 5 to 7 seconds, watch for trains, in other words—be aware, stay alert.

## CHILD SAFETY SEAT

For those traveling with small children, it's important to review the proper installation for a child safety seat. Many motorhomes do not have a secure, forward-facing seat with a belt other than ones on the driver's and passenger seat.

Some owners choose to use the passenger seat for the installation of the child safety seat while the adults sit on the sofa. Some dealers are now offering modifications with aftermarket options. Check with your local dealer or law enforcement agency. Many will inspect and recommend alterations for such applications.

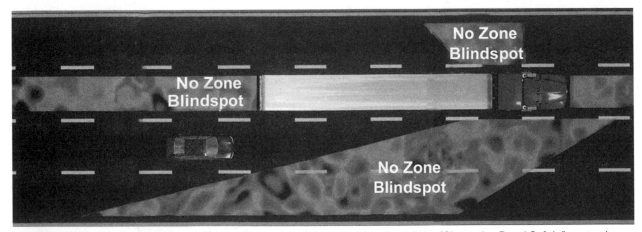

**FIGURE 15.16** The Federal Motor Carrier Safety Administration developed the "Share the Road Safely" campaign.

CHAPTER SIXTEEN

# Fire Safety

**Fire Classifications**
**Fire Extinguishers**
**Smoke Detectors**
**Carbon Monoxide Detectors**
**A Plan of Action**

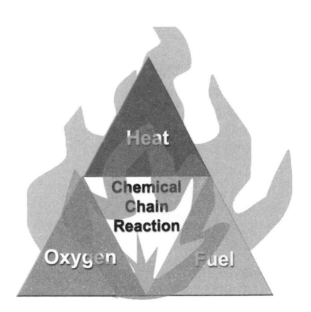

Fire plays an important role in your RV experience—internal combustion provides the force for movement of your tow vehicle or motorhome. It's used to heat your water, cook your food, and keep you warm. It's even used to help cool items in your refrigerator. This is all in a controlled environment. However, uncontrolled, fire is dangerous and deadly, and understanding what to do in case of an emergency is the first step in preventing a disaster.

Four components are necessary for a fire to occur and continue to burn. These are commonly referred to as the *fire tetrahedron.*

- *Fuel*—combustibles, such as wood, carpet, furniture, and flammable liquids
- *Oxygen*—always present in the air
- *Heat source*—heat raises the temperature of the fuel to produce combustible gas. Open flames, sparks, overheating appliances, and electrical wiring can all be a source of heat.
- *Chemical reaction*—some believe that all you need is fuel, oxygen, and heat to create a fire; however, we have all three present in our lives on a daily basis. There needs to be a chemical reaction among them to create a fire.

## FIRE CLASSIFICATIONS

Fire is classified in three types, so it's important to understand and identify the type of fire and use the appropriate fire extinguisher **(Figure 16.1)**. Throwing water on a grease fire only makes it

Combustibles that leave an ash: Wood-Carpet-Fabric

Combustibles Liquids: Motor fuels-propane

Energized electrical component: Wiring-outlet-motor

**FIGURE 16.1** Fires are identified in three classifications: Class A, Class B, and Class C.

splatter and spread, while putting water on an electrical fire creates an electrical hazard. Learning the ABCs of fire provides a better understanding of the type of extinguisher needed.

### CLASS A

Class A combustibles consist of materials that leave an ash when they burn.

Material examples include carpet, fabrics, and wood.

Clothing examples would include fiberglass and rubber.

### CLASS B

Class B combustibles are flammable liquids, gases, and solvents. Examples include: gasoline, diesel fuel, propane, lighter fluid, motor oil, and transmission fluid.

### CLASS C

A Class C fire is any energized electrical component. Fires can start from wiring, controls, motors, appliances, shore power, generators, and battery chargers,

A Class C fire can easily become a Class A or Class B fire.

## FIRE EXTINGUISHERS

An important aspect of RV safety is to know what to do in case of emergency—in this case, a fire.

Most RVs come with a 10-BC-rated fire extinguisher, which indicates it will help extinguish a liquid (B) or electrical (C) fire in a 10-square-foot area. Knowing where your fire extinguisher is located, how to use it, and its limitations is critical.

**FIGURE 16.2** A 10-BC fire extinguisher is generally standard safety equipment in an RV.

## DETERMINING THE RATING OF THE OEM FIRE EXTINGUISHER IN YOUR VEHICLE

Since your vehicle is registered using the chassis VIN number it falls under DOT code for a 10-BC extinguisher **(Figure 16.2)**. With a 10-BC-rated fire extinguisher, you will be limited from extinguishing a Class A fire, and most of what your RV contains consists of combustible materials and clothing. It is recommended that you purchase an additional 10-ABC extinguisher.

Locate the extinguisher in your RV. Most fire extinguishers are placed immediately inside the entrance door for easy access; however, this may not always be the case. Some diesel-pusher models do not have wall space for mounting; some trailers will place them inside a compartment. Make sure the dealer or previous owner has not moved the extinguisher.

It is a good idea to install additional extinguishers in easily accessed areas, such as exterior compartments, in a towed vehicle, in a tow vehicle, or inside the RV's bedroom.

It is highly recommended by fire prevention experts that you get hands-on training before operating a fire extinguisher **(Figure 16.3)**. Most local fire departments offer this service. Also, read

P.A.S.S
Pull the pin

Aim and squeeze

Sweep

**FIGURE 16.3** Learn how to use your fire extinguisher before you need it.

the instructions printed on the extinguisher as different types have a variable recommended distance according to OSHA.

Think of the the acronym PASS when using a fire extinguisher:

**P**ull the pin and hold the unit upright.
**A**im at the base of the fire, not the flames. (You should stand back at least 6 feet.)
**S**queeze the lever slowly. This will release the extinguishing agent.
**S**weep from side to side.

When the extinguisher agent comes in contact with the flame initially, the fire will generally

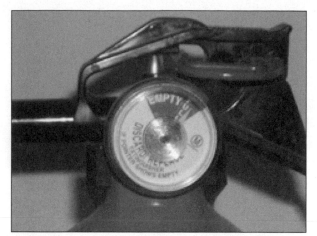

**FIGURE 16.4** Check your fire extinguisher each month.

**FIGURE 16.5** It is a good idea to install additional smoke detectors and change batteries each year.

flare up and appear to grow larger. This is normal and temporary as the agent will suppress the fire. Keep the trigger squeezed and continue to discharge the contents.

## FIRE-EXTINGUISHER MAINTENANCE

Check the pressure indicator and inspect the extinguisher monthly **(Figure 16.4)**. The indicator must be in the green area, and all pins, nozzle opening, trigger, and equipment free of defects. Also, once a year, remove the extinguisher from the harness, turn it upside down, and either shake or strike the bottom with your hand to dislodge the agent. And finally, check the service date.

## SMOKE DETECTORS

The National Fire Protection Association (NFPA) requires one smoke detector in every RV. This is generally placed in the kitchen area in typical floor plans. With today's divided or sectional floor-plan designs, it is a good idea to install additional detectors in each bedroom. Choose only Underwriters Laboratory (UL) RV-approved smoke detectors.

Smoke detectors are intended to alert you when there is a dangerous concentration of smoke in your RV. Most are powered by a small 9-volt

battery. Both the battery and detector should tested regularly **(Figure 16.5)**. The NFPA campaign suggests you change smoke-detector batteries twice a year when you change your clocks to and from daylight savings time.

Since most RVs are relatively confined spaces, the slightest cooking smoke can set off an alarm and become annoying. Rather than disable the alarm and risk the potential to forget to place it back into service, you may wish to install one with a temporary shutoff button. Simply press the button, and the unit will be disabled for approximately 15 minutes, at which time it automatically resets and chirps to let you know it is working. It will operate as designed even during the 15-minute period if heavy smoke is present.

## CARBON MONOXIDE DETECTORS

Carbon monoxide (CO) is an odorless, invisible, and deadly gas that can result from a leaky generator or engine exhaust or even a furnace. CO can also come from another vehicle's exhaust that may be parked next to you **(Figure 16.6)**. The U.S. Consumer Product Safety Commission (CPSC) recommends placing the CO detector

**FIGURE 16.6** Carbon monoxide (CO) can infiltrate an RV from a neighbor's exhaust.

in the bedroom. CO is approximately the same weight as air, but it generally comes from a warm-air source (generator or furnace exhaust) and will rise with that air. Therefore, it is best to place the detector at a considerable height, either on the ceiling or on a wall at least 8 inches from the ceiling and at least 5 feet off the floor.

## A PLAN OF ACTION

Recognizing the causes of common RV fires is the first step in preparation and developing a plan of action. A monthly inspection can be helpful in preventing a fire or allowing you to respond appropriately in case of an emergency.

Periodically inspect the following:

- *Propane lines and connections.* Visually inspect propane connections using a detergent soap-and-water solution as described in Chapter 12, "Propane Use and Safety." Bubbles around a connection or line indicate a leak. Every year have a qualified technician run a water-column or other professional pressure test on your system.
- *Electrical outlets, wiring, connections.* Use an inexpensive circuit tester to check inside outlets for power, to determine if the outlet is grounded, and whether the hot and common wires are reversed. This can also be used to check cords by plugging the cord into an outlet that has been checked and plugging the tester in the end of the cord. Extension cords and cords of tools and appliances should also be checked for cracks, cuts, exposed wires, and loose or broken prongs, and properly repaired or discarded if they are damaged. Don't try to tape them up.
- Three-prong tools or appliances can be tested for proper grounding. Extension cords and tool cords can be marked by wrapping colored electrical tape at the male end of the cord to show that they've been inspected and tested. Use different colored tape on the next periodic check.
- Also check to ensure all flammables outside the RV are secure and away from a fire or heat source.

Once you identify the elements that can create a fire hazard, a plan of action is needed. Identify the emergency escape routes in your RV such as escape windows, doors, or even windows large enough to crawl through (**Figure 16.7**). If you have a fifth-wheel trailer, consider moving a picnic table under the bedroom window, making it easier to crawl out and get to the ground. Prepare an emergency escape plan and make sure everyone knows how to use it and where they are to go in case of an emergency.

**FIGURE 16.7** Be prepared. Develop a plan of action and emergency escape route, such as a window large enough to crawl through.

Being prepared is essential in RV safety and critical in case of a fire because a small flame can become completely out of control in less than 30 seconds. It only takes a minute for thick, black smoke to fill an RV. During a fire, the ceiling traps the smoke and hot gases, and fire uses up the oxygen you need and produces deadly smoke and poisonous gas. Breathing even small amounts of smoke and toxic gas can make you drowsy, disoriented, and short of breath. The odorless, colorless fumes can quickly lull you into a deep sleep.

Once a smoke detector goes off, get out of the RV immediately. Do not stop to take anything with you. Remember, things can be replaced, people cannot. Go to the nearest exit, which could be the main door or a large window. If the only way out is through the smoke, crawl under the smoke as low as you can because the hot smoke and gases will rise and there may be breathable air near the floor.

After everyone has safely exited the RV, make sure the fire department has been called.

# CHAPTER SEVENTEEN

# Personal Safety

## Awareness/Preparation
## First Aid
## Medication
## In Case of Emergency (ICE)
## Emergency Road Service
## Staying in Touch

**T**here is more to personal safety than just protecting yourselves from criminals. In fact, the RV lifestyle generally affords an exceptionally safe environment. Several years ago, Gaylord Maxwell, the nationally known RV writer, educator, and enthusiast, penned this quote in *MotorHome* magazine:

Personal safety is an issue to which every RVer should give some attention. Not that we live in a dangerous lifestyle—the reality is just the opposite. The fact that so few crimes are committed in campgrounds or in other RV-related activities is strong testimony that people who spend a great deal of time in recreational vehicles live in an exceptionally safe environment. Bad guys just don't seem to go for RVing, so they aren't in the campgrounds or other gathering places for those of us who like rolling homes.

That article was written over ten years ago, and although Gaylord has since passed away, the words still ring true. Caravans, rallies, and campgrounds are full of people with the same goal in mind—*recreation*. Maxwell was dedicated to educating RV enthusiasts to provide a more enjoyable and safe RV experience **(Figure 17.1)**. His Life on Wheels seminars throughout the country were attended by thousands of RV owners and those looking to venture into the journey as well. This section of *The RV Handbook* will take a look at personal safety from an awareness and preparation, health, and emergency approach and is dedicated to the legacy that Gaylord Maxwell created.

## AWARENESS/PREPARATION

One underlying factor in RV safety is awareness and preparation. Whether it's maintaining your vehicle and trailer, understanding driving conditions and characteristics, or knowing what to do in case of an emergency, preparation and awareness can make a world of difference.

## VEHICLE PREPARATION

Every airplane pilot has a strict checklist of items that require verification prior to takeoff. Every RVer

**FIGURE 17.1** The RV lifestyle is exciting and relatively safe.

should have a pretrip checklist to verify all compartments are closed, systems are operating normally, and fluid levels are correct **(Figure 17.2)**. There are several lists available through *MotorHome* and *Trailer Life* magazines and the Good Sam Club, and a version in the appendix. However, as you become more seasoned, you will want to tweak the list to add the items and cargo you bring along. It's certain that you'll add that aftermarket satellite dish to the list after you knock it off the roof the first time!

## TOOLS

Throughout this handbook there are references to several different test devices and tools that are required to maintain and troubleshoot your RV. Identifying your comfort and skill level will help in determining the tools you may require to tackle the various tests and checks **(Figure 17.3)**.

A basic RV tool kit should include the following items:

- Socket set—⅜-inch-drive metric and (standard) Society of Automotive Engineers (SAE)
- Screwdriver(s)—flat head, Phillips, and star or torx head. An assortment of sizes and lengths should be carried.
- Pliers—Assortment of standard, c-channel, and needle-nose
- Crescent wrenches (2)—a 6-inch and a 12-inch
- Combination wrench set—metric and SAE
- Duct tape/electrical tape
- Hammer
- Rescue Tape
- Certified tire gauge
- Jumper cables
- Flashlight

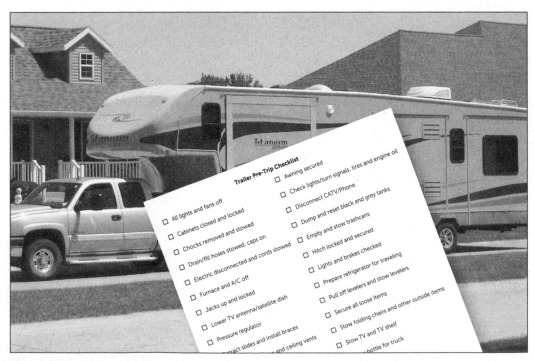

**FIGURE 17.2** A thorough checklist and proper maintenance are keys to reducing breakdowns and preventing putting yourself in a dangerous situation,.

**FIGURE 17.3** A well-stocked tool kit includes items specific to your RV, such as fuses, cabinet latches, and bulbs

As you become comfortable in your ability to diagnose and troubleshoot, you will add advanced tools and equipment to your tool kit, such as voltage meters and test lights. Keep in mind the space, or lack of, you have available for tools and other cargo. It is also important to bring along extra screws, hoses, belts, and fluids that are specific to your RV and engine, such as an assortment of automotive fuses. And your list will grow as you find the need for cabinet latches, proper sealant, clearance-light lenses, and other items.

## RESCUE TAPE

Rescue Tape is a self-fusing silicone repair product with infinite uses. First used by the U.S. mil-

itary and now seen at consumer and industrial trade shows across America, this is the most versatile and easy-to-use emergency repair product available. You can repair leaks in plumbing (950 psi tensile strength) and hoses (withstands 500°F) in a flash, insulate electrical wiring (insulates 8,000 volts per layer) or use as shrink wrap, wrap for tool handles, and much more. Distributors are available at most RV shows and rallies, or go directly to www.rescuetape.com.

## TRIP PLANNING

Learning everything you can about your next trip not only makes it more enjoyable but can also help identify areas of concern on highways, campground limitations, and can help with preventative measures. There are several great resources to help in trip planning, starting with *Trailer Life's RV Park, Campground, & Services Directory,* the most comprehensive, accurate, and reliable source for campground information available, with full descriptions and details for more than 11,500 private and public campgrounds, RV service centers, LP-gas locations, and tourist attractions. For advanced planning, use the *Trailer Life RV Parks & Campground Navigator.* This interactive two-CD set provides complete trip planning software for the United States and Canada.

## FIRST AID

No matter what type of roughing it you are doing, a well-stocked and readily accessible first aid kit is a must. Whether you buy a first aid kit or put one together yourself, make sure it has all the right components as recommended by the American Red Cross. There are kits that are specifically designed for camping and contain items that may be designed for outdoor activities.

Here is a list provided by the American Red Cross:

- Two absorbent compress dressings (5 × 9 inches)
- Twenty-five adhesive bandages (assorted sizes)
- One adhesive cloth tape (10 yards × 1 inch)
- Five antibiotic ointment packets (approximately 1 gram)
- Five antiseptic wipe packets
- Two packets of aspirin (81 mg each)
- One space blanket
- One breathing barrier (with one-way valve)
- One instant cold compress
- Two pair of large-size nonlatex gloves
- Two hydrocortisone ointment packets (approximately 1 gram each)
- Scissors
- 1 roller bandage (3 inches wide)
- 1 roller bandage (4 inches wide)
- 5 sterile gauze pads (3 × 3 inches)
- 5 sterile gauze pads (4 × 4 inches)
- Oral thermometer (non-mercury/ nonglass)
- Two triangular bandages
- Tweezers
- First aid instruction booklet

Include any personal items such as prescription medications or other items your health care provider may recommend.

## HEART ATTACK WARNING SIGNS

- Chest discomfort
- Discomfort in other parts of the upper body
- Shortness of breath
- Clammy perspiration

Learn the signs, but remember this: Even if you're not sure it's a heart attack, have it checked out (tell a doctor about your symptoms). Minutes matter! Fast action can save lives—maybe your own. Don't wait more than 5 minutes to call 911 or your emergency response number.

## STROKE WARNING SIGNS

If you or someone with you has one or more of these signs, don't delay!

- Sudden numbness or weakness of the face, arm, or leg, especially on one side of the body
- Sudden confusion, trouble speaking or understanding
- Sudden trouble seeing in one or both eyes
- Sudden trouble walking, dizziness, loss of balance or coordination

- Sudden, severe headache with no known cause

## MEDICATION

Most of us feel we are prepared for emergencies, both medical and roadside. However, if an accident or medical emergency situation happened right now, would you or your traveling companion be able to identify what prescription medication you are taking and how much? The trend today is to take all our medications and place them in a pillbox labeled Sunday, Monday, Tuesday, etc. Emergency medical technicians arriving at the scene of an accident or medical emergency have no idea what is in each compartment and do not have access to the label on the prescription bottle **(Figure 17.4)**. It is important to always carry an emergency medical card identifying medications and medical conditions, along with emergency phone numbers for physicians, people to call in case of emergency, and other valuable information. Medical cards are available online at www .medids.com where you can obtain and print

out a card as well as update it as needed. These medical cards can be placed above the visor so they are readily available to hand to EMTs for proper care **(Figure 17.5)**.

## IN CASE OF EMERGENCY (ICE)

We all have the "In case of emergency" phone number we wish to have called. But is it easily available in case of emergency? It is recommended that you program this number in your cell phone under ICE (In Case of Emergency) so the number can be called immediately.

### EMERGENCY HIGHWAY NUMBERS

Most states have an emergency system in place, the most common being 911. However, every state is different and it's important to identify each state's emergency numbers **(Figure 17.6)**. For example, Florida is 911 or star (*)FHP (347) on a cellular phone. The star button is usually

**FIGURE 17.4** Keeping medication in a weekly dispenser container without identification makes treatment in an emergency difficult.

## Medical Information Card

Name: _____

Address _____

City _____

DOB _____

Emergency Contacts:

Physicians:

Medical Conditions:

FIGURE 17.5  Always carry an up-to-date medical information card.

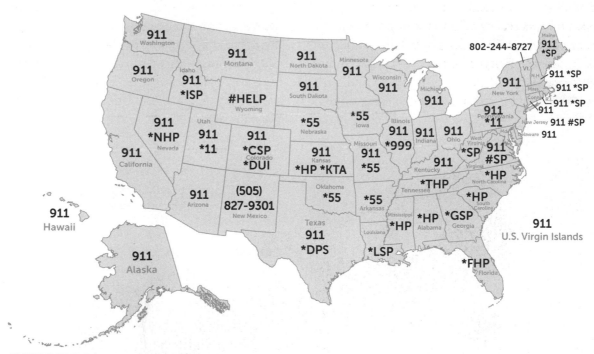

FIGURE 17.6  Become familiar with proper emergency numbers. Not all states use 911.

located on the lower left of the keypad and the 3 button, 4 button, and 7 button stand for Florida Highway Patrol (FHP). Many states, such as New Hampshire, Nebraska, Iowa, and Texas, use 1-800-525-5555 for their emergency phone response. A complete, updated listing can be obtained from your state Department of Transportation Web site.

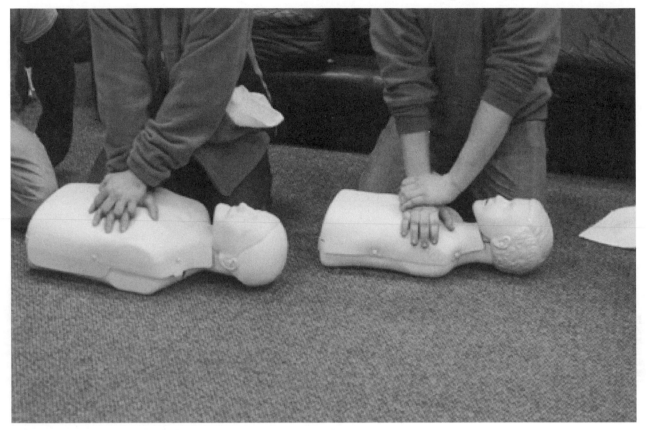

**FIGURE 17.7** Local American Red Cross agencies offer CPR classes.

## CPR

According to the American Red Cross, CPR should be given to a person who is not breathing and does not have a pulse **(Figure 17.7)**.

- Find hand position in center of chest over breastbone.
- Position shoulders over hands. Compress chest 15 times in about 10 seconds.
- Give 2 slow breaths.
- Do 3 more sets of 15 compressions and 2 breaths.

Coronary heart disease is the number one cause of death in the United States. Stroke is the number three cause of death in the United States and a leading cause of serious disability. That's why it's so important to reduce your risk factors, know the warning signs, and know how to respond quickly and properly if warning signs occur.

## EMERGENCY ROAD SERVICE

The Good Sam Club, as well as others, offers an emergency roadside assistance program. The Good Sam ERS provides twenty-four-hour customer service dispatch and technical support as well as access to a network of repair and towing service providers.

Often a breakdown is due to misunderstanding how the system works, or simply a switch in the off position. A certified technical support team can help in troubleshooting the problem and possibly assist in getting you back on the road. If not, a network of qualified towing professionals can bring you and your vehicle back to a safe and secure location. After all, you don't want just anyone hooking up to your rig and pulling it down the road.

## STAYING IN TOUCH

With today's technology, there are literally dozens of inexpensive methods of staying in touch with friends and loved ones. It's important to let people know where you are going and to provide a travel itinerary in case of an emergency situation.

### INTERNET

Most campgrounds now offer some form of Internet service either via WiFi (wireless), cable connection at the site, or a dedicated computer at the office.

Several cell phone service providers also offer various forms of wireless connections so that you can send and receive e-mail. Several retail operations such as national bookstore chains, coffee shops, and even shopping malls are providing wireless Internet access.

You don't need an expensive and extended contract to stay connected by cell phone. Trac-Phone® and other pay-as-you-go services offer prepaid calling cards that are inexpensive and allow for occasional use.

### RV CLUBS

Many manufacturers' clubs and Good Sam provide several services to help keep in touch while on the road, such as mail forwarding and even trip routing, which allows you to send an itinerary to friends and family to stay in touch.

The following charts, graphs, maps, and troubleshooting guides have been provided by various original equipment manufacturers (OEMs) and are designed to provide a quick reference or can be cut out of this book, copied, and stored in your RV. For example, the pre-trip checklist should be cut out, laminated, and placed in an easy-to-find location for reference. The weight charts should be cut out, copied, and used each time you weigh your RV or tow/towed vehicle to record specific weights. And the medical card should be cut out, copied, filled in with the proper information and stored in your wallet in case of emergency.

# RV Terminology

Following is a glossary of commonly used terms featured in *Trailer Life* magazine and reprinted by permission.

**Adjustable Ball Mount**   An adjustable ball mount allows the ball to be raised, lowered, and tilted in small increments to allow fine tuning of the spring bar setup and to compensate for tow vehicle "squat," which occurs after the trailer coupler is lowered onto the ball.

**Axle Ratio**   The final drive gear ratio created by the relationship between the ring and pinion gears and the rotation of the driveshaft. In a 4.10:1 axle ratio, for example, the driveshaft will rotate 4.1 times for each rotation of the axle shaft (wheel).

**Ball Mount**   The part of the hitch system that supports the hitch ball and connects it to the trailer coupler. Ball mounts are available in load-carrying and weight-distributing configurations.

**Brake Controller**   A control unit mounted inside the vehicle that allows electric trailer brakes to become activated in harmony with the braking of the tow vehicle. This device can be used to adjust trailer brake intensity, or to manually activate the trailer brakes.

**Breakaway Switch**   A safety device that activates the trailer brakes in the event the trailer becomes accidentally disconnected from the hitch while traveling.

**Bumper-Mount Hitch**   This type of hitch is available in two configurations: A bracket with a ball mounted to the bumper or a ball is attached to the bumper (typically on pickup trucks). These hitches have very limited RV applications.

**Class A Motorhome**   An RV with the living accommodations built on or as an integral part of a self-propelled motor vehicle. Models range from 24 to 40 feet long.

**Class B Motorhome**   Also known as a *camping van conversion*. These RVs are built within the dimensions of a van, but with a raised roof to provide additional headroom. Basic living accommodations inside are ideal for short vacations or weekend trips. Models usually range from 16 to 21 feet.

**Class C Motorhome**   An RV with the living accommodations built on a cutaway van chassis. A full–size bed in the cabover section allows for ample seating, galley, and bathroom facilities in the coach. Also called a *mini–motorhome* or *mini*. Lengths range from approximately 16 to 32 feet.

**Coupler**   The part of a trailer A–frame that attaches to the hitch ball.

**Detonation**   Also known as *knock* or *ping*, this is a condition in which some of the unburned air/fuel in the combustion chamber explodes at the wrong time in the ignition cycle, increasing mechanical and thermal stress on the engine.

**Dinghy**   A vehicle towed behind a motorhome, sometimes with two wheels on a special trailer called a *tow dolly*, but often with all four wheels on the ground.

**DW (Dry Weight)**   The manufacturer's listing of the approximate weight of the RV with no supplies, water, fuel, or passengers.

**Engine Oil Cooler**   A heat exchanger, similar to a small radiator, through which engine oil passes and is cooled by airflow.

**Fifth–Wheel Trailers**   Fifth–wheel trailers are designed to be coupled to a special hitch that is mounted over the rear axle in the bed of a pickup truck. These trailers can have one, two, or three axles and are the largest type of trailer built. Because of their special hitch requirements, fifth-wheel trailers can only be towed by trucks or specialized vehicles prepared for fifth-wheel trailer compatibility.

**Final Drive Ratio**   The reduction ratio found in the gearset that is located farthest from the engine. This is the same as the axle ratio.

**Frame–Mount Hitch**   Class II and higher hitches are designed to be bolted to the vehicle frame or cross members. This type of hitch may have a permanent ball mount, or may have a square-tube receiver into which a removable hitch bar or shank is installed.

## RV Terminology, *continued*

**GAWR (Gross Axle Weight Rating)**   The manufacturer's rating for the maximum allowable weight that an axle is designed to carry. GAWR applies to tow vehicle, trailer, fifth-wheel, and motorhome axles.

**GCWR (Gross Combination Weight Rating)**   The maximum allowable weight of the combination of tow vehicle and trailer/fifth-wheel, or motorhome and dinghy. It includes the weight of the vehicle, trailer/fifth-wheel (or dinghy), cargo, passengers, and a full load of fluids (fresh water, propane, fuel, etc.).

**GTWR (Gross Trailer Weight Rating)**   Maximum allowable weight of a trailer, fully loaded with cargo and fluids.

**GVWR (Gross Vehicle Weight Rating)**   The total allowable weight of a vehicle, including passengers, cargo, fluids, and hitch weight.

**Hitch Ratings**   Hitches are rated by the manufacturer according to the maximum amount of weight they are engineered to handle. Class I travel trailer hitches are rated for towing as much as 2,000 pounds. Class II units are for loads up to 3,500 pounds. Class III has a rating of 7,500 pounds, and Class IV is for loads of up to 10,000 pounds. Class V hitches are designed for towing loads up to 14,000 pounds. These ratings based on class category may vary depending on the manufacturer. Fifth-wheel ratings range to 25,000 pounds. The weight rating refers to the total weight of the trailer/fifth-wheel, with freshwater tank full, propane tanks full, all supplies onboard, and ready to travel.

**Hitch Weight**   The amount of weight imposed on the hitch when the trailer/fifth-wheel is coupled. Sometimes referred to as conventional trailer "tongue weight." Hitch weight for a travel trailer can be 10 to 15 percent of overall weight; fifth-wheel hitch weight is usually 18 to 20 percent of the overall weight.

**Limited-Slip Differential**   A differential that is designed with a mechanism that limits the speed and torque differences between its two outputs, ensuring that torque is distributed to both drive wheels, even when one is on a slippery surface.

**NCC (Net Carrying Capacity)**   Maximum weight of all passengers (if applicable), personal belongings, food, fresh water, supplies derived by subtracting the UVW from the GVWR.

**Payload Capacity**   The maximum allowable weight that can be placed in or on a vehicle, including cargo, passengers, fluids, and fifth-wheel or conventional hitch loads.

**Receiver**   The portion of a hitch that permits a hitch bar or shank to be inserted. The receiver may be either $1^1/_2$-, $1^5/_8$- or 2-inch square; the smallest being termed a *mini–hitch*.

**Safety Chains**   A set of chains that are attached to the trailer A-frame and must be connected to the tow vehicle while towing. Safety chains are intended to keep the trailer attached to the tow vehicle in the event of hitch failure, preventing the trailer from complete separation. They should be installed using an X-pattern, so the coupler is held off the road in the event of a separation.

**Shank**   Also called a *hitch bar* or *stinger*, the shank is a removable portion of the hitch system that carries the ball or adjustable ball mount, and slides into the receiver. Hit your leg on this as you walk by and you'll understand why it's sometimes called a *stinger*!

**Spring Bar**   Component parts of a weight–distributing hitch system, the spring bars are installed and tensioned in such a manner as to distribute a portion of the trailer's hitch weight to the front axle of the tow vehicle and to the axles of the trailer.

**Stinger**   See, shank.

**Sway**   Fishtailing action of the trailer caused by external forces that set the trailer's mass into a lateral (side-to-side) motion. The trailer's wheels serve as the axis or pivot point. Also known as "yaw."

**Sway Control**   Devices designed to damp the swaying action of a trailer, either through a friction system or a "cam action" system that slows and absorbs the pivotal articulating action between tow vehicle and trailer.

**Tail Swing**   Motorhomes built on chassis with short wheelbases and long overhangs behind the rear axle are susceptible to tail swing when turning sharply. As the motorhome moves in reverse or turns a corner, the extreme rear of the coach can move horizontally and strike objects nearby (typically road signs and walls). Drivers need to be aware of the amount of tail swing in order to prevent accidents.

## RV Terminology, *continued*

**Tongue Weight**   The amount of weight imposed on the hitch when the trailer is coupled. See, hitch weight.

**Tow Bar**   A device used for connecting a dinghy vehicle to the motorhome when it is towed with all four wheels on the ground.

**Tow Rating**   The manufacturer's rating of the maximum weight limit that can be safely towed by a particular vehicle. Tow ratings are related to overall trailer weight, not trailer size, in most cases. However, some tow ratings impose limits as to frontal area of the trailer and overall length. Tow ratings are determined by the vehicle manufacturer according to several criteria, including engine size, transmission, axle ratio, brakes, chassis, cooling systems, and other special equipment.

**Trailer Brakes**   Brakes that are built into the trailer axle systems and are activated either by electric impulse or by a surge mechanism. The overwhelming majority of RVs utilize electric trailer brakes that are actuated when the tow vehicle's brakes are operated, or when a brake controller is manually activated. Surge brakes utilize a mechanism that is positioned at the coupler that detects when the tow vehicle is slowing or stopping, and activates the trailer brakes via a hydraulic system (typically used on boats).

**Transmission Cooler**   A heat exchanger similar to a small radiator through which automatic transmission fluid passes and is cooled by airflow.

**Travel Trailer**   Also referred to as *conventional trailers*, these types of rigs have an A-frame and coupler and are attached to a ball mount on the tow vehicle. Travel trailers are available with one, two, or three axles. Depending upon tow ratings, conventional trailers can be towed by trucks, cars, or sport-utility vehicles.

**Umbilical Cord**   The wiring harness that connects the tow vehicle to the trailer, supplying electricity to the trailer's clearance and brake lights, electric brakes, and a 12–volt DC power line to charge the trailer's batteries. An umbilical cord can also be the power cable that is used to connect to campground 120-volt AC electrical hookups.

**UVW (Unloaded Vehicle Weight)**   Weight of the vehicle without manufacturer's or dealer-installed options and before adding fuel, water, or supplies.

**UTQGL (Uniform Tire Quality Grade Labeling)**   A program that is directed by the government to provide consumers with information about three characteristics of the tire: tread wear, traction, and temperature. Following government prescribed test procedures, tire manufacturers perform their own evaluations for these characteristics. Each manufacturer then labels the tire according to grade.

**Weight-Carrying Hitch**   Also known as a *dead-weight* hitch, this category includes any system that accepts the entire hitch weight of the trailer. In the strictest sense, even a weight-distributing hitch can act as a load-carrying hitch if the spring bars are not installed and placed under tension.

**Weight-Distributing Hitch**   Also known as an *equalizing* hitch, this category includes hitch systems that utilize spring bars that can be placed under tension to distribute a portion of the trailer's hitch weight to the tow vehicle's front axle and the trailer's axles.

**YAW**   Fishtailing action of the trailer caused by external forces that set the trailer's mass into a lateral (side-to-side) motion. The trailer's wheels serve as the axis or pivot point. Also known as *sway*.

# Michelin Inflation Charts for RV Usage

For RV use only, Michelin displays tire loads per axle end in the load and inflation tables, as we recommend weighing each axle end separately and using the heaviest end weight to determine the axle's cold inflation tire pressure. For control of your RV, it is critical the tire pressures be the same across an axle, while NEVER exceeding the maximum air pressure limit stamped on the wheels.

To select the proper load and inflation table, locate your tire size in the following pages, then match your

tire's sidewall markings to the table with the same sidewall markings. If your tire's sidewall markings do not match any table listed, please contact your Michelin dealer for the applicable load and inflation table.

Industry load and inflation standards are in a constant state of change, and Michelin continually updates its product information to reflect these changes. Printed material may not reflect the latest load and inflation

**In the load and inflation tables, SINGLE means an axle with one tire mounted on each end, while DUAL means an axle with two tires mounted on each end. The loads indicated represent the total weight of an axle end, in an RV application. When one axle end weighs more than the other, use the heaviest of the two end weights to determine the unique tire pressure for all tires on the axle. The maximum cold air pressure for each axle may vary, depending on their weights. These tables are applicable for all RV axles, whether or not they are power-driven.**

## WHEEL DIAMETER - 16"

### LT215/85R16 LRE — XPS RIB®

| PSI | | 35 | 40 | 45 | 50 | 55 | 60 | 65 | 70 | 75 | 80 | | MAXIMUM LOAD AND PRESSURE ON SIDEWALL | | | |
|---|---|---|---|---|---|---|---|---|---|---|---|---|---|---|---|---|
| kPa | | 240 | 280 | 310 | 340 | 380 | 410 | 450 | 480 | 520 | 550 | | | | | |
| LBS | SINGLE | 1495 | 1640 | 1785 | 1940 | 2055 | 2180 | 2335 | 2430 | 2550 | 2680 | S | 2680 | LBS at | 80 | PSI |
| | DUAL | 2720 | 2980 | 3250 | 3530 | 3723 | 3970 | 4300 | 4420 | 4640 | 4940 | D | 2470 | LBS at | 80 | PSI |
| kPa | SINGLE | 678 | 744 | 809 | 880 | 932 | 989 | 1059 | 1102 | 1156 | 1215 | S | 1215 | KG at | 550 | kPa |
| | DUAL | 1234 | 1351 | 1474 | 1601 | 1689 | 1801 | 1950 | 2005 | 2104 | 2240 | D | 1120 | KG at | 550 | kPa |

### LT225/75R16 LRE — XPS RIB®

| PSI | | 40 | 45 | 50 | 55 | 60 | 65 | 70 | 75 | 80 | | | MAXIMUM LOAD AND PRESSURE ON SIDEWALL | | | |
|---|---|---|---|---|---|---|---|---|---|---|---|---|---|---|---|---|
| kPa | | 280 | 310 | 350 | 380 | 410 | 450 | 480 | 520 | 550 | | | | | | |
| LBS | SINGLE | 1650 | 1790 | 1940 | 2060 | 2190 | 2335 | 2440 | 2560 | 2680 | | S | 2680 | LBS at | 80 | PSI |
| | DUAL | 3000 | 3260 | 3530 | 3750 | 3990 | 4300 | 4440 | 4660 | 4940 | | D | 2470 | LBS at | 80 | PSI |
| kPa | SINGLE | 748 | 812 | 880 | 934 | 993 | 1059 | 1107 | 1161 | 1215 | | S | 1215 | KG at | 550 | kPa |
| | DUAL | 1361 | 1478 | 1601 | 1701 | 1810 | 1950 | 2014 | 2114 | 2241 | | D | 1120 | KG at | 550 | kPa |

### LT235/85R16 LRE — XPS RIB®

| PSI | | 35 | 40 | 45 | 50 | 55 | 60 | 65 | 70 | 75 | 80 | | MAXIMUM LOAD AND PRESSURE ON SIDEWALL | | | |
|---|---|---|---|---|---|---|---|---|---|---|---|---|---|---|---|---|
| kPa | | 250 | 280 | 310 | 350 | 380 | 410 | 450 | 480 | 520 | 550 | | | | | |
| LBS | SINGLE | 1740 | 1862 | 1985 | 2205 | 2315 | 2425 | 2623 | 2755 | 2910 | 3042 | S | 3042 | LBS at | 80 | PSI |
| | DUAL | 3170 | 3390 | 3610 | 4012 | 4211 | 4410 | 4762 | 5014 | 5296 | 5556 | D | 2778 | LBS at | 80 | PSI |
| kPa | SINGLE | 790 | 845 | 900 | 1000 | 1050 | 1100 | 1190 | 1250 | 1320 | 1380 | S | 1380 | KG at | 550 | kPa |
| | DUAL | 1440 | 1540 | 1640 | 1820 | 1910 | 2000 | 2160 | 2270 | 2400 | 2520 | D | 1260 | KG at | 550 | kPa |

### LT245/75R16 LRE — XPS RIB®

| PSI | | 35 | 40 | 45 | 50 | 55 | 60 | 65 | 70 | 75 | 80 | | MAXIMUM LOAD AND PRESSURE ON SIDEWALL | | | |
|---|---|---|---|---|---|---|---|---|---|---|---|---|---|---|---|---|
| kPa | | 250 | 280 | 310 | 350 | 380 | 410 | 450 | 480 | 520 | 550 | | | | | |
| LBS | SINGLE | 1700 | 1865 | 2030 | 2205 | 2335 | 2480 | 2625 | 2765 | 2900 | 3042 | S | 3042 | LBS at | 80 | PSI |
| | DUAL | 3090 | 3390 | 3690 | 4012 | 4250 | 4510 | 4762 | 5030 | 5280 | 5556 | D | 2778 | LBS at | 80 | PSI |
| kPa | SINGLE | 790 | 845 | 920 | 1000 | 1060 | 1125 | 1190 | 1255 | 1315 | 1380 | S | 1380 | KG at | 550 | kPa |
| | DUAL | 1440 | 1537 | 1675 | 1820 | 1927 | 2045 | 2160 | 2280 | 2395 | 2520 | D | 1260 | KG at | 550 | kPa |

## WHEEL DIAMETER - 17"

### 7.50R17 LRD — XCA

| PSI | | 45 | 50 | 55 | 60 | 65 | 70 | 75 | | MAXIMUM LOAD AND PRESSURE ON SIDEWALL | | | |
|---|---|---|---|---|---|---|---|---|---|---|---|---|---|
| kPa | | 310 | 340 | 380 | 410 | 450 | 480 | 520 | | | | | |
| LBS | SINGLE | 1860 | 2025 | 2185 | 2340 | 2495 | 2650 | 2800 | S | 2800 | LBS at | 75 | PSI |
| | DUAL | 3460 | 3760 | 4060 | 4350 | 4640 | 4920 | 5200 | D | 2600 | LBS at | 75 | PSI |
| kPa | SINGLE | 840 | 900 | 990 | 1050 | 1130 | 1190 | 1270 | S | 1270 | KG at | 520 | kPa |
| | DUAL | 1560 | 1680 | 1840 | 1960 | 2100 | 2220 | 2360 | D | 1180 | KG at | 520 | kPa |

# Michelin Inflation Charts, *continued*

## 10R17.5 LRG   XZA®

| PSI | | 85 | 90 | 95 | 100 | 105 | 110 | 115 | | | MAXIMUM LOAD AND PRESSURE ON SIDEWALL | | | |
|---|---|---|---|---|---|---|---|---|---|---|---|---|---|---|
| kPa | | 590 | 620 | 660 | 690 | 720 | 760 | 790 | | | | | | |
| LBS | SINGLE | 3860 | 4005 | 4150 | 4300 | 4470 | 4640 | 4805 | | S | 4805 | LBS at | 115 | PSI |
| | DUAL | 7280 | 7570 | 7860 | 8160 | 8470 | 8780 | 9080 | | D | 4540 | LBS at | 115 | PSI |
| kPa | SINGLE | 1750 | 1820 | 1890 | 1950 | 2030 | 2110 | 2180 | | S | 2180 | KG at | 790 | kPa |
| | DUAL | 3300 | 3440 | 3580 | 3700 | 3840 | 3980 | 4120 | | D | 2060 | KG at | 790 | kPa |

## WHEEL DIAMETER - 19.5"

## 8R19.5 LRF   XZA®

| PSI | | 70 | 75 | 80 | 85 | 90 | 95 | 100 | 105 | 110 | | | MAXIMUM LOAD AND PRESSURE ON SIDEWALL | | | |
|---|---|---|---|---|---|---|---|---|---|---|---|---|---|---|---|---|
| kPa | | 480 | 520 | 550 | 590 | 620 | 660 | 690 | 720 | 760 | | | | | | |
| LBS | SINGLE | 2540 | 2680 | 2835 | 2955 | 3075 | 3195 | 3305 | 3415 | 3525 | | S | 3525 | LBS at | 110 | PSI |
| | DUAL | 4920 | 5140 | 5360 | 5570 | 5780 | 6000 | 6200 | 6400 | 6610 | | D | 3305 | LBS at | 110 | PSI |
| kPa | SINGLE | 1150 | 1220 | 1285 | 1340 | 1400 | 1450 | 1500 | 1550 | 1600 | | S | 1600 | KG at | 760 | kPa |
| | DUAL | 2240 | 2340 | 2430 | 2520 | 2620 | 2720 | 2820 | 2920 | 3000 | | D | 1500 | KG at | 760 | kPa |

## 225/70R19.5 LRF   XZE®, XRV®

| PSI | | 65 | 70 | 75 | 80 | 85 | 90 | 95 | | | MAXIMUM LOAD AND PRESSURE ON SIDEWALL | | | |
|---|---|---|---|---|---|---|---|---|---|---|---|---|---|---|
| kPa | | 450 | 480 | 520 | 550 | 590 | 620 | 660 | | | | | | |
| LBS | SINGLE | 2755 | 2895 | 3040 | 3195 | 3315 | 3450 | 3640 | | S | 3640 | LBS at | 95 | PSI |
| | DUAL | 5200 | 5440 | 5720 | 6000 | 6230 | 6490 | 6830 | | D | 3415 | LBS at | 95 | PSI |
| kPa | SINGLE | 1250 | 1310 | 1380 | 1450 | 1500 | 1570 | 1650 | | S | 1650 | KG at | 660 | kPa |
| | DUAL | 2360 | 2460 | 2600 | 2720 | 2820 | 2940 | 3100 | | D | 1550 | KG at | 660 | kPa |

## 225/70R19.5 LRG   XZE®

| PSI | | 65 | 70 | 75 | 80 | 85 | 90 | 95 | 100 | 105 | 110 | | MAXIMUM LOAD AND PRESSURE ON SIDEWALL | | | |
|---|---|---|---|---|---|---|---|---|---|---|---|---|---|---|---|---|
| kPa | | 450 | 480 | 520 | 550 | 590 | 620 | 660 | 690 | 720 | 760 | | | | | |
| LBS | SINGLE | 2755 | 2895 | 3040 | 3195 | 3315 | 3450 | 3640 | 3715 | 3845 | 3970 | S | 3970 | LBS at | 110 | PSI |
| | DUAL | 5200 | 5440 | 5720 | 6000 | 6230 | 6490 | 6830 | 6980 | 7230 | 7500 | D | 3750 | LBS at | 110 | PSI |
| kPa | SINGLE | 1250 | 1310 | 1380 | 1450 | 1500 | 1570 | 1650 | 1690 | 1740 | 1800 | S | 1800 | KG at | 760 | kPa |
| | DUAL | 2360 | 2460 | 2600 | 2720 | 2820 | 2940 | 3100 | 3160 | 3280 | 3400 | D | 1700 | KG at | 760 | kPa |

## 245/70R19.5 LRF   XZE®, XRV®

| PSI | | 80 | 85 | 90 | 95 | | | MAXIMUM LOAD AND PRESSURE ON SIDEWALL | | | |
|---|---|---|---|---|---|---|---|---|---|---|---|
| kPa | | 550 | 590 | 620 | 660 | | | | | | |
| LBS | SINGLE | 3640 | 3740 | 3890 | 4080 | | S | 4080 | LBS at | 95 | PSI |
| | DUAL | 6830 | 7030 | 7310 | 7720 | | D | 3860 | LBS at | 95 | PSI |
| kPa | SINGLE | 1650 | 1700 | 1770 | 1850 | | S | 1850 | KG at | 660 | kPa |
| | DUAL | 3100 | 3180 | 3320 | 3500 | | D | 1750 | KG at | 660 | kPa |

## 245/70R19.5 LRG   XZE®

| PSI | | 80 | 85 | 90 | 95 | 100 | 105 | 110 | | | MAXIMUM LOAD AND PRESSURE ON SIDEWALL | | | |
|---|---|---|---|---|---|---|---|---|---|---|---|---|---|---|
| kPa | | 550 | 590 | 620 | 660 | 690 | 720 | 760 | | | | | | |
| LBS | SINGLE | 3640 | 3740 | 3890 | 4080 | 4190 | 4335 | 4540 | | S | 4540 | LBS at | 110 | PSI |
| | DUAL | 6830 | 7030 | 7310 | 7720 | 7880 | 8150 | 8600 | | D | 4300 | LBS at | 110 | PSI |
| kPa | SINGLE | 1650 | 1700 | 1770 | 1850 | 1900 | 1970 | 2060 | | S | 2060 | KG at | 760 | kPa |
| | DUAL | 3100 | 3180 | 3320 | 3500 | 3580 | 3700 | 3900 | | D | 1950 | KG at | 760 | kPa |

## 245/70R19.5 LRH   XZE®

| PSI | | 75 | 80 | 85 | 90 | 95 | 100 | 105 | 110 | 115 | 120 | | MAXIMUM LOAD AND PRESSURE ON SIDEWALL | | | |
|---|---|---|---|---|---|---|---|---|---|---|---|---|---|---|---|---|
| kPa | | 520 | 550 | 590 | 620 | 660 | 690 | 720 | 760 | 790 | 830 | | | | | |
| LBS | SINGLE | 3390 | 3570 | 3750 | 3925 | 4100 | 4270 | 4440 | 4610 | 4775 | 4940 | S | 4940 | LBS at | 120 | PSI |
| | DUAL | 6420 | 6760 | 7100 | 7430 | 7760 | 8080 | 8400 | 8720 | 9040 | 9350 | D | 4675 | LBS at | 120 | PSI |
| kPa | SINGLE | 1540 | 1610 | 1700 | 1770 | 1860 | 1930 | 2000 | 2090 | 2150 | 2240 | S | 2240 | KG at | 830 | kPa |
| | DUAL | 2920 | 3060 | 3220 | 3360 | 3520 | 3660 | 3780 | 3960 | 4080 | 4240 | D | 2120 | KG at | 830 | kPa |

228

## Michelin Inflation Charts, *continued*

### 9R22.5 LRF — XZE®

| PSI | | 70 | 75 | 80 | 85 | 90 | 95 | 100 | 105 | | MAXIMUM LOAD AND PRESSURE ON SIDEWALL | | | |
|---|---|---|---|---|---|---|---|---|---|---|---|---|---|---|
| kPa | | 480 | 520 | 550 | 590 | 620 | 660 | 690 | 720 | | | | | |
| LBS | SINGLE | 3370 | 3560 | 3730 | 3890 | 4080 | 4235 | 4390 | 4540 | S | 4540 | LBS at | 105 | PSI |
| | DUAL | 6540 | 6820 | 7100 | 7380 | 7720 | 8010 | 8300 | 8600 | D | 4300 | LBS at | 105 | PSI |
| kPa | SINGLE | 1530 | 1615 | 1690 | 1760 | 1850 | 1920 | 1990 | 2060 | S | 2060 | KG at | 720 | kPa |
| | DUAL | 2960 | 3100 | 3220 | 3340 | 3500 | 3640 | 3780 | 3900 | D | 1950 | KG at | 720 | kPa |

### 10R22.5 LRF — XZE®

| PSI | | 70 | 75 | 80 | 85 | 90 | 95 | 100 | | MAXIMUM LOAD AND PRESSURE ON SIDEWALL | | | |
|---|---|---|---|---|---|---|---|---|---|---|---|---|---|
| kPa | | 480 | 520 | 550 | 590 | 620 | 660 | 690 | | | | | |
| LBS | SINGLE | 4080 | 4280 | 4480 | 4675 | 4850 | 5025 | 5205 | S | 5205 | LBS at | 100 | PSI |
| | DUAL | 7720 | 8090 | 8460 | 8820 | 9170 | 9520 | 9880 | D | 4940 | LBS at | 100 | PSI |
| kPa | SINGLE | 1850 | 1940 | 2030 | 2120 | 2200 | 2280 | 2360 | S | 2360 | KG at | 690 | kPa |
| | DUAL | 3500 | 3660 | 3820 | 4000 | 4160 | 4320 | 4480 | D | 2240 | KG at | 690 | kPa |

### 10R22.5 LRG — XZE®

| PSI | | 70 | 75 | 80 | 85 | 90 | 95 | 100 | 105 | 110 | 115 | MAXIMUM LOAD AND PRESSURE ON SIDEWALL | | | |
|---|---|---|---|---|---|---|---|---|---|---|---|---|---|---|---|
| kPa | | 480 | 520 | 550 | 590 | 620 | 660 | 690 | 720 | 760 | 790 | | | | |
| LBS | SINGLE | 4080 | 4280 | 4480 | 4675 | 4850 | 5025 | 5205 | 5360 | 5515 | 5675 | S | 5675 | LBS at | 115 | PSI |
| | DUAL | 7720 | 8090 | 8460 | 8820 | 9170 | 9520 | 9880 | 10150 | 10420 | 10710 | D | 5355 | LBS at | 115 | PSI |
| kPa | SINGLE | 1850 | 1940 | 2030 | 2120 | 2200 | 2280 | 2360 | 2430 | 2500 | 2575 | S | 2575 | KG at | 790 | kPa |
| | DUAL | 3500 | 3660 | 3820 | 4000 | 4160 | 4320 | 4480 | 4600 | 4720 | 4860 | D | 2430 | KG at | 790 | kPa |

### 11R22.5 LRG — XZA3®

| PSI | | 70 | 75 | 80 | 85 | 90 | 95 | 100 | 105 | | MAXIMUM LOAD AND PRESSURE ON SIDEWALL | | | |
|---|---|---|---|---|---|---|---|---|---|---|---|---|---|---|
| kPa | | 480 | 520 | 550 | 590 | 620 | 660 | 690 | 720 | | | | | |
| LBS | SINGLE | 4530 | 4770 | 4990 | 5220 | 5510 | 5730 | 5950 | 6175 | S | 6175 | LBS at | 105 | PSI |
| | DUAL | 8760 | 9160 | 9520 | 9900 | 10410 | 10830 | 11250 | 11680 | D | 5840 | LBS at | 105 | PSI |
| kPa | SINGLE | 2050 | 2160 | 2260 | 2370 | 2500 | 2600 | 2700 | 2800 | S | 2800 | KG at | 720 | kPa |
| | DUAL | 3980 | 4160 | 4320 | 4500 | 4720 | 4920 | 5120 | 5300 | D | 2650 | KG at | 720 | kPa |

### 11R22.5 LRH — XZA3®

| PSI | | 75 | 80 | 85 | 90 | 95 | 100 | 105 | 110 | 115 | 120 | MAXIMUM LOAD AND PRESSURE ON SIDEWALL | | | |
|---|---|---|---|---|---|---|---|---|---|---|---|---|---|---|---|
| kPa | | 520 | 550 | 590 | 620 | 660 | 690 | 720 | 760 | 790 | 830 | | | | |
| LBS | SINGLE | 4770 | 4990 | 5220 | 5510 | 5730 | 5950 | 6175 | 6320 | 6465 | 6610 | S | 6610 | LBS at | 120 | PSI |
| | DUAL | 9160 | 9520 | 9900 | 10410 | 10830 | 11250 | 11680 | 11790 | 11900 | 12010 | D | 6005 | LBS at | 120 | PSI |
| kPa | SINGLE | 2160 | 2260 | 2370 | 2500 | 2600 | 2700 | 2800 | 2870 | 2940 | 3000 | S | 3000 | KG at | 830 | kPa |
| | DUAL | 4160 | 4320 | 4500 | 4720 | 4920 | 5120 | 5300 | 5360 | 5420 | 5450 | D | 2725 | KG at | 830 | kPa |

### 235/80R22.5 LRG — XZE®, XRV®

| PSI | | 70 | 75 | 80 | 85 | 90 | 95 | 100 | 105 | 110 | MAXIMUM LOAD AND PRESSURE ON SIDEWALL | | | |
|---|---|---|---|---|---|---|---|---|---|---|---|---|---|---|
| kPa | | 480 | 520 | 550 | 590 | 620 | 660 | 690 | 720 | 760 | | | | |
| LBS | SINGLE | 3470 | 3645 | 3860 | 3975 | 4140 | 4300 | 4455 | 4610 | 4675 | S | 4675 | LBS at | 110 | PSI |
| | DUAL | 6320 | 6630 | 7050 | 7230 | 7530 | 7940 | 8110 | 8390 | 8820 | D | 4410 | LBS at | 110 | PSI |
| kPa | SINGLE | 1570 | 1650 | 1750 | 1800 | 1880 | 1950 | 2020 | 2090 | 2120 | S | 2120 | KG at | 760 | kPa |
| | DUAL | 2860 | 3000 | 3200 | 3280 | 3420 | 3600 | 3680 | 3800 | 4000 | D | 2000 | KG at | 760 | kPa |

### 255/80R22.5 LRG — XZE®, XRV®

| PSI | | 70 | 75 | 80 | 85 | 90 | 95 | 100 | 105 | 110 | MAXIMUM LOAD AND PRESSURE ON SIDEWALL | | | |
|---|---|---|---|---|---|---|---|---|---|---|---|---|---|---|
| kPa | | 480 | 520 | 550 | 590 | 620 | 660 | 690 | 720 | 760 | | | | |
| LBS | SINGLE | 3875 | 4070 | 4300 | 4440 | 4620 | 4805 | 4975 | 5150 | 5205 | S | 5205 | LBS at | 110 | PSI |
| | DUAL | 7050 | 7410 | 7720 | 8080 | 8410 | 8820 | 9050 | 9370 | 9610 | D | 4805 | LBS at | 110 | PSI |
| kPa | SINGLE | 1760 | 1850 | 1950 | 2010 | 2100 | 2180 | 2260 | 2340 | 2360 | S | 2360 | KG at | 760 | kPa |
| | DUAL | 3200 | 3360 | 3500 | 3660 | 3820 | 4000 | 4100 | 4260 | 4360 | D | 2180 | KG at | 760 | kPa |

### 255/70R22.5 LRH — XZE® *

| PSI | | 80 | 85 | 90 | 95 | 100 | 105 | 110 | 115 | 120 | MAXIMUM LOAD AND PRESSURE ON SIDEWALL | | | |
|---|---|---|---|---|---|---|---|---|---|---|---|---|---|---|
| kPa | | 550 | 590 | 620 | 660 | 690 | 720 | 760 | 790 | 830 | | | | |
| LBS | SINGLE | 4190 | 4370 | 4550 | 4675 | 4895 | 5065 | 5205 | 5400 | 5510 | S | 5510 | LBS at | 120 | PSI |
| | DUAL | 7940 | 8220 | 8550 | 8820 | 8910 | 9220 | 9350 | 9830 | 10140 | D | 5070 | LBS at | 120 | PSI |
| kPa | SINGLE | 1900 | 1980 | 2060 | 2120 | 2220 | 2300 | 2360 | 2450 | 2500 | S | 2500 | KG at | 830 | kPa |
| | DUAL | 3600 | 3720 | 3880 | 4000 | 4040 | 4180 | 4240 | 4460 | 4600 | D | 2300 | KG at | 830 | kPa |

## Michelin Inflation Charts, *continued*

### 275/80R22.5 LRG   XZA3®

| PSI | | 70 | 75 | 80 | 85 | 90 | 95 | 100 | 105 | 110 | | MAXIMUM LOAD AND PRESSURE ON SIDEWALL | | | |
|---|---|---|---|---|---|---|---|---|---|---|---|---|---|---|---|
| kPa | | 480 | 520 | 550 | 590 | 620 | 660 | 690 | 720 | 760 | | | | | |
| LBS | SINGLE | 4500 | 4725 | 4940 | 5155 | 5370 | 5510 | 5780 | 5980 | 6175 | S | 6175 | LBS at | 110 | PSI |
| | DUAL | 8190 | 8600 | 9080 | 9380 | 9770 | 10140 | 10520 | 10880 | 11350 | D | 5675 | LBS at | 110 | PSI |
| kPa | SINGLE | 2040 | 2140 | 2240 | 2340 | 2440 | 2500 | 2620 | 2710 | 2800 | S | 2800 | KG at | 760 | kPa |
| | DUAL | 3720 | 3900 | 4120 | 4260 | 4440 | 4600 | 4780 | 4940 | 5150 | D | 2575 | KG at | 760 | kPa |

### 275/80R22.5 LRH   XZE®, XZA3®

| PSI | | 75 | 80 | 85 | 90 | 95 | 100 | 105 | 110 | 115 | 120 | MAXIMUM LOAD AND PRESSURE ON SIDEWALL | | | |
|---|---|---|---|---|---|---|---|---|---|---|---|---|---|---|---|
| kPa | | 520 | 550 | 590 | 620 | 660 | 690 | 720 | 760 | 790 | 830 | | | | |
| LBS | SINGLE | 4915 | 5175 | 5435 | 5690 | 5940 | 6190 | 6435 | 6680 | 6920 | 7160 | S | 7160 | LBS at | 120 PSI |
| | DUAL | 9080 | 9560 | 10030 | 10500 | 10970 | 11430 | 11880 | 12330 | 12780 | 13220 | D | 6610 | LBS at | 120 PSI |
| kPa | SINGLE | 2240 | 2340 | 2470 | 2570 | 2710 | 2800 | 2900 | 3030 | 3120 | 3250 | S | 3250 | KG at | 830 kPa |
| | DUAL | 4120 | 4320 | 4560 | 4760 | 5000 | 5180 | 5360 | 5600 | 5760 | 6000 | D | 3000 | KG at | 830 kPa |

### 275/70R22.5 LRJ   XZA2® Energy™

| PSI | | 85 | 90 | 95 | 100 | 105 | 110 | 115 | 120 | 125 | 130 | MAXIMUM LOAD AND PRESSURE ON SIDEWALL | | | |
|---|---|---|---|---|---|---|---|---|---|---|---|---|---|---|---|
| kPa | | 590 | 620 | 660 | 690 | 720 | 760 | 790 | 830 | 860 | 900 | | | | |
| LBS | SINGLE | 4940 | 5170 | 5400 | 5625 | 5850 | 6070 | 6290 | 6510 | 6730 | 6940 | S | 6940 | LBS at | 130 PSI |
| | DUAL | 9710 | 10160 | 10610 | 11050 | 11490 | 11930 | 12360 | 12790 | | | D | 6395 | LBS at | 120 PSI |
| kPa | SINGLE | 2240 | 2345 | 2450 | 2550 | 2655 | 2755 | 2855 | 2955 | 3055 | 3150 | S | 3150 | KG at | 900 kPa |
| | DUAL | 4405 | 4610 | 4815 | 5010 | 5210 | 5410 | 5605 | 5800 | | | D | 2900 | KG at | 830 kPa |

### 295/80R22.5 LRH   XZA2® Energy™

| PSI | | 75 | 80 | 85 | 90 | 95 | 100 | 105 | 110 | 115 | 120 | MAXIMUM LOAD AND PRESSURE ON SIDEWALL | | | |
|---|---|---|---|---|---|---|---|---|---|---|---|---|---|---|---|
| kPa | | 520 | 550 | 590 | 620 | 660 | 690 | 720 | 760 | 790 | 830 | | | | |
| LBS | SINGLE | 5375 | 5660 | 5940 | 6220 | 6495 | 6770 | 7040 | 7300 | 7570 | 7830 | S | 7830 | LBS at | 120 PSI |
| | DUAL | 9530 | 10030 | 10530 | 11030 | 11510 | 12000 | 12470 | 12950 | 13420 | 13880 | D | 6940 | LBS at | 120 PSI |
| kPa | SINGLE | 2440 | 2550 | 2700 | 2810 | 2960 | 3060 | 3170 | 3310 | 3410 | 3550 | S | 3550 | KG at | 830 kPa |
| | DUAL | 4340 | 4540 | 4800 | 4980 | 5240 | 5440 | 5620 | 5880 | 6060 | 6300 | D | 3150 | KG at | 830 kPa |

### 295/60R22.5 LRJ   XZA2® Energy™

| PSI | | 85 | 90 | 95 | 100 | 105 | 110 | 115 | 120 | 125 | 130 | MAXIMUM LOAD AND PRESSURE ON SIDEWALL | | | |
|---|---|---|---|---|---|---|---|---|---|---|---|---|---|---|---|
| kPa | | 590 | 620 | 660 | 690 | 720 | 760 | 790 | 830 | 860 | 900 | | | | |
| LBS | SINGLE | 5260 | 5505 | 5750 | 5990 | 6230 | 6465 | 6700 | 6930 | 7160 | 7390 | S | 7390 | LBS at | 130 PSI |
| | DUAL | 9650 | 10100 | 10550 | 10990 | 11430 | 11860 | 12290 | 12720 | 13140 | 13560 | D | 6780 | LBS at | 130 PSI |
| kPa | SINGLE | 2390 | 2490 | 2610 | 2710 | 2800 | 2930 | 3020 | 3140 | 3230 | 3350 | S | 3350 | KG at | 900 kPa |
| | DUAL | 4380 | 4560 | 4800 | 4980 | 5140 | 5380 | 5540 | 5760 | 5940 | 6150 | D | 3075 | KG at | 900 kPa |

### 305/70R22.5 LRL   XRV®

| PSI | | 75 | 80 | 85 | 90 | 95 | 100 | 105 | 110 | 115 | 120 | MAXIMUM LOAD AND PRESSURE ON SIDEWALL | | | |
|---|---|---|---|---|---|---|---|---|---|---|---|---|---|---|---|
| kPa | | 520 | 550 | 590 | 620 | 660 | 690 | 720 | 760 | 790 | 830 | | | | |
| LBS | SINGLE | 5375 | 5660 | 5940 | 6220 | 6495 | 6770 | 7040 | 7300 | 7570 | 7830 | S | 7830 | LBS at | 120 PSI |
| | DUAL | 9530 | 10030 | 10530 | 11030 | 11510 | 12000 | 12470 | 12950 | 13420 | 13880 | D | 6940 | LBS at | 120 PSI |
| kPa | SINGLE | 2440 | 2550 | 2700 | 2810 | 2960 | 3060 | 3170 | 3310 | 3410 | 3550 | S | 3550 | KG at | 830 kPa |
| | DUAL | 4340 | 4540 | 4800 | 4980 | 5240 | 5440 | 5620 | 5880 | 6060 | 6300 | D | 3150 | KG at | 830 kPa |

### 315/80R22.5 LRL   XZA2® Energy™, XZA®1

| PSI | | 85 | 90 | 95 | 100 | 105 | 110 | 115 | 120 | 125 | 130 | MAXIMUM LOAD AND PRESSURE ON SIDEWALL | | | |
|---|---|---|---|---|---|---|---|---|---|---|---|---|---|---|---|
| kPa | | 590 | 620 | 660 | 690 | 720 | 760 | 790 | 830 | 860 | 900 | | | | |
| LBS | SINGLE | 6415 | 6670 | 6940 | 7190 | 7440 | 7610 | 7920 | 8270 | 8810 | 9090 | S | 9090 | LBS at | 130 PSI |
| | DUAL | 11680 | 12140 | 12790 | 13090 | 13540 | 13880 | 14420 | 15220 | 16020 | 16540 | D | 8270 | LBS at | 130 PSI |
| kPa | SINGLE | 2910 | 3030 | 3150 | 3260 | 3370 | 3450 | 3590 | 3750 | 3980 | 4125 | S | 4125 | KG at | 900 kPa |
| | DUAL | 5300 | 5500 | 5800 | 5940 | 6140 | 6300 | 6540 | 6900 | 7240 | 7500 | D | 3750 | KG at | 900 kPa |

### 365/70R22.5 LRL   XZA®

| PSI | | 80 | 85 | 90 | 95 | 100 | 105 | 110 | 115 | 120 | 125 | MAXIMUM LOAD AND PRESSURE ON SIDEWALL | | | |
|---|---|---|---|---|---|---|---|---|---|---|---|---|---|---|---|
| kPa | | 550 | 590 | 620 | 660 | 690 | 720 | 760 | 790 | 830 | 860 | | | | |
| LBS | SINGLE | 7350 | 7710 | 8070 | 8430 | 8780 | 9130 | 9480 | 9820 | 10200 | 10500 | S | 10500 | LBS at | 125 PSI |
| | DUAL | | | | | | | | | | | D | | LBS at | PSI |
| kPa | SINGLE | 3320 | 3510 | 3660 | 3840 | 3980 | 4120 | 4300 | 4440 | 4620 | 4750 | S | 4750 | KG at | 860 kPa |
| | DUAL | | | | | | | | | | | D | | KG at | kPa |

## Michelin Inflation Charts, *continued*

### 445/50R22.5 LRL    X One® XRV®

| PSI | | 75 | 80 | 85 | 90 | 95 | 100 | 105 | 110 | 115 | 120 | | MAXIMUM LOAD AND PRESSURE ON SIDEWALL | | | |
|---|---|---|---|---|---|---|---|---|---|---|---|---|---|---|---|---|
| kPa | | 520 | 550 | 590 | 620 | 660 | 690 | 720 | 760 | 790 | 830 | | | | | |
| LBS | SINGLE | 6940 | 7310 | 7680 | 8030 | 8390 | 8740 | 9090 | 9370 | 9780 | 10200 | S | 10200 | LBS at | 120 | PSI |
| | DUAL | | | | | | | | | | | D | | LBS at | | PSI |
| kPa | SINGLE | 3150 | 3320 | 3480 | 3640 | 3810 | 3970 | 4120 | 4250 | 4430 | 4625 | S | 4625 | KG at | 830 | kPa |
| | DUAL | | | | | | | | | | | D | | KG at | | kPa |

## WHEEL DIAMETER - 24.5"

### 11R24.5 LRG    XZA3®

| PSI | | 70 | 75 | 80 | 85 | 90 | 95 | 100 | 105 | | MAXIMUM LOAD AND PRESSURE ON SIDEWALL | | | |
|---|---|---|---|---|---|---|---|---|---|---|---|---|---|---|
| kPa | | 480 | 520 | 550 | 590 | 620 | 660 | 690 | 720 | | | | | |
| LBS | SINGLE | 4820 | 5070 | 5310 | 5550 | 5840 | 6095 | 6350 | 6610 | S | 6610 | LBS at | 105 | PSI |
| | DUAL | 9320 | 9740 | 10140 | 10520 | 11020 | 11350 | 11680 | 12010 | D | 6005 | LBS at | 105 | PSI |
| kPa | SINGLE | 2190 | 2300 | 2410 | 2520 | 2650 | 2770 | 2890 | 3000 | S | 3000 | KG at | 720 | kPa |
| | DUAL | 4220 | 4420 | 4600 | 4780 | 5000 | 5160 | 5320 | 5450 | D | 2725 | KG at | 720 | kPa |

### 275/80R24.5 LRG    XZA3®

| PSI | | 70 | 75 | 80 | 85 | 90 | 95 | 100 | 105 | 110 | | MAXIMUM LOAD AND PRESSURE ON SIDEWALL | | | |
|---|---|---|---|---|---|---|---|---|---|---|---|---|---|---|---|
| kPa | | 480 | 520 | 550 | 590 | 620 | 660 | 690 | 720 | 760 | | | | | |
| LBS | SINGLE | 4545 | 4770 | 4940 | 5210 | 5420 | 5675 | 5835 | 6040 | 6175 | S | 6175 | LBS at | 110 | PSI |
| | DUAL | 8270 | 8680 | 9080 | 9480 | 9860 | 10410 | 10620 | 10990 | 11350 | D | 5675 | LBS at | 110 | PSI |
| kPa | SINGLE | 2060 | 2160 | 2240 | 2360 | 2460 | 2575 | 2650 | 2740 | 2800 | S | 2800 | KG at | 760 | kPa |
| | DUAL | 3740 | 3940 | 4120 | 4300 | 4480 | 4720 | 4820 | 4980 | 5150 | D | 2575 | KG at | 760 | kPa |

# Goodyear Tire Inflation Charts

## LOAD/INFLATION INFORMATION FOR RV ST METRIC TIRES
TIRE LOAD LIMITS (LBS) AT VARIOUS COLD INFLATION PRESSURES (PSI) HIGHWAY STEER AND ALL POSITION TREAD DESIGNS USED IN NORMAL HIGHWAY SERVICE*

| Tire Size | Max Speed Rating (MPH) | Inflation Pressure - PSI | | | | | | | | | | |
|---|---|---|---|---|---|---|---|---|---|---|---|---|
| | | 15 | 20 | 25 | 30 | 35 | 40 | 45 | 50 | 55 | 60 | 65 |
| ST175/80R13 | 65 | 670 | 795 | 905 | 1000 | **1100(B)** | 1190 | 1270 | **1360(C)** | | | |
| ST185/80R13 | 65 | 740 | 870 | 990 | 1100 | **1200(B)** | 1300 | 1400 | **1480(C)** | | | |
| ST205/75R14 | 65 | 860 | 1030 | 1170 | 1300 | **1430(B)** | 1530 | 1640 | **1760(C)** | | | |
| ST215/75R14 | 65 | 953 | 1110 | 1270 | 1410 | **1520(B)** | 1660 | 1790 | **1870(C)** | | | |
| ST205/75R15 | 65 | 905 | 1070 | 1220 | 1360 | **1480(B)** | 1610 | 1720 | **1820(C)** | | | |
| ST225/75R15 | 65 | 1060 | 1260 | 1430 | 1600 | 1760 | 1880 | 2020 | **2150(C)** | 2270 | 2380 | **2540(D)** |
| ST235/80R16 | 65 | | | 1720 | 1920 | 2090 | 2270 | 2430 | 2600 | 2730 | 2870 | **3000(D)** |

## LOAD/INFLATION INFORMATION FOR RV TIRES
TIRE LOAD LIMITS (LBS) AT VARIOUS COLD INFLATION PRESSURES (PSI) HIGHWAY STEER AND ALL POSITION TREAD DESIGNS USED IN NORMAL HIGHWAY SERVICE*

| Tire Size | Single (S) Dual (D) | Inflation Pressure - PSI | | | | | | | | | | | | | | | |
|---|---|---|---|---|---|---|---|---|---|---|---|---|---|---|---|---|---|
| | | 35 | 40 | 45 | 50 | 55 | 60 | 65 | 70 | 75 | 80 | 85 | 90 | 95 | 100 | 105 | 110 |
| LT215/75R15 | S | 1345 | 1475 | 1600 | **1765(C)** | 1845 | 1960 | **2095(D)** | | | | | | | | | |
| | D | 1225 | 1340 | 1455 | **1610(C)** | 1680 | 1785 | **1930(D)** | | | | | | | | | |
| LT235/75R15 | S | 1530 | 1680 | 1825 | **1895(C)** | 2100 | 2230 | **2335(D)** | | | | | | | | | |
| | D | 1390 | 1530 | 1660 | **1820(C)** | 1910 | 2030 | **2150(D)** | | | | | | | | | |
| LT225/75R16 | S | 1500 | 1650 | 1790 | **1940(C)** | 2060 | 2190 | **2335(D)** | 2440 | 2560 | **2680(E)** | | | | | | |
| | D | 1365 | 1500 | 1630 | **1765(C)** | 1875 | 1995 | **2150(D)** | 2200 | 2330 | **2470(E)** | | | | | | |
| LT245/75R16 | S | 1700 | 1865 | 2030 | **2205(C)** | 2335 | 2480 | **2623(D)** | 2765 | 2900 | **3042(E)** | | | | | | |
| | D | 1545 | 1695 | 1845 | **2006(C)** | 2125 | 2255 | **2381(D)** | 2515 | 2640 | **2778(E)** | | | | | | |
| LT215/85R16 | S | 1495 | 1640 | 1785 | **1940(C)** | 2050 | 2180 | **2335(D)** | 2430 | 2550 | **2680(E)** | | | | | | |
| | D | 1360 | 1490 | 1625 | **1765(C)** | 1865 | 1985 | **2150(D)** | 2210 | 2320 | **2470(E)** | | | | | | |
| LT235/85R16 | S | 1700 | 1870 | 2030 | 2205 | 2335 | 2485 | **2623(D)** | 2765 | 2905 | **3042(E)** | 3170 | 3300 | 3415 | 3550 | 3675 | **3750(G)** |
| | D | 1545 | 1700 | 1845 | 2006 | 2125 | 2260 | **2381(D)** | 2515 | 2645 | **2778(E)** | 2885 | 3005 | 3085 | 3230 | 3345 | **3415(G)** |
| 7.50R16LT | S | 1620 | 1770 | 1930 | **2040(C)** | 2190 | 2310 | **2470(D)** | 2560 | 2670 | **2755(E)** | | | | | | |
| | D | 1430 | 1565 | 1690 | **1820(C)** | 1930 | 2040 | **2150(D)** | 2245 | 2345 | **2470(E)** | | | | | | |
| 8.75R16.5 | S | | | | | | 2240 | 2405 | 2470 | 2570 | **2680(E)** | | | | | | |
| | D | | | | | | 1970 | 2095 | 2175 | 2260 | **2405(E)** | | | | | | |

*Industry standards for load & inflation are in the process of being revised. These tables are current as of 01/01/05. For the most current information, please visit the RV Tire section of Goodyear's Web site at www.goodyear.com/rv.*

## Goodyear Tire Inflation Charts, *continued*

## LOAD/INFLATION INFORMATION FOR RV TIRES
**TIRE LOAD LIMITS (LBS) AT VARIOUS COLD INFLATION PRESSURES (PSI) TRAILER DESIGNS USED IN NORMAL HIGHWAY SERVICE\***

| Tire Size | Max Speed Rating (MPH) | Single (S) Dual (D) | Inflation Pressure - PSI | | | | | | | | | | | |
|---|---|---|---|---|---|---|---|---|---|---|---|---|---|---|
| | | | 70 | 75 | 80 | 85 | 90 | 95 | 100 | 105 | 110 | 115 | 120 | 125 |
| 215/17.5 | 75 | S | | | | | 3695 | 3860 | 4020 | 4180 | 4340 | 4495 | 4650 | **4806(H)** |
| | | D | | | | | 3490 | 3645 | 3800 | 3950 | 4100 | 4245 | 4395 | **4540(H)** |

## LOAD/INFLATION INFORMATION FOR RV TIRES
**TIRE LOAD LIMITS (LBS) AT VARIOUS COLD INFLATION PRESSURES (PSI) HIGHWAY STEER AND ALL-POSITION TREAD DESIGNS USED IN NORMAL HIGHWAY SERVICE\***

| Tire Size | Max Speed Rating (MPH) | Single (S) Dual (D) | Inflation Pressure - PSI | | | | | | | | | | |
|---|---|---|---|---|---|---|---|---|---|---|---|---|---|
| | | | 65 | 70 | 75 | 80 | 85 | 90 | 95 | 100 | 105 | 110 | 115 | 120 |
| 8R19.5 | 75 | S | 2410 | 2540 | 2680 | 2835 | 2955 | 3075 | 3195 | 3305 | 3415 | **3525(F)** | | |
| | | D | 2350 | 2460 | 2610 | 2755 | 2865 | 2975 | 3085 | 3195 | 3305 | **3415(F)** | | |
| 225/70R19.5 | 75 | S | | 2895 | 3040 | 3195 | 3315 | 3450 | **3640(F)** | 3715 | 3845 | **3970(G)** | | |
| | | D | | 2720 | 2860 | 3000 | 3115 | 3245 | **3415(F)** | 3490 | 3615 | **3750(G)** | | |
| 245/70R19.5 | 75 | S | | 3640 | 3740 | 3890 | **4080(F)** | 4190 | 4335 | **4540(G)** | | | | |
| | | D | | 3415 | 3515 | 3655 | **3970(F)** | 4115 | 4265 | **4410(G)** | | | | |
| †245/70R19.5 | 75 | S | | | | 3640 | 3740 | 3890 | **4080(F)** | 4190 | 4335 | **4540(G)** | | |
| | | D | | | | 3415 | 3515 | 3655 | **3970(F)** | 4115 | 4265 | **4410(G)** | | |
| 265/70R19.5 | 75 | S | | | | 3970 | 4180 | 4355 | 4540 | 4685 | 4850 | 5070 | 5170 | **5355(G)** |
| | | D | | | | 3750 | 3930 | 4095 | 4300 | 4405 | 4560 | 4805 | 4860 | **5070(G)** |

†Tires produced after 2/28/06.

| Tire Size | Max Speed Rating (MPH) | Single (S) Dual (D) | Inflation Pressure - PSI | | | | | | | | | | |
|---|---|---|---|---|---|---|---|---|---|---|---|---|---|
| | | | 70 | 75 | 80 | 85 | 90 | 95 | 100 | 105 | 110 | 115 | 120 |
| 9R22.5 | 75 | S | 3370 | 3560 | 3730 | 3890 | 4080 | 4235 | 4390 | **4540(F)** | | | |
| | | D | 3270 | 3410 | 3550 | 3690 | 3860 | 4005 | 4150 | **4300(F)** | | | |
| 10R22.5 | 65 | S | 4080 | 4280 | 4480 | 4675 | 4850 | 5025 | **5205(F)** | 5360 | 5515 | **5675(G)** | |
| | | D | 3860 | 4045 | 4230 | 4410 | 4585 | 4760 | **4940(F)** | 5075 | 5210 | **5355(G)** | |
| 11R22.5 | 75 | S | 4530 | 4770 | 4990 | 5220 | 5510 | 5730 | 5950 | **6175(G)** | 6320 | 6465 | **6610(H)** |
| | | D | 4380 | 4580 | 4760 | 4950 | 5205 | 5415 | 5625 | **5840(G)** | 5895 | 5950 | **6005(H)** |
| 12R22.5 | 75 | S | 4940 | 5200 | 5450 | 5690 | 6005 | 6205 | 6405 | 6610 | 6870 | 7130 | **7390(H)** |
| | | D | 4780 | 4990 | 5190 | 5390 | 5675 | 5785 | 5895 | 6005 | 6265 | 6525 | **6780(H)** |
| 245/75R22.5 | 75 | S | 3470 | 3645 | 3860 | 3980 | 4140 | 4300 | 4455 | 4610 | **4675(G)** | | |
| | | D | 3260 | 3425 | 3640 | 3740 | 3890 | 4080 | 4190 | 4335 | **4410(G)** | | |

## LOAD/INFLATION INFORMATION FOR RV TIRES
**TIRE LOAD LIMITS (LBS) AT VARIOUS COLD INFLATION PRESSURES (PSI) HIGHWAY STEER AND ALL-POSITION TREAD DESIGNS USED IN NORMAL HIGHWAY SERVICE***

| Tire Size | Max Speed Rating (MPH) | Single (S) Dual (D) | Inflation Pressure - PSI | | | | | | | | | | | |
|---|---|---|---|---|---|---|---|---|---|---|---|---|---|---|
| | | | 70 | 75 | 80 | 85 | 90 | 95 | 100 | 105 | 110 | 115 | 120 | 125 |
| 255/70R22.5 | 75 | S | | | 4190 | 4370 | 4550 | 4675 | 4895 | 5065 | 5205 | 5400 | **5510(H)** | |
| | | D | | | 3970 | 4110 | 4275 | 4410 | 4455 | 4610 | 4675 | 4915 | **5070(H)** | |
| 265/75R22.5 | 75 | S | 3875 | 4070 | 4255 | 4440 | 4620 | 4800 | 4975 | 5150 | **5205(G)** | | | |
| | | D | 3870 | 4040 | 4205 | 4370 | 4525 | 4685 | **4805(G)** | | | | | |
| 275/70R22.5 | 75 | S | | | | 5170 | 5400 | 5630 | 5850 | 6070 | 6290 | 6510 | 6730 | **6940(H)** |
| | | D | | | | 4770 | 4980 | 5180 | 5390 | 5590 | 5800 | 6000 | 6200 | **6395(H)** |
| 275/70R22.5 (G159) | 75 | S | | | | 4885 | 5080 | 5305 | 5530 | 5750 | 5965 | 6185 | 6400 | **6610(H)** |
| | | D | | | | 4535 | 4750 | 4960 | 5165 | 5370 | 5575 | 5775 | 5975 | **6175(H)** |
| 275/80R22.5 | 75 | S | | | | | 5500 | 5745 | 5985 | 6225 | 6460 | 6700 | 6930 | **7160(H)** |
| | | D | | | | | 5080 | 5305 | 5530 | 5750 | 5965 | 6185 | 6400 | **6610(H)** |

| Tire Size | Max Speed Rating (MPH) | Single (S) Dual (D) | Inflation Pressure - PSI | | | | | | | | | | | |
|---|---|---|---|---|---|---|---|---|---|---|---|---|---|---|
| | | | 75 | 80 | 85 | 90 | 95 | 100 | 105 | 110 | 115 | 120 | 125 | 130 |
| 295/75R22.5 | 75 | S | 4725 | 4940 | 5155 | 5370 | 5510 | 5780 | 5980 | **6175(G)** | 6370 | **6610(H)** | | |
| | | D | 4690 | 4885 | 5070 | 5260 | 5440 | **5675(G)** | 5800 | **6005(H)** | | | | |
| 295/80R22.5 | 75 | S | | 5480 | 5750 | 6020 | 6285 | 6550 | 6810 | 7070 | 7320 | 7580 | **7830(H)** | |
| | | D | | 4855 | 5100 | 5335 | 5570 | 5805 | 6035 | 6265 | 6490 | 6720 | **6940(H)** | |
| 315/80R22.5 | 75 | S | | | 6415 | 6670 | 6940 | 7190 | 7440 | 7610 | 7920 | 8270 | 8680 | **9090(L)** |
| | | D | | | 5840 | 6070 | 6395 | 6540 | 6770 | 6940 | 7210 | 7610 | 7940 | **8270(L)** |
| 11R24.5 | 75 | S | | 5310 | 5550 | 5840 | 6095 | 6350 | **6610(G)** | 6790 | 6970 | **7160(H)** | | |
| | | D | | 5070 | 5260 | 5510 | 5675 | 5840 | **6005(G)** | 6205 | 6405 | **6610(H)** | | |

*Industry standards for load & inflation are in the process of being revised. These tables are current as of 01/01/05. For the most current information, please visit the RV Tire section of Goodyear's Web site at www.goodyear.com/rv.*

# Pre-Trip Checklist

- ❏ All lights and fans off
- ❏ Cabinets closed and locked
- ❏ Chocks removed and stowed
- ❏ Drain/fill hoses stowed, caps on
- ❏ Electric disconnected/cords stowed
- ❏ Furnace and A/C off
- ❏ Jacks up and locked
- ❏ Lower TV antenna/satellite dish
- ❏ Pressure regulator
- ❏ Retract slides and install braces
- ❏ Secure all windows and ceiling vents
- ❏ Stow shower and bathroom supplies
- ❏ Turn off propane
- ❏ Water heater off
- ❏ Wheels torqued
- ❏ Retract entry step
- ❏ Make sure inside weight is evenly distributed

- ❏ Awning secured
- ❏ Check lights/turn signals/engine oil
- ❏ Disconnect CATV/phone
- ❏ Dump and reset black and gray tanks
- ❏ Empty and stow trashcans
- ❏ Hitch locked and secured
- ❏ Lights and brakes checked
- ❏ Prepare refrigerator for traveling
- ❏ Pull off levelers and stow levelers
- ❏ Secure all loose items
- ❏ Stow folding chairs and other outside items
- ❏ Stow TV and TV shelf
- ❏ Water bottle for truck
- ❏ Water pump off
- ❏ Check roof rack or storage pod
- ❏ Shut off all gas pilot lights
- ❏ **Never, ever back trailer without first posting a lookout with a radio!**

# Motorhome Weight Worksheet

| Front Axle | Rear Axle | Towed Vehicle |
|---|---|---|
| 1. MFG GAWR_____ | 3. MFG GAWR_____ | Towing Capacity_____ |
| 2. Actual GAWR_____ | 4. Actual GAWR_____ | Actual Weight _____ |

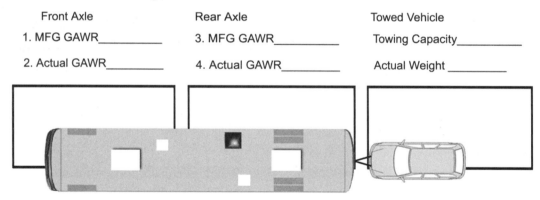

1 minus 2 = _____     3 minus 4 = _____

5. MFG Gross Vehicle Weight Rating_____     6. Actual Weight  (2 + 4)_____

## Weigh Individual Wheel Position

| Front Axle | Rear Axle | Towed Vehicle |
|---|---|---|
| 1. MFG GAWR_____ | 3. MFG GAWR_____ | Towing Capacity_____ |
| 2. Actual GAWR_____ | 4. Actual GAWR_____ | Actual Weight _____ |

**\*Note\*** Individual wheel weights are best obtained by using individual weights on a flat surface.  This service is provided by RV Safety & Education Foundation. Refer to Chapter 2 for more information.

# Trailer Weight Worksheet

Tow Vehicle Front Axle
1. MFG GAWR_____
2. Actual GAWR_____

Tow Vehicle Rear Axle
3. MFG GAWR_____
4. Actual GAWR_____

Trailer Weight
5. MFG GVWR_____
6. Actual Weight_____

**Weigh Individual Wheel Position**

## Trailer Weight Worksheet

Tow Vehicle Front Axle
1. MFG GAWR_____
2. Actual GAWR_____

Tow Vehicle Rear Axle
3. MFG GAWR_____
4. Actual GAWR_____

Trailer Weight
5. MFG GVWR_____
6. Actual Weight_____

**\*Note\* Individual wheel weights are best obtained by using individual weights on a flat surface.  This service is provided by RV Safety & Education Foundation. Refer to Chapter 2 for more information.**

# Towing Glossary

Provided by Roadmaster

**Binding**   When the tow bar is difficult to detach because of excessive pressure, the tow bar is said to be "bound."

**Car-Mounted**  Refers to a tow bar that is designed to be mounted and stored on the towed vehicle.

**Curb Weight**   The total weight of a vehicle when not loaded with either passengers or cargo.

**Diode**   Diodes allow the towed vehicle's brake and turn signal lights to mimic the motorhome's (which is required by law) without damaging the towed vehicle's electrical system. They allow current to flow in only one direction, thereby eliminating electrical feedback, which could damage the towed vehicle's wiring, fuses, or other electrical components.

**Gross Vehicle Weight Rating (GVWR)**   How much weight a vehicle is designed to carry. The GVWR includes the net weight of the vehicle, plus the weight of passengers, fuel, cargo, and any additional accessories. The GVWR is a safety standard used to prevent overloading.

**Hitch (receiver hitch)**   The tubular shaft extending from the motorhome which is used to attach a motorhome-mounted tow bar to the motorhome.

**Motorhome-Mounted**   Refers to a tow bar that is designed to be mounted and stored on the motorhome.

**Mounting Bracket (or bracket)**   Connects the towed vehicle to the tow bar. All mounting brackets are bolted to the towed vehicle.

**Proportional Braking**   A supplemental braking system (see below) which brakes at the same time and intensity as the motorhome is said to be *proportional*.

**Quick-Disconnects (QDs)**   The components which attach the tow bar to the bracket. The quick-disconnects allow the tow bar to be quickly connected and disconnected. There is one QD for the driver's side and one for the passenger side.

**Quick Links**   Used to attach the safety cables. They look like one link in a chain, and have a nut which can be threaded up or down to open or close the link.

**Removable Bracket Arms**   All mounting brackets have arms which extend out from the vehicle. Some models have arms that can be easily removed, making the bracket virtually invisible.

**Safety Cables**   Required by law in most states, safety cables connect the towed vehicle to the towing vehicle. They are a secondary safety device to hold the vehicles together, if the towing system fails.

**Stinger**   The tubular shaft extending from the tow bar which is used to attach the tow bar to the motorhome. The stinger is attached to the hitch (see above).

**Supplemental Braking**   An independent braking system for the towed vehicle.

# Towing Safety Checklist

**Provided by Blue Ox**

Inspect the tow bar, dolly, or trailer for loose bolts and worn parts. Tighten the loose bolts and replace any worn parts before hooking up. If you have bolts that are consistently coming loose, use Locktite or put a double nut on to keep them tight.

During hook up:

1. Hook up on a flat, smooth surface.

2. If you have a coupler-style tow bar; check the fit of the coupler on the ball and adjust the coupler as necessary.

3. Hook up the tow bar.

4. Set up the towed vehicle's steering and transmission to tow.

5. Check your parking brake to ensure it is disengaged

6. Latch the legs on a self-aligning tow bar.

7. Attach the safety cables. Cross the cables between the vehicles.

8. Attach the electrical cable.

9. Check the functioning of all lights on both vehicles.

10. Locate your spare key and lock the towed vehicle's doors.

11. Drive with care and remember your vehicle will be about 25-feet longer while you are towing.

Each time you stop, check the tow bar, baseplate, and cables to make sure they are still properly attached. Check the tires of the towed vehicle to make sure they are not going flat. If you are using a dolly or trailer, check the wheels to make sure they are not hot to the touch. If the wheels are hot, it may indicate a brake or bearing problem. Each day before you start, check the lights to make sure they are working properly. Between trips, clean the tow bar and cables to keep them in good shape. Also, clean and lubricate the tow bar as recommended in the manufacturer's instructions.

# Weight limits for towing without supplemental brakes

**Towing and Suspension Solutions**

ROADMASTER

## It's required!

The states in red require supplemental brakes if the towed weight exceeds 3,000 pounds. The color key for the other states, as well as state-by-state weight limits, is listed below.

### SPECIFIC WEIGHT LIMITS — UNITED STATES

If the towed weight exceeds the following, a supplemental braking device is required.

| | |
|---|---|
| 1 | 1,000 pounds (New York) |
| 1.5 | 1,500 pounds (Cal., ID, NV) |
| 2 | 2,000 pounds (Miss., Ohio) |
| 3 | 3,000 pounds (29 states & DC) |
| 4 | 4,000 pounds (Del., NC, RI) |
| 4.5 | 4,500 pounds (Texas) |
| 5 | 5,000 pounds (Alaska) |
| 10 | 10,000 pounds (Massachusetts) |

### OTHER CATEGORIES

| | |
|---|---|
| A | Must stop within a specified distance |
| B | Not stated or no requirement |
| C | Supplemental brakes always required |

### KEY

'A' **Must stop within a specified distance**

'B' **Not stated or no requirement**

'C' **Supplemental brakes always required**

*Important!* Every reasonable effort was made to verify the accuracy of this information; however, ROADMASTER, Inc. does not warrant its accuracy and disclaims all liability for any claims or damages which may result from errors or omissions.

## United States

| | WEIGHT LIMIT IN POUNDS OR OTHER RESTRICTION (SEE 'KEY') |
|---|---|
| Alabama | 3,000 |
| Alaska | 5,000 |
| Arizona | 3,000 |
| Arkansas | 3,000 |
| California | 1,500 |
| Colorado | 3,000 |
| Connecticut | 3,000 |
| Delaware | 4,000 |
| District of Columbia | 3,000 |
| Florida | 3,000 |
| Georgia | 3,000 |
| Hawaii | 3,000 |
| Idaho | 1,500 |
| Illinois | 'C' |
| Indiana | 3,000 |
| Iowa | 3,000 |
| Kansas | 'A' |

| | WEIGHT LIMIT IN POUNDS OR OTHER RESTRICTION (SEE 'KEY') |
|---|---|
| Kentucky | 'A' |
| Louisiana | 3,000 |
| Maine | 3,000 |
| Maryland | 3,000 |
| Massachusetts | 10,000 |
| Michigan | 3,000 |
| Minnesota | 3,000 |
| Mississippi | 2,000 |
| Missouri | 'B' |
| Montana | 3,000 |
| Nebraska | 3,000 |
| Nevada | 1,500 |
| New Hampshire | 'A' |
| New Jersey | 3,000 |
| New Mexico | 'C' |
| New York | 1,000 |
| North Carolina | 4,000 |

| | WEIGHT LIMIT IN POUNDS OR OTHER RESTRICTION (SEE 'KEY') |
|---|---|
| North Dakota | 'C' |
| Ohio | 2,000 |
| Oklahoma | 3,000 |
| Oregon | 'B' |
| Pennsylvania | 'A' |
| Rhode Island | 4,000 |
| South Carolina | 'C' |
| South Dakota | 3,000 |
| Tennessee | 3,000 |
| Texas | 4,500 |
| Utah | 'A' |
| Vermont | 3,000 |
| Virginia | 3,000 |
| Washington | 3,000 |
| West Virginia | 3,000 |
| Wisconsin | 1,000 |
| Wyoming | 4,000 |

## Federal Regulations

Title 49 (49CFR571) of the Federal Motor Vehicle Safety Standards (10-01-08 edition) defines a 'trailer' as follows: "Trailer means a motor vehicle with or without motive power, designed for carrying persons or property and for being drawn by another motor vehicle."

## Canada

| | WEIGHT LIMIT IN POUNDS OR OTHER RESTRICTION (SEE 'KEY') |
|---|---|
| Alberta | 2,000 |
| British Columbia | 4,400 |
| Manitoba | 'A' |
| New Brunswick | 3,000 |
| Newfoundland | 'A' |
| Northwest Territories | 'C' |
| Nova Scotia | 4,000 |
| Ontario | 3,000 |
| Prince Edward Island | 3,300 |
| Quebec | 2,860 |
| Saskatchewan | 3,000 |
| Yukon Territory | 2,000 |

Source:
American Automobile Association
Digest of Motor Laws, 2010 edition

*Note: This was was originally produced in a color scale and has been modified for black & white printing.

A full color copy is available for download at www.roadmasterinc.com  Click on products/supplemental towing/articles.

# Maintenance Record*

Record all periodic and unscheduled maintenance and service. See *Periodic Maintenance* (Page 12).

| DATE | HOUR METER READING | MAINTENANCE OR SERVICE PERFORMED |
|---|---|---|
| | | |
| | | |
| | | |
| | | |
| | | |
| | | |
| | | |
| | | |
| | | |
| | | |
| | | |
| | | |
| | | |
| | | |
| | | |
| | | |
| | | |
| | | |
| | | |
| | | |
| | | |
| | | |
| | | |
| | | |
| | | |

Record the name, address, and phone number of your authorized Onan service center.

| |
|---|
| |
| |
| |
| |

° Please ignore the reference to pages in this chart. This graphic was taken directly from the manufacturer's manual and does not refer to the pagination in this book.

# Norcold Troubleshootiing

Most Norcold refrigerators are equipped with diagnostic indicators located on the operating controls. Units with this type of display use alphanumeric codes while others provide flashing LEDs.

The codes assist service technicians in troubleshooting and help alert owners to a problem in any mode of operation. These diagnostic indicators are listed in the owners manual.

For example, models with a single display like the N82X have the following fault codes:

No Display indicates that either DC voltage is unavailable to the control panel, or the refrigerator is off.

If the door is left open for more than 2 minutes, the interior light will shut off and the fault code will display the letter "d."

If the burner does not ignite, or re-ignite an "F" appears.

An "A" indicates AC voltage is unavailable.

A "C" indicates DC voltage to the control panel is too low.

If the temperature setting flashes for 10 seconds and the mode appears, the refrigerator is operating on the backup operating system. This system provides a means for the refrigerator to cool in the event of a temperature sensor failure. It will provide adjustable cooling until the unit can be serviced and restored to normal operation by a Norcold Service Center.

Other models will have similar fault codes and meanings such as "dr" for an open door, and often have an audible alarm as well.

"No" "FL" indicates a burner ignition failure, "no" "AC" for power loss, and more. Check your owner's manual for fault codes specific to your model or visit www.norcold.com

**Burner Flame Inspection**

The efficiency of your refrigerator while operating in the gas mode is dependent upon the correct burner flame. The burner flame provides energy to heat or "percolate" the solution properly.

A proper flame is a combination of the correct LP gas pressure, air input, and a clean burner and orifice. It is recommended that you visually inspect the flame periodically using the following procedure:

While in GAS operation, turn the temperature setting to the coldest position. Open the lower intake vent. Caution must be taken as the burner box may be hot. It is recommended that you use gloves or a tool such as a screwdriver to open the burner box door. Look at the flame. It may be necessary to remove the burner box for a better view.

The flame should be a darker blue inside and a lighter blue outside and should be a constant and steady shape. If the flame is yellow or has an erratic and unstable shape, contact your dealer or Norcold Service Center.

Make sure the flame does not touch the inside of the flue tube, if it does, contact your dealer or Norcold Service Center.

**Electrode**

Do a visual check for cracks or breaks on the ceramic insulator. If you find either, replace the electrode. The spark gap must be set at 3/16" of an inch and the tip of the electrode above the slots in the burner.

**The Igniter**

The igniter is an electronic device that produces high voltage to create a spark at the burner when the refrigerator is in GAS mode. To test the igniter, you must first verify that the 12-volt DC power is within 1 volt of the supply voltage at the main power block during the trial for ignition phase of the starting sequence. A drop of more than 1 volt indicates a loose connection or a circuit board problem.

Next, disconnect the DC power at the main 12-volt power block, remove the high-voltage cable from the igniter, and reconnect the 12-volt DC power. The refrigerator will go into the trial for ignition phase of

## Norcold Troubleshooting, *continued*

the starting sequence and you should hear a sparking sound coming from the igniter block. If not, you will need to replace the igniter.

### Flame Blow-out

If the flame blows out under especially windy conditions, try to position the RV to avoid the wind blowing against the wall vents. Make sure the metal shield is around the burner box and secured Confirm that the burner and flame are adjusted correctly. If the problem persists, set the temperature to max. This measure can only be temporary because after a few hours, items in the refrigerator compartment will freeze. Do not cover the vents to prevent flame blow-out. Circulation of air is necessary for proper and safe operation.

### Gas Safety Valve

To test the gas safety valve, start the refrigerator in the LP mode, open the lower intake vent and remove one wire from the gas safety valve. Within 30 seconds, the flame should extinguish.

### Cooling Unit

Before diagnosing a cooling unit, make sure the unit is level, you have proper ventilation in the back compartment, and you have proper power and gas.

If the refrigerator cools in one mode of operation but not the other, the cooling unit is not the problem.

Operate the unit for approximately one hour and carefully touch the unit at the boiler box and the absorber area. This is the start and finish of the solution and should have a similar temperature which would indicate proper circulation.

Caution must be taken as high temperatures can be experienced at the burner assembly!

If you have little or no warmth at the absorber, circulation is limited in the cooling unit.

If the boiler is warm and the absorber is extremely hot, there is a circulation of hot gas only and the evidence of a leak as the ammonia is being boiled but there is not hydrogen for evaporation.

### Ticking Noise When Running on Electricity.

The ticking sound is most likely a product of dirty DC voltage used to operate the refrigerator-control system. This could be a control-wire hookup problem. Make sure the control wire is hooked to the battery side of the converter. When in doubt connect this wire directly to the battery. Make sure this wire is fused at the source; a 3-amp fuse should be sufficient.

If there is a voltage variation to the control panel, the relay in the circuit board will chatter—the ticking sound. It could be an erratic ground. Pull the ground wires, clean them, and reattach.

### Should I turn the refrigerator off while not in use?

Because there are no moving parts in an absorption system, leaving the refrigerator on while the RV is stored will not shorten it's life, however it makes no sense to leave it on. It is wise to clean it thoroughly and leave it cracked open during storage. Possibly leave a box of open baking soda.

### Interference from Lights

Sometime while running the fluorescent lights, the ref begins to click and search from gas to electricity and makes an annoying sound.

# Dometic Troubleshooting

The Dometic panel provides information on the power mode and the level of cooling and is fitted with an on/off switch and a check light in case of an equipment failure. It does not provide diagnostic codes, therefore troubleshooting must be performed at individual components.

### Electrode

If the electrode does not spark, first, make sure the igniter is receiving 12-volts. If not, turn the refrigerator off and remove the wire between the electrode and igniter. Turn the refrigerator to the gas mode. If no internal clicking sound is heard the igniter is defective.

### Cooling Unit

Cooling units are sometimes diagnosed as being defective when the actual problem is something else. Cooling units are expensive to replace, so it is important to make the correct diagnosis. By using the proper test procedures, you can eliminate all other possibilities before condemning the cooling unit.

### Preliminary Checks

Check for an ammonia smell around the cooling unit and inside the refrigerator. This could indicate a possible refrigerant leak. Check for any deposits of yellow powder on the tubing which will sometimes form around the area of a leak.

Determine if the refrigerator works on one heat source but not another by testing it in the alternate modes. If so, or if there is better cooling results from one source than another, the problem is not the cooling unit.

Make sure the refrigerator is level. Sometimes the vehicle is level but the refrigerator is not due to installation issues. Place a level on the bottom of the freezer compartment and check side-to-side and front-to-back levels.

Carefully check door gaskets for proper seat. A leaking gasket can allow enough warm air inside the refrigerator to overcome most of the cooling being produced.

Check the venting system to insure that ample air flow is provided at the back of the refrigerator.

Run the refrigerator for at least two hours, then check the boiler enclosure and absorber coil for temperature at the back of the cooling unit with your hand.

Under normal operation the temperature at these spots should be the same. If the temperature at the absorber coils is much hotter, it indicates loss of refrigerant and the cooling unit must be replaced.

If the temperature at the boiler is very hot and the absorber coils are cool, it indicates poor circulation which could be liquid trapped in the evaporator sections caused by out-of-level operation. Shut the unit off, let it cool down, allowing the liquid to settle back in the absorber vessel. Then restart the refrigerator and check temperatures after 2 hours.

### Burner Flame Inspection

The efficiency of your refrigerator while operating in the gas mode is dependent upon the correct burner flame. The burner flame provides energy to heat or "percolate" the solution properly.

A proper flame is a combination of the correct LP gas pressure, air input, and a clean burner and orifice. It is recommended that you visually inspect the flame periodically using the following procedure:

While in GAS operation, turn the temperature setting to the coldest position. Open the lower intake vent. Caution must be taken as the burner box may be hot. It is recommended that you use gloves or a tool such as a screwdriver to open the burner box door. Look at the flame. It may be necessary to remove the burner box for a better view.

The flame should be a darker blue inside and a lighter blue outside and should be a constant and steady shape. If the flame is yellow or has an erratic and unstable shape, contact your dealer or Dometic Service Center.

Make sure the flame does not touch the inside of the flue tube, if it does, contact your dealer or Dometic Service Center.

## Dometic Troubleshooting, *continued*

### Clean DC Power

Sometimes erratic operation can be caused by an AC "ripple" into the DC power supply. Clean direct current (DC) power is mandatory for high tech circuits to operate as designed. The sources for DC power are a battery and converter. A battery will provide recharging of the battery by the converter or the alternator.

AC ripple can be measured by a voltmeter set on the AC scale at the main terminal block connections. Six volts AC or less is acceptable.

A brief interruption of the DC power supply while refrigerator is operating on gas can cause a check light; for example: Turning the refrigerator OFF-ON while operating in the gas mode can cause a check light. The switching of relays from converter power to battery power when unplugging from shore power or shutting down of the generator could interrupt DC power long enough to cause a check light.

### Ticking Noise When Running on Electricity.

The ticking sound is most likely a product of dirty DC voltage used to operate the refrigerator-control system. Could be a control-wire hookup problem. Make sure the control wire is hooked to the battery side of the converter. When in doubt connect this wire directly to the battery. Make sure this wire is fused at the source; a 3-amp fuse should be sufficient.

If there is a voltage variation to the control panel, the relay in the circuit board will chatter-the ticking sound. It could be an erratic ground. Pull the ground wires, clean them, and reattach.

### Should I turn the refrigerator off while not in use?

Because there are no moving parts in an absorption system, leaving the refrigerator on while the RV is stored will not shorten it's life, however it makes no sense to leave it on. It is wise to clean it thoroughly and leave it cracked open during storage. Possibly leave a box of open baking soda.

### Interference from Lights

Sometime while running the fluorescent lights, the ref begins to click and search from gas to electricity and makes an annoying sound.

Radio frequencies from the ballasts in the lights are causing the circuit board to go haywire. This is especially a problem with older ref. Turn on one light at a time to identify the culprit and replace the ballast or fixture itself.

### Excess Heat

Adding a 12-Volt DC fan to the back coils from Radio Shack can help dissipate heat. Install in the outside compartment, wire to a 12-volt source, or to the gas solenoid valve.

### Sticky Door

A door that is hard to open or close could be sagging and need realignment. Use a 1/8" nylon washer shimmed to the bottom hinge.

### A Few Last Suggestions

If bugs or spiders creep into the exhaust vent, remove the vent and place a piece of screen inside and reinstall the vent. Make sure it's small enough to keep the critters out, but does not block airflow.

If cans and bottles slide around inside the refrigerator, use slip-resistant matting for grip.

To verify the temperature inside your refrigerator, place a remote temperature sensor inside with the receiver outside. Camping World also offers a temperature sensor that records highs and lows to indicate if your refrigerator went out while you were gone.

# Load Management Basics

To determine your power needs for a 15–amp, 30–amp, or 50–amp system, use the following chart to estimate the total combined watts of all the appliances, lamps, battery chargers, air conditioners and other electrical products you typically use at the same time. (All electrical appliances and lights are labeled with their power requirements expressed in watts or amps). You can use any number of appliances simultaneously, as long as their combined wattage doesn't exceed the electrical output of your RV's circuit breaker rating.

| Appliances | Average Required | Wattage Amps |
| --- | --- | --- |
| Air Conditioner | 1400–2400 | 9–20 |
| Battery Charger | Up to 3000 | 6–28 |
| Blender | 600 | 5.5 |
| Broiler | 1350 | 12 |
| Broom/Vacuum | 200–500 | 1.5–4 |
| Coffeepot | 550–1000 | 4–8 |
| Compact Disc Player & Speakers | 50–100 | 0.5–0.9 |
| Computer | 50–100 | 0.5–0.9 |
| Converter | 500–1000 | 4–8 |
| Curling Iron | 20–50 | 0.2–0.5 |
| Drill | 250–750 | 2–6 |
| Electric Blanket | 50–200 | 0.5–1.5 |
| Fan | 25–100 | 0.2–0.9 |
| Frying Pan/Wok | 1000–1350 | 8–11 |
| Hair Dryer | 350–1500 | 3–13 |
| Iron | 500–1200 | 4–10 |
| Lightbulbs | 40–100 ea. | 0.36–0.9 |
| Microwave/Convection Oven | 700–1500 | 6–13 |
| Radio | 50–200 | 0.5–1.5 |
| Refrigerator | 400–1000 | 3–8 |
| Space Heater | 1000–1500 | 8–13 |
| Stove (per element) | 350–1000 | 3–8 |
| Television | 200–600 | 1.5–4 |
| Toaster | 750–1200 | 6.5–10 |
| VCR | 150–200 | 1.15 |
| Washer/Dryer | 2000–2250 | 16 |
| Water Heater | 1000–1500 | 8–13 |
| Water Pump | 500–600 | 4–5 |

# Periodic Maintenance—Gas*

Periodic maintenance is essential for top performance and long genset life. Use Table 4 as a guide for normal periodic maintenance. In hot and dusty environments some maintenance procedures should be performed more frequently, as indicated by the footnotes in the table. Keeping a log of maintenance performed and hours run will help you keep genset maintenance regular and provide a basis for supporting warranty claims (Page 33).

Maintenance, replacement or repair of emission control devices and systems may be performed by any engine repair establishment or individual. However, warranty work must be completed by an authorized Onan dealer.

**TABLE 4. PERIODIC MAINTENANCE SCHEDULE**

| MAINTENANCE PROCEDURE | MAINTENANCE FREQUENCY | | | | | | |
|---|---|---|---|---|---|---|---|
| | Every Day or Every 8 Hours | After First 20 Hours | Every Month | Every 50 Hours | Every 150 Hours | Every 450 Hours | Page |
| General Inspections | X | | | | | | 16 |
| Check Engine Oil Level | X | | | | | | 17 |
| Clean and Check Battery | | | $X^3$ | | | | 19 |
| Clean Spark Arrestor | | | | X | | | 21 |
| Change Engine Oil & Oil Filter | | $X^1$ | | | $X^{2, 3, 4}$ | | 18 |
| Replace Air Filter Element | | | | | $X^2$ | | 19 |
| Replace Spark Plugs | | | | | | $X^5$ | 20 |
| Clean Engine Cooling Fins | | | | | | $X^2$ | – |
| Replace Fuel Filter | | | | | | $X^{5, 6}$ | – |
| Adjust Valve Lash | | | | | | $X^6$ | – |
| Clean or Replace Cylinder Heads | | | | | | $X^6$ | – |

1 – As a part of engine break-in, change the engine oil after the first 20 hours of operation.
2 – Perform more often when operating in dusty environments.
3 – Perform more often when operating in hot weather.
4 – Perform at least once a year.
5 – Perform sooner if engine performance deteriorates.
6 – Must be performed by a qualified mechanic (authorized Onan dealer).

° Please ignore the reference to pages in this chart. This graphic was taken directly from the manufacturer's manual and does not refer to the pagination in this book.

# Periodic Maintenance—Diesel*

Periodic maintenance is essential for top performance and long genset life. Use Table 3 as a guide for normal periodic maintenance. In hot and dusty environments some maintenance procedures should be performed more frequently, as indicated by the footnotes in the table. Keeping a log of maintenance performed and hours run (Page 34) will help you keep genset maintenance regular and provide a basis for supporting warranty claims.

Maintenance, replacement or repair of emission control devices and systems may be performed by any engine repair establishment or individual. However, warranty work must be completed by an authorized Onan dealer.

## TABLE 3. PERIODIC MAINTENANCE SCHEDULE

| MAINTENANCE PROCEDURE | MAINTENANCE FREQUENCY | | | | | | Page |
|---|---|---|---|---|---|---|---|
| | Every Day | After First 50 Hours | Every Month | Every 150 Hours | Every 500 Hours | Every 1000 Hours | |
| General Inspection | X | | | | | | 13 |
| Check Engine Oil Level | X | | | | | | 14 |
| Check Engine Coolant Level | X | | | | | | 19 |
| Clean and Check Battery | | | $X^3$ | | | | 16 |
| Change Engine Oil and Filter | | $X^1$ | | $X^{2,3,4}$ | | | 15 |
| Clean Spark Arrestor | | | | $X^4$ | | | 17 |
| Replace Engine Air Filter | | | | | $X^{2,4}$ | | 16 |
| Replace Fuel Filter | | | | | X | | 18 |
| Check Coolant Anti-freeze Protection | | | | | X | | 19 |
| Flush Coolant System | | | | | | $X^5$ | 19 |
| Replace Coolant Pressure Cap | | | | | | $X^5$ | 19 |
| Replace Engine V-belt | | | | | | $X^{6,7}$ | – |
| Clean Crankcase Breather | | | | | | $X^{6,7}$ | – |
| Replace Coolant Hoses and Thermostat | | | | | | $X^{6,7}$ | – |

1 – As a part of engine break-in, change the engine oil after the first 50 hours of operation.
2 – Perform more often when operating in dusty conditions.
3 – Perform more often when operating in hot weather.
4 – Perform at least once a year.
5 – Perform at least once every two years.
6 – Perform at least once every five years.
7 – Must be performed by a qualified mechanic (authorized Onan dealer).

° Please ignore the reference to pages in this chart. This graphic was taken directly from the manufacturer's manual and does not refer to the pagination in this book.

# State Driver's License Summary

Provided by www.changingears.com. Reprinted with permission

This section contains a summary of non–commercial RV driver's license requirements of the fifty states plus Washington DC

**Legend:**

**State**   State or Washington DC code

**CDL**   Indicates if CDL is required for non–commercial RV's

**Special** Indicates if special driver's license is required

**DL**   Abbreviation for driver's license

**Review** Date of information review

> = Greater than

Y = Yes

N = No

k = 1,000

| STATE | CDL | SPECIAL | DL WEB SITE | COMMENTS | REVIEW |
|-------|-----|---------|-------------|----------|--------|
| AK | N | N | DL Web Site | | Jul 05 |
| AL | N | N | DL Web Site | | Jul 05 |
| AR | N | N | DL Web Site | Driver's license manual states that a Class D license is valid up to 26,000 lb GVWR. We confirmed by phone that the Class D license is valid for all RV's. | Jul 05 |
| AZ | N | N | DL Web Site | Driver's license and CDL manuals imply that a CDL is required above 26,000 lb GVWR. However, A.R.S. 28–3102 exempts RVs from CDL requirement. | Mar 09 |
| CA | N | Y > 10k lb or > 40' | DL Web Site | Motor homes over 40' but not longer than 45' require non–commercial Class B. Trailers over 10,000 lb GVWR and fifth wheels over 15,000 lb GVWR require non–commercial Class A. See Recreational Vehicles and Trailers Handbook. | Oct 08 |
| CO | N | N | DL Web Site | While CDL manual states that a CDL is required for trucks above 6,500 lb, we confirmed by phone that CDL is not required for any RV. | Jul 05 |
| CT | N | Y > 10k lb | DL Web Site | Class 2 license required for trailers above 10,000 lb GVW | Jul 05 |
| DC | Y > 26k lb | N | DL Web Site | According to officials, a CDL is required above 26,000 lb.Must pass the CDL knowledge test, but the road test is *not* required. | Jan 06 |
| DE | N | N | DL Web Site | | Jul 05 |
| FL | N | N | DL Web Site | Driver's license manual states that a Class E license is valid up to 26,000 lb GVWR. We confirmed by phone that the Class E license is valid for *all* RV's. | Jul 05 |
| GA | N | N | DL Web Site | | Jul 05 |

| STATE | CDL | SPECIAL | DL WEB SITE | COMMENTS | REVIEW |
|-------|-----|---------|-------------|----------|--------|
| HI | Y > 26k lb | Y > 15k lb | DL Web Site | Class 4 license required for trailers weighing more than 15,000 lb and less than 26,000 lb CDL implied above 26,000 lb | Jul 05 |
| IA | N | N | DL Web Site | | Jul 05 |
| ID | N | N | DL Web Site | | Jul 05 |
| IL | N | Y > 16k lb | DL Web Site | Above 16,000 lb GVWR or GCWR, or towing above 10,000 lb, requires non–commercial Class A, B, or C | Aug 07 |
| IN | Y > 45′ | N | DL Web Site | | Aug 09 |
| KS | N | Y > 26k lb | DL Web Site | Above 26,000 lb GVWR or GCWR requires non–commercial Class A or B | Jul 05 |
| KY | N | N | DL Web Site | | Jul 05 |
| LA | N | N | DL Web Site | | Jul 05 |
| MA | N | N | DL Web Site | Driver's license manual states that a Class D license is valid up to 26,000 lb registered weight. We confirmed by phone that the Class D license is valid for *all* RV's. | Jul 05 |
| MD | N | Y > 26k lb | DL Web Site | Above 26,000 lb GVW requires non–commercial Class A or B | Jul 05 |
| ME | N | N | DL Web Site | | Jul 05 |
| MI | N | Y > 1 trailer | DL Web Site | "R" endorsement required if pulling two trailers | Jul 05 |
| MN | N | N | DL Web Site | | Jul 05 |
| MO | N | N | DL Web Site | | Jul 05 |
| MS | N | N | DL Web Site | | |
| | Jul 05 | | | | |
| MT | N | N | DL Web Site | Driver's license manual states that a Class D license is valid up to 26,000 lb GVW. We confirmed by phone that the Class D license is valid for *all* RV's. | Dec 05 |
| NC | N | Y > 26k lb | DL Web Site | Above 26,000 lb GVWR or GCWR requires non–commercial Class A or B | Jul 05 |
| ND | N | N | DL Web Site | | Jul 05 |
| NE | N | N | DL Web Site | | Jul 05 |
| NH | N | N | DL Web Site | Driver's license manual states that a Class D license is valid up to 26,000 lb GVW. We confirmed by phone that the Class D license is valid for *all* RV's. | Jan 06 |
| NJ | N | N | DL Web Site | | Jul 05 |
| NM | N | Y > 26k lb | DL Web Site | Above 26,000 lb GVW requires class E. See sections 18.19.5.30 and 18.19.5.112 in TRD Publication 18.18 & 18.19 NMAC. | Oct 08 |
| NV | N | Y > 10k lb | DL Web Site | When towing a trailer above 10,000 lb GVWR, requires "J" endorsement. Above 26,000 lb GVWR or GCWR requires non–commercial Class A or B. | Jul 05 |

| STATE | CDL | SPECIAL | DL WEB SITE | COMMENTS | REVIEW |
|---|---|---|---|---|---|
| NY | N | Y > 26k lb | DL Web Site | Above 26,000 lb GVWR requires "R" endorsement. A new law enacted 7/2005 has eliminated the non–CDL class C. See The Elimination of the Non–CDL Class C License. | Jan 07 |
| OH | N | N | DL Web Site | | Jul 05 |
| OK | N | N | DL Web Site | | Jul 05 |
| OR | N | N | DL Web Site | | Jul 05 |
| PA | N | Y > 26k lb | DL Web Site | Above 26,000 lb GVWR or GCWR requires non–commercial Class A or B | Sep 09 |
| RI | N | N | DL Web Site | According to DL officials, above 26,000 lb GVWR or GCWR requires commercial Class A or B. However, *RI statute 31–10.3–16 (5)* specifically exempts RV's. | Aug 07 |
| SC | N | Y > 26k lb | DL Web Site | Above 26,000 lb GVW requires Class E or F | Jan 07 |
| SD | N | N | DL Web Site | | Jul 05 |
| TN | N | N | DL Web Site | | Jul 05 |
| TX | N | Y > 26k lb | DL Web Site | Above 26,000 lb GVWR or GCWR (while towing > 10,000 lb) requires non–commercial Class A or B | Aug 07 |
| UT | N | N | DL Web Site | Also see the License Class section in the *Utah Investigators Vehicle Crash Report Instruction Manual*. | Jun 10 |
| VA | N | N | DL Web Site | Information confirmed by a VA state trooper. | Jun 08 |
| VT | N | N | DL Web Site | | Jul 05 |
| WA | N | N | DL Web Site | | Jul 05 |
| WI | Y > 45' | N | DL Web Site | RV exemption in CDL manual: "motor home, fifth–wheel mobile home—provided it isn't longer than 45 feet" | Jul 05 |
| WV | N | N | DL Web Site | | Jul 05 |
| WY | N | Y > 26k lb | DL Web Site | Above 26,000 lb GVWR or GCWR requires non–commercial Class A or B | Jul 05 |

# Motorhome Buyer's Worksheet

Use this worksheet to record each motorhome you are interested in. Write down what you liked, disliked, or would like changed in the + and − column of each section. Staple or paperclip it to a brochure if possible. Make sure you write down where you saw it! Use the back for additional notes, sketches, or to help draw a map location if attending a show.

Date _____     Brand/Year _____     Location _____

Manufacturer _____     Model _____     Actual Length _____

GVWR _____     CCC _____     Towing Capacity _____

_____ New                    _____ Used                    Mileage _____

**Chassis**                    **Floorplan/Sliderooms**          **Exterior Style**

Drivetrain _____     Desc _____     Desc _____

   +        −        +               −                              +          −


     **Galley**                    **Living Room**                **Drivers/Passenger Area**

   +        −               +          −                    +          −


   **Bathroom**                    **Bedroom**                    **Color/Décor**

   +        −               +          −                    +          −


Options Included:                              Price: _____


Impressive Features:


Dislikes:


Dealership/Sales Professional:

# Trailer Buyer's Worksheet

Use this worksheet to record each travel trailer you are interested in. Write down what you liked, disliked, or would like changed in the + and − column of each section. Staple or paperclip it to a brochure if possible. Make sure you write down where you saw it! Use the back for additional notes, sketches, or to help draw a map location if attending a show.

Date _____     Brand/Year _____     Location _____

Manufacturer _____     Model _____     Actual Length _____

GVWR _____     CCC _____     Towing Capacity _____

_____ New                    _____ Used                    Mileage _____

**Chassis**                    **Floorplan/Sliderooms**          **Exterior Style**

Drivetrain _____     Desc _____            Desc _____

   +        −        +                   −              +      −


    **Galley**                    **Living Room**                **Storage**

   +       −               +       −               +       −


  **Bathroom**                    **Bedroom**                    **Color/Décor**

   +       −               +       −               +       −


Options Included:                              Price: _____


Impressive Features:


Dislikes:


Dealership/Sales Professional:

# Top Ten RV Breakdowns

**As Reported to the Good Sam Emergency Road Service Technical Line**

| Failure | Prevention Tip |
| --- | --- |
| 1. Tire Failure | Check inflation regularly, understand weight ratings, and check lug nut torque |
| 2. Dead House Batteries | Proper maintenance, charging, and battery isolation system check |
| 3. Dead Engine Battery | Check charging system, engine belts, and parasitic drain |
| 4. Out of Gas | It doesn't cost any more to keep the tank full! |
| 5. Windshield Crack | Cover chips immediately with tape, ensure tight seals on gaskets, and have them fixed |
| 6. Entrance Steps Damaged | Use your checklist, check door/frame sensor, and have the engine start over-ride verified |
| 7. 120-Volt | Verify that campground breakers are on, check GFCI reset, and that voltage coming from the campground source is 110-volt AC or higher |
| 8. Refrigerator | Verify operation on all power, check ventilation, check house batteries for more than 10.5 volts, check that propane is on and full |
| 9. Roof AC | Check filters regularly, remote AC needs 120-volt and 12-volt power to operate, *know your height!* |
| 10. Generator | Check fuel level, maintain, start generator every 2 weeks and run under load to prevent varnish buildup, and verify breakers on the genset |

## Medical Information Card

Medical Conditions:

Name: _____

Address _____

City _____

DOB _____

Emergency Contacts:

Physicians:

# Index